WOMEN AND PLAYWRITING IN NINETEENTH-CENTURY BRITAIN

EDITED BY

TRACY C. DAVIS AND ELLEN DONKIN

CAMBRIDGE
UNIVERSITY PRESS

PUBLISHED BY THE PRESS SYNDICATE OF THE UNIVERSITY OF CAMBRIDGE
The Pitt Building, Trumpington Street, Cambridge CB2 1RP, United Kingdom

CAMBRIDGE UNIVERSITY PRESS
The Edinburgh Building, Cambridge, CB2 2RU, UK   http://www.cup.cam.ac.uk
40 West 20th Street, New York, NY 10011–4211, USA   http://www.cup.org
10 Stamford Road, Oakleigh, Melbourne 3166, Australia

© Tracy C. Davis and Ellen Donkin 1999

First published 1999

Printed in the United Kingdom at the University Press, Cambridge

Typeset in Baskerville 11/12.5pt   [CE]

A catalogue record for this book is available from the British Library

Library of Congress cataloging in publication data
Women and playwriting in nineteenth-century Britain /edited by Tracy C. Davis and Ellen Donkin.
p.   cm.
Includes bibliographical references and index.
Contents: The sociable playwright and representative citizen / Tracy C. Davis – To be public as a genius and private as a woman / Gay Gibson Cima – Mrs. Gore gives tit for tat / Ellen Donkin – Jane Scott, the writer/manager / Jacky Bratton – Staging the state / Beth H. Friedman–Romell – The lady playwrights and the wild tribes of the East / Heidi J. Holder – From a female pen / Katherine Newy – Genre trouble / Susan Bennett – Sappho in the closet / Denise A. Walen – Conflicted politics and circumspect comedy / Susan Carlson.
ISBN 0 521 57413 7 (hardback) – ISBN 0 521 65982 5 (paperback)
1. English drama – Women authors – History and criticism.
2. Women and literature – Great Britain – History – nineteenth century.
3. English drama – nineteenth century – History and criticism.
I. Davis, Tracy C., 1960– .   II. Donkin, Ellen, 1949– .
PR728.w6w66   1999
822′.8099287 – dc21   98–38099   CIP

ISBN 0 521 57413 7 hardback
ISBN 0 521 65982 5 paperback

Of Genius wild & savage Nature spring
The Drama rose, when that & mind were young.
Rose, such as now, o'ercanopied by trees
And lighted by the Sun, the Indian sees:
An uncouth Pantomime of mingling foes,
Ear-piercing war-cries, long-resounding blows,
Mimicry that abjures the aid of speech,
And brainless jest which thought disdains to reach.
Such was the Drama when its course began;
So impotent! so rude! – for such was Man.
    . . .
Secure that here all flames you may defy,
Except th' unburning flames of Woman's eye.

(Mary Russell Mitford, ms poem entered for the 1812 Drury Lane
opening address)

Contents

Illustrations

Contributors

SUSAN BENNETT is Professor of English at the University of Calgary, Canada. Among her recent publications are *Performing Nostalgia: Shifting Shakespeare and the Contemporary Past* (1996) and *Theatre Audiences: A Theory of Production and Reception* (second edition, 1997). She is currently working on a study of genre in the context of women's dramatic writing.

JACKY BRATTON is Professor of Theatre and Cultural History at Royal Holloway, University of London. Her field is nineteenth-century performance, with a cultural-materialist/feminist approach. She is editor, with Jim Cook and Christine Gledhill, of *Melodrama: Stage, Picture, Screen* (1994), and sole editor of *Acts of Supremacy* (1991). She is currently editing *King Lear* on CD-ROM for Cambridge University Press, and serves as editor of the journal *Nineteenth Century Theatre*.

SUSAN CARLSON is Professor of English at Iowa State University, where she teaches courses in drama, literature, and women's studies. She is the author of *Women and Comedy: Rewriting the British Theatrical Tradition* (1991), as well as recent essays on Aphra Behn, the Omaha Magic Theatre, and *The Taming of the Shrew*. She is currently writing *Shakespeare and the Suffragettes*, a study of suffrage theatre and early twentieth-century stagings of Shakespearean comedy.

GAY GIBSON CIMA is Professor of English at Georgetown University, and has published widely on feminist performance issues and theatre history. Her book *Performing Women: Female Characters, Male Playwrights, and the Modern Stage* was published by Cornell University Press in 1993. She is currently writing a history of women critics in the United States from the eighteenth to the early twentieth century.

JIM DAVIS is Associate Professor and Head of the School of Theatre, Film and Dance at the University of New South Wales. He has published a number of articles on the Britannia Theatre, Hoxton, and edited the diaries of the Britannia's stage manager, Frederick Wilton, for publication (1992). He is currently engaged in a research project on nineteenth-century London theatre audiences.

TRACY C. DAVIS is Associate Professor of Theatre, English, and Performance Studies at Northwestern University. She is the author of *Actresses as Working Women: Their Social Identity in Victorian Culture* (1991), *George Bernard Shaw and the Socialist Theatre* (1994), dozens of articles on nineteenth- and twentieth-century performance and culture, and is presently writing a book for Cambridge University Press on the economics of nineteenth-century British theatre which investigates the theoretical and pragmatic intersections of capital and performance.

ELLEN DONKIN is Professor of Theatre at Hampshire College in Amherst, Massachusetts. She publishes on feminist directing and feminist theatre history. Her work includes essays on Sarah Siddons, Eleonora Duse, Gertrude Stein, and Sarah Bernhardt. She is coeditor of *Upstaging Big Daddy* with Susan Clement (1993), and author of *Getting Into the Act: Women Playwrights in London, 1776–1829* (1995).

BETH H. FRIEDMAN-ROMELL is currently completing her doctorate in Theatre and Drama at Northwestern University, where she is researching gendered constructions of national identity in British theatrical performance in the Age of Revolutions. Her publications include essays for *Theatre Journal* on theatrical cross-dressing in eighteenth-century London, and for *Nineteenth Century Theatre* on Joanna Baillie's *The Family Legend*. Friedman-Romell is a recipient of the Society for Theatre Research's Kathleen Barker Award.

HEIDI HOLDER is Assistant Professor of English at Central Michigan University. She has published articles in *Essays in Theatre, University of Toronto Quarterly*, and *Journal of Modern Literature*; she also contributed a chapter on melodrama and empire to *Acts of Supremacy: the British Empire and the Stage, 1790–1930*, edited by Jacky Bratton. She is currently completing a manuscript on genre and censorship in the Victorian and Edwardian theatre.

JANE MOODY until recently held a Research Fellowship at Girton College, Cambridge University, and now is Lecturer in the Department of English and Related Literature at the University of York. She has published articles in *Shakespeare Survey*, *Texas Studies in Literature and Language*, and *Nineteenth Century Theatre*. Her monograph on illegitimate theatre in early nineteenth-century London is being published by Cambridge University Press.

KATHERINE NEWEY teaches theatre at Lancaster University. She has published on melodrama, nineteenth-century theatre reviewing, Jane Austen, and Mary Shelley. She is currently engaged in a major study of nineteenth-century women playwrights, funded by the Australian Research Council.

DENISE WALEN is an Assistant Professor in the Drama Department at Vassar College, where she teaches theatre history and dramatic literature. Her work focuses on the historical context of homoerotic representations in both texts and performances. She has contributed articles and reviews to *Text and Presentation*, *Theatre History Studies*, *Theatre Journal*, and *Theatre Studies*. Her article on Charlotte Cushman will appear in *Gays and Lesbians in American Theatre History*.

Acknowledgements

When we undertook to edit this volume, we realized that to rethink how this period has been historicized we would need to deploy a new kind of process. We commissioned ten essays and set out a time-scale which allowed for collecting and distributing everyone's work in preparation for a symposium held at Northwestern University. Substantive revisions came about as a result of our discussions. The editors thank the authors for taking the original leap of faith with us, commencing their research in *terra incognita*, and for their subsequent patience and persistence in thinking through each essay. The symposium was attended not only by the authors of this volume but also by invited scholars who came as respondents. So, in a very real sense, they are also contributors to this book and need to be acknowledged as such. Special thanks are due to Tom Crochunis, Amy Partridge, Esther Beth Sullivan, Judith Drummond, Catherine Burroughs, and Kerry Powell. We are also indebted to the people who joined this symposium on their own initiative and generously contributed their ideas: Richard Fotheringham, Angela Escott, Brian Artese, Maureen A. Dowd, Rachel LoCascio, Amy Kritzer, and Beverly Boyd. Special thanks also to David Downs, whose performances as John Phillip Kemble and Samuel Whitbread will never be forgotten by those privileged to be witnesses.

Earlier in 1997, a group of graduate students at Northwestern participated in what might have been the first class on the subject of nineteenth-century British women playwrights, and Tracy C. Davis acknowledges the lively and engaging afternoons spent discussing many of the texts treated in this book with Brian Artese, Jennifer Berzansky, Anthea Kraut, Julie Leavitt, Rachel LoCascio, John Martin, Amy Partridge, and Leslie Waddell-Harris. Anna Altman, a graduating senior, also braved the fray. This class was made possible through a generous grant from the Alumni Fund of Northwestern

University, which helped finance the acquisition of many important resources gathered from libraries and archives in Britain and America. In addition, the School of Speech, College of Arts and Sciences, Department of Theatre, and Department of English contributed funds that ensured the symposium was hospitably catered and graciously housed.

The editors also thank Victoria Cooper of Cambridge University Press, whose savvy reading of the field is matched by perspicacity and boundless tact. The kind efforts of Hilary Hammond and Jayne Matthews are also acknowledged. Annette Fern shepherded many of the contributors through the labyrinths of riches of the Harvard Theatre Collection.

Both editors thank Max Shapey and Elly's long-suffering family – Larry Winship, Molly Donkin Winship, and Grace Cobb Winship – and their respective (and sometimes overlapping) communities of great women friends.

Introduction

Tracy C. Davis and Ellen Donkin

> To understand the workings of the social memory it may be
> worth investigating the social organization of forgetting, the
> rules of exclusion, suppression or repression, and the question
> of who wants whom to forget what, and why. In a phrase, social
> amnesia. Amnesia is related to "amnesty," to what used to be
> called "acts of oblivion," the official erasure of memories of
> conflict in the interests of social cohesion.
>
> (Burke 1997: 56–57)

Nineteenth-century British women playwrights stubbornly refuse to
comply with any of the tropes of feminist historiography that
Margaret Ezell identifies as the historical constructions of second-
wave feminist scholarship (Ezell 1993). We do not see, in their work
or their lives, growing rebellion (either individual or collective)
leading to a feminist consciousness. We do not see an evolution from
Aphra Behn, Delarivière Manley, and Mary Pix in the 1690s to the
next century's flowering of Hannah Cowley, Elizabeth Inchbald, and
Hannah More paving the way for legions (or even a trickle) of more
confident and assured nineteenth-century women taking up the
drama as if it belonged more comfortably in their hands. And we do
not see simple models of women playwrights as outcasts, for many
were heralded with welcome praise even though they often found
long-term success less easy to come by. Nor do we see them shut out
of writing altogether by the vicissitudes of a theatre and culture
where masculine prerogative stacked the deck against them, for
many persisted in writing for theatre or forging careers that involved
writing in various genres and forms. What we do see, however, is
that the vast range of activity which women undertook in writing
plays has disappeared from the historical consciousness of theatre
historians, literary critics, and feminist scholars of all kinds, despite
their very solid presence in the annals, calendars, bibliographies,

and handbooks of the stage (Mann and Mann 1996; Davis and Joyce
1992; Mullin 1987; Ellis 1985; Wearing 1976; Nicoll 1952, 1955 and
1959). Kerry Powell capitalizes on some of this research to detail the
prohibitions on dramatic theory which mask gender prejudice, and
the deeply buried subversive subtexts in some late-Victorian drama
by women (1997). But by and large, scholarship has corrected some
of the record though not yet its historicization.

As the epigraph from Peter Burke suggests, it is as if there is
organized forgetting, patterns of exclusion, suppression, or repression, and a widespread social and scholarly amnesia about them. It is
not only intuitively true but also factually true that women – who
were so prominent amongst the ranks of novelists, poets, and essayists
– also wrote plays, and not only for the mass medium of professional
theatres but also for the growing market in amateur theatres (home,
school, and community groups) and for a reading public. So far, the
scholarship has concentrated on women playwrights in relation to
Romanticism (Burroughs 1997; Cox 1992; Purinton 1992), and
especially on Joanna Baillie, "the Shakespeare of her Age," comple-
mented by John Franceschina's anthology of Gothic melodramas,
including plays by Miss Burke, Harriet Lee, Jane Scott, Margaret
Harvey, Elizabeth Polack, and Catherine Gore (1997). Adrienne
Scullion's anthology broadens the scope by providing a more tempo-
rally diverse group of writers, including Teresa de Camp, Fanny
Kemble, Florence Bell and Elizabeth Robins, and Pearl Craigie
(1996). But readily available research resources provide a goldmine of
additional texts by hundreds more women. The Readex series
English and American Drama of the Nineteenth Century (on micro-
card and microfiche) aspires to include every known play in every
known version, the Frank Pettingell Collection of East End plays (on
microfilm) includes many promptbooks and play manuscripts, the
English Verse Drama Database created at the University of Michigan
so far includes plays by Joanna Baillie, Felicia Hemans, Mary Russell
Mitford, Frances Kemble, Emmeline Stuart-Wortley, Pearl Craigie,
and Michael Field (http://www.hti. umich.edu/english/evd), and in
time the website British Women Playwrights Around 1800 will
include more and more dramatic texts (http://www-sul.stanford.
edu/mirrors/romnet/wp1800), opening up this field to the vast
research possibilities that exist simply amongst textual resources.
What have been "acts of oblivion" in terms of the scholarly memory
of these women need not be perpetuated a moment longer.

What this book aims to do, in part, is to explore a number of reasons why there has been such widespread amnesia about women's playwriting activity, and the ways that this amnesia touches other types of women's theatrical work, writing work, and official participation in nineteenth-century culture. Their oblivion has been orchestrated, both in the nineteenth and twentieth centuries, in ways unique to their sex. Historians and critics have consistently leapt over the nineteenth century (and sometimes the entire eighteenth too), forgetting all the generations between Aphra Behn and Caryl Churchill, with a nod to Edwardian suffragists (Fitzsimmons and Gardner 1991; Spender and Hayman 1985). This amounts to acceptance of, and complicity with, the ideological forces that preferred to keep women in the background, that rightly or wrongly perpetuated the antitheatrical prejudice, and that undervalued the drama (and its slightly less prestigious cousins, the mere "play-scripts") as a writing pursuit secondary to novels, poetry, expository prose, and even translation.

Instead, when we reopen the inquiry, we discover that writing plays (whether they are intended for page or stage, closet or theatre) is inherently a kind of "free space" for invention. The persistent anxiety over rejuvenating the National Drama – an indigenously written and theorized product that could be proudly hailed – offered in principle a field open to all comers who might somehow make this mass medium as praiseworthy at the height of the British Empire's world dominion as it was in the era of its formation, when Shakespeare (or so Britons recalled) came to the fore. The accomplishments of the culture were manifestly out of balance with the accomplishments of the nation, and a flowering of Genius was sought with desperate longing (Gamer 1997). What the heralds of culture got instead was a patch of tangled weeds.

But could Genius be a woman? Despite the rhetoric of scrupulous fairness and evenhandedness from the managers, it seemed that nothing from a woman's hand could, on a stage deemed worthy of legitimate drama, satisfy the critics. Ultimately, no men were fully satisfactory either, but women's trials were complicated by more factors, including the abiding belief that respectability, dramatic genius, and playwriting skill were uneasily if not impossibly reconciled in a woman. The stage was rough enough for gentlemen – Byron, Coleridge, and Tennyson all fare badly in theatrical posterity – but quite impossible for ladies.

As long as the criterion for success is synonymous with the legitimate theatres, the scope of the question is unnaturally narrow. For until the Theatres Regulation Act of 1843, the denominator of legitimate theatres limits the field in London to two patent houses (Covent Garden and Drury Lane) and the Haymarket, plus a handful of theatres royal scattered through the major English provincial, Scottish, and Irish cities. Everything else was "minor" or "illegitimate," constrained by the licensing laws from producing the valued genres of tragedy and comedy. After 1843, the situation officially loosened, but the hierarchy was retained through the artistic hegemony of London's West End and the second-class (or worse) status of any theatre beyond that boundary. Also devalued were dramatic endeavors directed at private theatricals, however genteel, as a matter of disdain for the champions of the National Drama and the still-dominant evolutionary bias in theatre and dramatic history that relentlessly seeks the English lineage leading from the sparkling by-play of Sheridan's dialogue to the comedies of Shaw and Wilde, ignoring the century in between. What if, for example, instead of identifying Tom Robertson as the most important stepping-stone between Richard Brinsley Sheridan and George Bernard Shaw we substituted Mary Russell Mitford as the link? Is there any obvious rationale for why the house dramatist at the fashionable Prince of Wales Theatre takes precedence over the highly acclaimed author of *Julian*, *Foscari*, and *Rienzi* as the standard-bearer between Sheridan and Shaw? Or is there any sound principle excluding a host of other women writing for the most popular of stages – Jane Scott, Catherine Gore, Sarah Lane, and Melinda Young – if Robertson takes such a rightful place? Can we tinker with the periodization of theatre history by focusing also on the work of women, or must we throw out the paradigms entirely?

Although Genius was the abiding criterion in the nineteenth century, it is patently misleading to hold to it now. The first order of questions, in a newly conceived nineteenth-century theatre history, might more productively focus not on Genius but on survival. Not on legitimacy but on activity. Far too much cultural weight has been given to far too few of the actants, and far too little of their endeavor. The new information that emerges simply by adjusting the lens to a different focal length suggests whole new patterns in the historiography. By selecting particular heroes, we achieved a particular version of the past in which art struggled to survive within the exigencies of business, and a succession of pretty good playwrights attracted crowds when produced by very good actor-managers who accurately judged and provided for the taste of the town. What we still find, when including women, is that playwrights are predominantly middle-class, and that particular kinds of learning and certain levels of prosperity are especially conducive to enabling (or motivating) the writing in the first place. We find that women worked almost everywhere men worked (in the East End, in the West End, in the provinces) and that they struggled with everything men encountered (genre prescriptions, staging conventions, indifferent audiences, and inept producers). But we also find some differences, which we offer with caution and anxiety, conscious that women authors experienced the world with the privileges and prescriptions of a different gender.

It is precisely these differences which have informed the shaping of this book. Difference is not only a fact of gender in the broadest sense, but equally an issue for the researcher and critic who would seek to understand how difference informs the process by which they work. This book is organized as a series of questions which intentionally undermine assumptions about where to look for evidence, what authorship means, why locale matters, and how genre functions. And yet in this collection, the first of its kind on this subject, there are also differences of interpretation. Most notably on the comedic competition of 1844 (won by Catherine Gore), the authorial ascription of a Britannia Theatre playwright (Sarah Lane), and the approaches toward the most canonized of nineteenth-century women dramatists (Joanna Baillie), we offer different interpretations. The idea is not to counter one monolithic narrative of the nineteenth century with another, but to make a case for the multivocality of history and the importance of staging emergent debates. But the first order of business is adjusting the lens so that theatrical activity by women snaps into focus.

The first part of the book, "In judgment," suggests that we look at how these women have been judged, not only by their own contemporaries, but also by historians. In the first chapter, Tracy C. Davis proposes "sociability" as a theoretical concept which makes a crucial lens adjustment possible. It is a shock to realize how the dichotomy between the so-called "public" and the so-called "private" has worked its way into the fabric of historical inquiry, with the result that women in the nineteenth century disappear behind its cloth. It is particularly egregious for feminist historians working in theatre, who by looking only at "public women" (published, produced) have inadvertently overlooked a huge and instructive groundswell of theatrical activity by women. Activity is the key word, whether in and for the closet or the public stage. Focusing on the realms of sociability requires that we detach ourselves from the convenient binary of public/private, and look instead at theatrical activity in its myriad of public and private forms – closet drama, salon readings, home theatricals, school plays, political pageants – in an effort to understand it as a form of cultural participation. In this new scenario, it does not matter any longer whether or not a woman was published, reviewed or produced. It matters that something theatrical was in circulation, that it shaped opinion, a sense of the self, or a sense of community. Theatrical activity framed in these terms reveals not only the fluidity of these imaginary borders between public and private, but also the women themselves, who now appear before us in legions, from all classes and all geographical corners. Their connecting thread is theatre, not necessarily as a profession or even as a primary source of identification, but as an activity. As Davis puts it, "Shall we let women succeed on their own terms?"

Being inside the profession, however, usually meant that a woman playwright was not allowed to succeed on her own terms. The terms were always controlled by other people. Gay Gibson Cima's chapter makes it clear that one of the hazards of the profession for women was journalistic notice. Reviews, Cima reports, were almost never written by women. They carried the double authority of being in print and being written by an (alleged) eyewitness. But whose eyes were watching these productions? Cima reveals many of them to be men who were themselves playwrights, subsidizing a precarious career in theatre by working as journalists. Their anonymous columns provided an unfiltered conduit for judgments not only of the woman's work, but of her social presence as playwright. Cima's chapter warns us as historians to consider the source before we cite the review. Ellen Donkin's chapter on Catherine Gore documents the devastating impact of those reviews, not only on a woman's professional momentum, but also on the way she is subsequently judged by historians who do not trouble to balance the evidence of the reviews against the length of the run. It is abundantly clear, at the close of this section, that professional theatre, situated in the respectable West End and bolstered by the historic legitimacy conferred by monopoly, was a toxic environment for women.

The second part of this book, "Wrighting the play," asks two important questions: do female-authored plays constitute the limits of female authorship?; and can playwrights "make" plays without necessarily "writing" them? Jacky Bratton coins the term "intertheatricality," a concept which intentionally expands and enlarges our notions of authorship. The specific case in point is Jane Scott, manager, playwright and performer. If we look at one of Scott's evenings as a totality, that is, not just at Scott's plays but also the sequence of songs she chose, and the juxtaposition of the animal acts with the dancing girls, important layers of cultural meaning emerge, ones that Scott seems to have engineered. Jane Moody takes this expanded notion of authorship and goes a step further by claiming that women who managed and performed could "author" a play by proxy. Moody looks at Vestris and Céleste as women who, by virtue of their highly distinctive performing styles, shaped their texts by a kind of ventriloquism. In other words, playwriting need not necessitate writing at all, but instead can be conceived as *wrighting* in the sense of shaping or fashioning. Jim Davis's chapter on Sarah Lane focuses on translation and adaptation, and while raising questions about Mrs. Lane's authorship of several plays ascribed to her, he demonstrates how her combined skills as manager and dramaturg require that here, too, we must rethink how the term *playwrighting* not only enlarges our notions of *playwriting*, but also more accurately accounts for the activities of women. Together, Bratton, Moody, and Davis complicate the idea of self-conscious authorship, authorial naming, networks of production, and serial collaboration to reevaluate what writing (or *wrighting*) entails (see also Bristol 1996: 38–43). Authorship, they argue, is not so much an ideological fiction as a matter of historical indeterminacy (Davis), multiplicity (Bratton), or collectivity (Moody).

Part III, "Geographies of production," considers how the legitimacy and acceptability of women playwrights and their work was contingent upon where (and if) that work was produced. Even if we were to momentarily revert back to the luxurious traditional notion of singular authorship, the idea of the author proves unstable in actual production. The important issue for women playwrights, as Beth Friedman-Romell points out in her chapter on Joanna Baillie's

Constantine Paleologus, is that a woman's play in production in the nineteenth century moved through a machine which was almost wholly male-controlled, and that these men, particularly the provincial managers, had license to make substantial interventions to that script, either in the service of local politics, practical considerations of personnel and resources, or by way of satisfying gender expectations. Heidi Holder's chapter moves out of the provincial theatres and into London's East End, drawing our attention to how the plays of Melinda Young and Sarah Lane created roles for women that featured extraordinarily robust and assertive female characters. Far from functioning as a kind of escapism, as historians have claimed, these melodramas may have modeled agency for the women in their audiences in a way to which nothing in the West End could lay claim. Katherine Newey's chapter takes us to the West End, and reflects soberly on what it cost a woman to scale the fortress of legitimate theatre on its own terms. She formulates the idea of the "lady" playwright, and how that uneasy compromise between privacy and professionalism had the effect of a double-edged sword, by permitting a woman and her work to be conflated and judged on the basis of socially "appropriate" behavior (which manifestly did not include playwriting to begin with).

The final part of the book, "Genre trouble," asks this question: Why is it that when women's work exceeds the informal boundaries of dramatic genre, it is condemned as inept, rather than praised as innovative? Susan Bennett's chapter looks at two tragedies by Baillie and two melodramas by the lesser-known playwright Elizabeth Polack, and considers how these scripts "pollute" received categories of genre by repeatedly moving away from the universal and in the direction of particularity and difference with respect to gender and ethnicity.

Denise A. Walen's chapter considers another locus of tragedy, that of closet drama, which in the context of "sociability" takes its place firmly among the varieties of theatrical activity. Walen reappropriates this kind of theatre, not as a category of deficiency but as a map of something suppressed – in this case, lesbianism – in culture. She argues that if the historian conceives of closet drama as a locus for radical imaginary enactment, then the women who wrote these plays emerge very differently, not as "lady" playwrights who shrank from the test of production, but as deliberate experimentalists working with inflammatory materials. The ascription "closet drama" has been used to name certain kinds of plays as also-rans: somehow deficient in the kind of practical theatre experience necessary for success on the professional stage. But Walen instead tries to determine what kinds of complex and various activities the term *closet* might be closeting. If we think of the women writing Sappho plays, and of the women reading them, as participating in the sociable act of making culture, then it matters as much that these verse dramas *were* "closeted" as it would if they were not. It is not necessarily a judgment by posterity, but instead can be an aesthetic option in its own time. After all, Mann and Mann (1996: 412–17) found virtually as many women's plays of 1800–42 to be unacted, closet dramas, or privately produced (46.4%) as were professionally produced (47.8%), out of a sample of 201 texts.

The final chapter of this book, which also brings us to the close of the nineteenth century, is Susan Carlson's. Where Powell focused on serious drama (1997: 122–45), Carlson focuses on comedy, a genre which she warns us is renowned for its reconfirmation of the status quo. Nonetheless, women playwrights at the close of the century found ways to deploy comedy both as a means of validating and of challenging their culture. In so doing, they repeatedly fell foul of the rules of genre, usually with devastating critical results. But Carlson also cautions us about something that is resonant for the volume as a whole: we cannot give in to understandable impulses to superimpose our own needs for valor and vision after the fact.

Mary Russell Mitford provides a powerful case in point. In 1812, while gaining fame as a poet but not yet embarked as a playwright, she offered an address to be read at the opening performance of the new Theatre Royal, Drury Lane. Along with dozens of other writers, she entered her poem into a contest, and lost to Lord Byron. The poet laureate, like most of the other entrants, eulogized the old Drury, narrated the fire, pumped up nationalist fervor, and lauded the noble – and entirely masculine – tradition of the British stage.

> Dear are the days which made our annals bright,
> Ere GARRICK fled, or BRINSLEY ceas'd to write;
> Heirs to their labours, like all high-born heirs,
> Vain of *our* ancestry, as they of theirs.
> While thus Remembrance borrows Banquo's glass,
> To claim the scepter'd Shadows as they pass,
> And we the mirror hold, where imag'd shine
> Immortal names, emblazon'd on our line:

> Pause – ere their feebler offspring you condemn;
> Reflect how hard the task to rival them.   (*Genuine Rejected* 1812: 2)

Mitford's defiance of this view is palpable. Her entry, reproduced as the epigraph to this book, virtually cringes at the "brainless jest" and dumb show of British drama which Byron praised, for she is mindful that it is watched over by the colonized peoples of the empire. The theatres may burn, she intimates, and their fare may perish, but not without her piercing judgment going down into eternity:

> Secure that here all flames you may defy,
> Except th' unburning flames of Woman's eye.   (Mitford 1812)

Two serious volumes of these rejected addresses were collected and published.[1] None of their selections overlap. Neither includes Mitford. Instead, a verse by "Laura Matilda," a composite of Hannah Cowley and Perdita Robinson – both dead – was included as a parody of their poetic school, the Della Cruscans (Boyle 1929: 152). It concludes:

> Blood in every vein is gushing
> Vixen vengeance lulls my heart;
> See, the Gorgon gang is rushing!
> Never, never let us part!   (Boyle 1929: 69)

As with this poetic analogy, so with the plays. Absence from the record does not mean abjuration of writing. And likewise, inclusion in the record may be compromised by the taint of literary prejudice, or worse. In either case – the women who wrote and the men who wrote about (or on behalf of) them – there is a point of view. What is at stake here is not Mitford, or anyone else, necessarily becoming part of the chronicle of famous men, but that Mitford, like so many women, had – and asserted – her point of view. Perhaps we agree with her view, or perhaps not, but there it is ready to be found and accounted for.

If we are going to adjust the lens through which we look at these women, we must have the courage to see what is actually there. The temptation is to create a triumphant countercanon of women's playwriting within a narrative of evolving mastery, but it is a temptation that should be resisted at all costs. Remembering women's outlets for sociability makes it possible for us to see more clearly the complexity, richness, and diversity of what was there, though it may not satisfy a certain persistent longing for greatness. It is our hope that this book be understood not as a compendium of definitive statements on nineteenth-century women playwrights, but as an invitation to scholars everywhere who have an abiding interest in British culture, theatre, and the social history of women to join us in reconsidering this enormously important century before we stumble into the next. The history of women playwrights in the nineteenth century has its own peculiar inflections and twists, but on no account can it be any longer considered a blank slate. If there are blanks, they are products of social amnesia, not of a failure to engage. The chapters of this book constitute our effort to reinterpret the century, and we invite historians, critics, directors, and theoreticians to enter in with us.

NOTES

1   A host of parodic and farcical addresses as well as single editions were also published (Arnott and Robinson 1970: 136–37).

REFERENCES

Arnott, James Fullarton, and John William Robinson 1970, *English Theatrical Literature 1559–1900: A Bibliography*, London: Society for Theatre Research.

Boyle, Andrew (introduction) [1812] 1929, *Rejected Addresses or The New Theatrum Poetarum*, London: Constable.

Bristol, Michael 1996, "How Good Does Evidence Have to Be?," *Textual and Theatrical Shakespeare: Questions of Evidence*, ed. Edward Pechter, Iowa City: University of Iowa Press, 22–43.

British Women Writers Around 1800, http://www-sol.stanford.edu/mirrors/romnet/wp1800

Burke, Peter 1997, *Varieties of Cultural History*, Ithaca, NY: Cornell University Press.

Burroughs, Catherine B. 1997, *Closet Stages: Joanna Baillie and the Theater Theory of British Romantic Women Writers*, Philadelphia: University of Pennsylvania Press.

Cox, Jeffrey N. (ed.) 1992, *Seven Gothic Dramas 1789–1825*, Athens, OH: Ohio University Press.

Davis, Gwenn, and Beverly A. Joyce 1992, *Drama by Women to 1900: A Bibliography of American and British Writers*, Toronto and Buffalo: University of Toronto Press.

Ellis, James 1985, *English Drama of the Nineteenth Century: An Index and Finding Guide*, New Canaan, CT: Readex.

English and American Drama of the Nineteenth Century, New York: Readex Microprint.

English Verse Drama Database, University of Michigan, http://www.hti.-umich.edu/english/evd.

Ezell, Margaret 1993, *Writing Women's Literary History*, Baltimore: Johns Hopkins University Press.

Fitzsimmons, Linda, and Viv Gardner (eds.) 1991, *New Woman Plays*, London: Methuen.

Franceschina, John (ed.) 1997, *Sisters of Gore: Seven Gothic Melodramas by British Women, 1790–1843*, New York and London: Garland.

Frank Pettingell Collection of Plays, University of Kent, Canterbury: Harvester Press Microform Publications.

Gamer, Michael 1997, "National Supernaturalism: Joanna Baillie, Germany, and the Gothic Drama," *Theatre Survey* 38.2: 49–88.

Genuine Rejected Addresses, Presented to the Committee of Management for Drury-Lane Theatre; Preceded by that Written by Lord Byron, and Adopted by the Committee 1812, London: McMillan.

Mann, David D., and Susan Garland Mann 1996, *Women Playwrights in England, Ireland, and Scotland 1660–1823*, Bloomington and Indianapolis: Indiana University Press.

Mitford, Mary Russell 1812, Add. MS 27899, British Library, London.

Mullin, Donald 1987, *Victorian Plays: A Record of Significant Productions on the London Stage, 1837–1901*, New York: Greenwood.

Nicoll, Allardyce 1952, *A History of English Drama 1660–1900*, 3rd edn, vol. IV, Cambridge: Cambridge University Press.

Nicoll, Allardyce 1959, *A History of English Drama 1660–1900*, 3rd edn, vol. V, Cambridge: Cambridge University Press.

Nicoll, Allardyce 1955, *A History of English Drama 1660–1900*, 3rd edn, vol. VI, Cambridge: Cambridge University Press.

Powell, Kerry 1997, *Women and Victorian Theatre*, Cambridge: Cambridge University Press.

Purinton, Marjean D. 1992, *Romantic Ideology Unmasked: The Mentally Constructed Tyrannies in Dramas of William Wordsworth, Lord Byron, Percy Shelley, and Joanna Baillie*, Newark, DE: University of Delaware Press.

Scullion, Adrienne (ed.) 1996, *Female Playwrights of the Nineteenth Century*, London: Everyman.

Spender, Dale, and Carole Hayman (eds.) 1985, *"How the Vote was Won" and Other Suffragette Plays*, London: Methuen.

Wearing, J. P. 1976, *London Stage 1890–1899: A Calendar of Plays and Players*, 2 vols., Metuchen, NJ: Scarecrow Press.

PART I

In judgment

CHAPTER I

The sociable playwright and representative citizen

Tracy C. Davis

Is there such a thing as what a "normative playwright" does? If we follow the historiography of John Russell Stephens, whose *Profession of the Playwright* is the best guide we have to the experience of being a nineteenth-century writer for the stage, evidently the playwright is a self-promoting entrepreneur who moves easily in the public realm seeking preferment, and whose chance at getting a return on the investment of time and energy put into writing a piece of drama depends on the fickle attentions of managers and the degraded and ever-shifting tastes of audiences. When educated by bitter experience to know that quality does not supersede such obstacles, the "normative playwright" either persists by writing for the stage, switches to another profession altogether, or moves to other genres because evidently there is as porous a boundary between forms (plays, novels, and journalism) as between the genres of comedy and burlesque (Stephens 1992).

If we read accounts of novice playwrights, such as Benjamin Frere's 1813 *Adventures of a Dramatist*, we might be inclined to regard the rank and file of names listed by Allardyce Nicoll (in *A History of English Drama*, 1930 and 1946) and Gwenn Davis and Beverly A. Joyce (in *Drama by Women to 1900*, 1992) as simply a legion of scribblers – some hacks, some talented – who wrote out of pecuniary need and probably answered the need all too precariously. Some might regard live performance as their best chance, while others (like Frere) also tried to have their plays published and sought the favor of men like William Lane, whose Minerva Press was "exceptionally active in cultivating the production and sale of women's material" (Turner 1992: 90). In either case, we envisage playwrights who literally go out in public and literally knock on doors trying to hawk their literary wares. Knowing that many women did get their plays produced and published, an account like the following (from a young woman's diary of 1801) might reinforce how thoroughly odd it would be to imagine a playwright doing anything other than what Stephens outlines. Jane Porter, herself an aspiring author, describes socializing in the family drawing room one day and hearing the unexpected news that Covent Garden's manager was calling upon her sister Maria.

> Mr. Harris of Covent Garden Theatre was announced ... He behaved profoundly polite; and told Maria if she would take the trouble to add songs to her play of *The Runaways*, he would bring it out early next season. She consented. He paid her many compliments on the pleasure which its perusal had afforded him; and on her judgement. After his departure, Mr. Mundan [*sic*: the actor] dropt in. On being told what Mr. Harris had said, he expressed his surprise, and declared, that he never knew such an attention as the Manager calling on an author before. (27 January 1801, Folger M.b. 15)

If Munden had never heard of a manager calling on playwrights before, presumably he meant playwrights of either gender. While the visitation is singular, there is no reason to suspect that Harris's subsequent request that he wished Maria Porter to turn *The Runaways*, by then a dramatic opera, into a farce singled out her literary product for any special disrespect (22 May 1801). We might simply infer that some playwrights – however literate – really did not understand the taste of the town, no matter how sound their dramaturgy, and benefited from the advice of professional producers. Knowledge, like success, may have nothing to do with the playwright's gender.

So, while there might be normative experiences of playwriting that cut across gender lines, are there normative experiences of putting a work forward that do not? Teresa de Lauretis suggests "the female subject is the site of differences; differences that are not only sexual or only racial, economic, or (sub)cultural, but all of these together" (1986: 14), yet in considering nineteenth-century women playwrights, which – if any – differences matter? The differences in the statistics of their frequency in being produced at major theatres? The differences in the statistics of their frequency as theatre managers and lessees, and thus their reduced chances for selecting repertoire, affecting taste, challenging public opinion, and putting forward their own vision, whatever that may be? The differences resulting in what constituted women's and men's prestige, their "rightful" claim to public debate, the ease with which media, genres, or locales were yielded up to them? By these measures, gender matters very much indeed.

There is knowledge to be gained from attempting to recognize or rule out intrinsic differences between men's and women's work, but on the whole dichotomous models mislead, whether we try to trace distinctions in the plays themselves, in playwrights' access to market-places, or in their reactions to exclusion. If we – collectively – are going to change how the nineteenth-century theatre is thought about, clearly we must come up with something other than essentia-lized gender differences, a catalogue of women's work, or lamenta-tions about the uneven playing field. It appears, for example, from the financial records of the new Drury Lane Theatre after 1812 that female authors received the privilege of free admission – both Marianne Chambers and Elizabeth Inchbald show up in the accounts (Folger W. B. 393 ff 62–63) – but is it necessary to understand them as exceptions to their sex, to quantify their appearance in relation to male authors, or to speculate on why other women with free admissions, such as actresses, did *not* write plays? Does this constitute an uneven playing field, and if so is this what matters most? Should we be looking, in the first place, for the incidence of women writing plays along with the meanings of this practice in terms of social relations? Setting literary professionalism in extraliterary contexts is crucial (Turner 1992: 2), and I propose we do this with modeling inspired by social theory. The debate amongst philosophers, political theorists, cultural historians, and literary historians over the constructions of civil society usefully frames a way to understand where women were in the cultural field of playwriting, and why.

I

I begin by responding to the blank stares and politely disingenuous incantations that I received when I first proposed to organize this volume of essays: "Ah, nineteenth-century British women play-wrights. *Such as?*" My vehement assertions that women did indeed write plays – lots of women wrote lots of plays – led me beyond the twentieth-century amnesia to the last century's critical tradition that "women can't write *good* plays," then to the charge that "women *shouldn't* write plays," and finally to the prevalent opinion that women should just keep out of the public eye altogether. Feminists

point out that the social division of public and private realms is
asymmetrical by gender – in structure, ideology, and practices – so
that women's proper domain was the domestic, and men's was the
marketplace. *Ergo*, women who took their plays to the marketplace
transgressed gender norms, and to avoid damage to their sensibilities
or reputations, they frequently conducted their pecuniary, contractual, and dramaturgical activities by male proxy (a husband, father,
brother, or helpful friend). But by accepting such an explanation,
and normatively relegating women to the domestic realm, scholars
replicate the oppressive ideology, for the domestic realm is a zone as
much marked by male-defined ideology as the public realm; this is
why the phrase "head of household" connotes a male, revealing how
male authority and female subordination pervade all realms of the
social, both at home and beyond (Weintraub 1997: 29–31; Davis
1994: 65–72).

Women had a great deal at stake in writing plays, for it
represented in the composition, publication, reading, and performance widespread and important modes of participating in the
political act of sociability, construing this as politics not in the sense
of the authority of administering the state, but as Jeff Weintraub
puts it: "discussion, debate, deliberation, collective decision making,
and action in concert" amounting to citizenship in the form of
"participatory self-determination, deliberation, and conscious cooperation" (1997: 11, 14). I argue that though it matters when women
playwrights did successfully take their work into the public realm, it
matters equally that many plied the craft within their homes or
schools, because the "intimate domain of family, friendships, and
the primary group" and the "instrumental domain of the market
and formal institutions," which are in constant tension with each
other, are merely a continuum of sociability (1997: 20–21). In this
model, akin to what Bruce Robbins calls "a more relaxed, decentered pluralism (publicness as something spread liberally through
many irreducibly different collectives)" (1993: xxi), "the public" is
not simply a place, a range of eligible activities, or even an *idea*;
and it is certainly not the antithesis of "the private." Neither the
public nor the private is bounded. Neither sphere is singular. One
may garner more prestige at a major metropolitan theatre, registering strongly enough to enter the historical record, but activity in
any realm was notable activity, and in many respects it was the *same*
activity.

A lot is at stake in positing this inclusive and diverse model of sociability, representativeness, and citizenship in the era before electronic media. The theatre and newspapers were, in the nineteenth century, the mass media. In 1865, at a point prior to the boom in theatre building but after the legitimation achieved through the Theatres Regulation Act of 1843, London theatres had a weekly capacity of 228,000, a figure which multiplies to 11,856,000 annually (*Report* 1866: 295).[1] Factoring in provincial theatres would easily triple this figure at a point when the population of England and Wales was approximately 21 million. This is a vast number of people for women playwrights *not* to reach. If we think of the public sphere as an undifferentiated entity, as with late twentieth-century television, it can, in Michael Warner's words, "represent difference as other, but as an available form of subjectivity it remains unmarked" by minority entrants such as women (1993: 241). But if we broaden the scope of investigation to include other realms of women's writing activity, we not only pull into focus the dynamics of the commercial stage as a domain of activity, we *shape* the public sphere rather than taking it as a given (Carpignano *et al.* 1993: 100). As Gay Gibson Cima shows in Chapter 2, the press (like its twin public, the commercial theatre) may claim objectivity but never achieves it. The marketplace may boast democracy, yet does not facilitate it. Everyone of a certain educational and privileged class may be free to think and write, yet does not have access to readers and spectators: that phantom public which is their audience. How might a more prodigiously conceived realm of women's playwriting have affected opinion making, and why has it been the custom of theatre historians to wipe this whole slate nearly clean? Why is something valorized as legitimate cultural work, and when might this apply to one group and not to another?

Throughout modern history, women have been told they cannot do certain things, and women have protested this in order to overcome the discursive bar. The prohibition moves from category to category – in the early seventeenth century it was against women practicing statecraft or acting, in the eighteenth century it was against women preaching or writing criticism, in the nineteenth century it was against women working for pay or playwriting, and in the twentieth century it was against women composing music or directing – but the history of self and group assertion in overcoming the psychological effect of these obstacles is very much a *laissez-faire* argument about what the market will bear. Nineteenth-century

poetry, like Greek scholarship in the eighteenth century, was the
domain of men. Nineteenth-century playwriting, like professional
sports in the twentieth century, was the domain of women *if we know
where to look for them*. Paid public authorship might have been a
taboo for women, but it was a taboo frequently breached and just as
real and important in the subversions of its strictures as in its
observances.

We can no longer safely claim that "Anonymous was a woman" or
that pseudonymity served to shield women uniquely from the
calumnies of public exposure, for Catherine Judd has demonstrated
that men were more likely than women to use cross-gender pseudonyms (1995: 250–68; see also Turner 1992: 79). But the seventeenth-
century concept of woman writer as whore does seem to have been
displaced in the nineteenth century by the concept of public woman
writer as man (or usurper of masculine prerogative) (Judd 1995:
260–61). Still, this is an uneasy claim as long as gender is isolated
from other aspects of social identity (Kaplan 1992: 13). We are
unlikely to forget Voltaire's dictum that "the composition of a
tragedy requires testicles," or Byron's gracious allowance that
Joanna Baillie might be freak enough to have, or at least borrow, a
pair (Finney 1989: 17; Byron 1976: 203). While I agree with Norma
Clarke that "the history of women's writing is a history of social,
cultural and personal interaction far more complex than any history
drawn from the trajectories of men's lives can possibly convey,"
Davidoff and Hall's concept of "structured inequality" must be
carefully and cautiously justified, based on sound evidentiary principles (Clarke 1990: 26; Davidoff and Hall 1987: 272), for sometimes
inequality allows women into domains at one point and not another,
as sociologists of reputations demonstrate. The "empty field
phenomenon," for example, which Tuchman and Fortin document
for the novel may only be true for their data. They demonstrate the
relationship between the maintenance and creation of exclusionary
practices: women were allowed to enter the socially and culturally
devalued realm of novel writing circa 1840–79, but during the
novel's late Victorian period of redefinition, and especially during
Edwardian institutionalization of the form into a high cultural
product, women were squeezed out (1989: *passim*). John Russell
Stephens's lack of attention to periodicity and assumptions about the
collapsibility of gender would not excuse us from mistaking the
frequent Georgian or mid-Victorian wail "Where are the good

British playwrights?" for an "empty field phenomenon" that made drama ripe for women's incursions. The invective leveled at Joanna Baillie for presuming to have the testicular tragic or Catherine Gore for channeling the comic muse suggests that sociology needs a very different paradigm for explaining the playwriting realm, a pursuit with a 2,500-year history. On the other hand, it is probably premature to surrender to Dorothy Mermin's remark that "drama had entered a long decline, so that the paucity of female playwrights did not materially affect the literary landscape" (1993: 43).

One of the most appealing aspects of sources like Frere's memoir *Adventures of a Dramatist* is that it characterizes London as the brokerage of art, and the production and/or publication of plays as being market driven. Arriving in the capital, he proclaims: "Hail, London! Universal Mart; the central place of traffic for talents, beauty, and reputation, where, at the sound of Folly's rattle, Fashion displays her wares and every vice finds customers" (1813: vol. II, 35). As critics and historians, we need to be constantly aware that playwriting existed in relation to marketplaces, whether those marketplaces were private, provincial, or nonremunerative (though perhaps garnering other marks of social status), whether they were solely through publishing, or in the volatile realm of professional public production. Eschewing the custom of theatre history by refusing to recognize the professional as more valid than the reading, amateur, home, or school markets; or refusing to stratify the major from minor playhouses; and valorizing the mere existence and survival of women's play texts in whatever form, we may lose sight of just how extraordinarily "unprotected" dramatic writing was in a financial sense from condemnation, oblivion, and censure, in the nineteenth century as well as now, conditions that affected all aspirants, except perhaps the male managers and their sons.

Eighteenth-century moral philosophy established *laissez-faire*'s inextricable linking of private and public activities in economic pursuits (through sentimentality and capitalism) (Marshall 1986). This "associative public sphere" (as distinct from a model of the purely mercantile or the purely governmental "public") is where socializing and cultural production both occurred. It draws a contrast between the "public" (be it a salon in which women predominated, or a men's club where women were banned) and the "solitary" (the private, as distinct from the domestic) (Klein 1995; Wach 1996; Benhabib 1995; Wolf 1997), for the public, in this formulation, aligns with what is perceptible as social intercourse. Thus, the authoring of a play is an act of the associative public sphere, necessarily implicating publicity (publicness), whether it was bound for publication, home theatricals, professional production – or utter obscurity – for in common with other kinds of public acts, playwriting "stands in opposition to both doing and keeping silent" (Huet 1994: 57), just as a thinker who neither legislates nor dictates still makes interventions into the public through ideas which may incur debate and perhaps inspire action in others. This is the concrete version of civil society in which a "theatrical" model of sociability exists through symbolic display and self-representation (Robbins 1993: xix; Ryan 1990) as well as in "the structural separation between performance and audience" in which "the ideological category of the public is constructed," whether the performance in question is a chat show or a democratic election (Carpignano *et al.* 1993: 95).

Placing women thus in the associative public realm forces the question of how to regard women playwrights as "representative citizenry" when, in an official sense, they are neither representative of citizens (enfranchised men) nor fully authorized as citizens who make representations of things (such as artists). Are they representative of women sharing their class and background, of other playwrights, or perhaps of women in general through the characters they created? Do they achieve the status of the bourgeois citizen because they adopt sanitized modes of address (Deem 1996: 527), passing censorship and eschewing what is recognizably radical? If the closet drama is supposed to designate that which is "not dramatic" or "not stageable," what is at stake in power and prestige, especially in recent claims by Catherine Burroughs that the closet celebrated women's cultural worth (1997: 143–68). Is the genteel authoress *more* of a representative citizen in not publishing or professionally producing her plays? Or is her niche – as an adaptor and translator, or a children's dramatist, or an author of recital pieces in dialect – indicative of the "broad church" which we will write into the historiography of representative citizenry? Shall we let women succeed on their own terms?

Finally, in considering the valences of public and private, how are women's plays used as platforms to debate (or to represent) things of concern? There is, of course, the likelihood that the major and minor issues of the day were dramatized by women, and that this variously supported and challenged the status quo (Burke 1996).

Elsewhere in this volume, Susan Carlson, Denise Walen, Beth Friedman-Romell, and Heidi Holder take up precisely this point. But additionally, how did women playwrights interpose themselves into the discursive realms of the public and private and of communities of speech and action which I am calling sociability? When Baillie writes to another woman about retiring to her study to prepare the last edition of her plays, she illustrates this issue beautifully:

I have been much occupied since last [J]une in correcting the proof sheets of my new publication. I thought I had done with all this business, but circumstances arose to make me desirous of leaving all my Dramas in print corrected under my own eye, so I was obliged to throw aside the indolence & desire of quiet & privacy so nature[al] to old aye [*sic*]. (12 December 1835)

In other words, retiring into her study to correct proofs constituted a public act, for it would result in publicity, publicness, and posterity over which she exerted agency. Even the housebound woman had many ways to be public. Jane Porter describes how, in theatricals put up by family and friends, an audience of twenty people made her fearful, yet the next night's crowd of fifty people "terrified to death all of us" because of the size of the audience and because it included individuals who were not part of the Porters' regular circle (25 and 26 May 1801). Thus, even within the home theatrical, varying degrees of exposure were incurred when audiences expanded beyond the close circles of everyday sociability.

This sets into context questions about the "significance" of women's dramatic activity (significant to whom, for what reasons, and with what chance of registering instrumentally on prevailing evolutionary models of historiography) and opens up questions about the "significance" of different kinds of data as well as individual figures themselves. At this point in our work charting this terrain, a knoll is as noteworthy as a mountain. I no more want to notice only "significant" women and judge them only by measures of professional notoriety and influence than to restrict myself to using nineteenth-century criteria of seeking "women of virtue" or "feminine writing" (Ezell 1993: 68–69, 94–96). But I still strive to understand how gender matters. The tropes in Frere's *Adventures of a Dramatist* which depict the playwright as eccentric in the eyes of fellow beings, or which depict high-flown ambition as noble in contrast to the crass exigencies of commerce, may have very different valences when we think of how the dramatist was a gendered person and what ensued from this fact. Frere's allusion, early on, that relatives questioned his soundness of mind when he became immersed in composing his play, to the extent that they considered committing him to a madhouse, might read comically from him while from a woman such as Georgina Weldon, who was committed by her husband to a lunatic asylum, it is deeply serious, potentially tragic, and ridden with the fear and loathing inherent in a deeply misogynist culture (Owen 1990: 160–67). Likewise, the dramatist's lengthy ruminations on ambition might amount to the flight of Icarus, aiming high but with a calamitous result, while the same ruminations on the part of Icarus's wife or mother might be regarded as a ludicrous display of conceit with no promise in either their conception or execution. The cartographer has an advantage over us by having absolute standards of measurement to distinguish the knoll from the mountain, the hillock from the promontory, and the forest from the bluff. For historians dealing with gender, there is no counterpart to sea level from which we can measure the striations of elevation, and no fully trustworthy classificatory or numerical standards for distinguishing one figure from another, or even the characteristics of an individual from a pack. What is genuinely safe and appropriate to assume or assert on gender grounds is entirely up for debate.

It is promising, I think, to consider how in the nineteenth century occupation became the core identity for men, and what it represented when women attempted to move in and claim something so prominently public as the identity of a dramatist when that dramatist's trajectory was toward the commercial stage. Scholarly learning and writerly ability had to be accounted for, and often explained away, in women. Elizabeth Carter's penchant for housekeeping warranted remarking alongside her translation of the Greek Stoic Epictetus, as much as Baillie's predeliction for making her own pies and puddings appears in an anecdote about Sotheby relaying the exciting news to her of a provincial revival of *De Monfort*: an anecdote related by none other than Frances Kemble (1878: vol. III, 272).[2] Even in the wake of Elizabeth Inchbald and Hannah Cowley – economically successful playwrights who could be regarded as prototypes – the woman playwright was neither a stable nor an uncontested category. Women made gains during the century's course, but the idea of separate spheres retained discursive force.

However elusive the realm of privacy, where an authentic self exists free from others' expectations, women's publicity in horizontal and vertical senses had official, if not real, borders.[3]

As Laura Thatcher Ulrich masterfully demonstrates, women's labour may exist as the uncelebrated, and even unpaid, warp to the woof threads of masculinized capitalism (1991). Bernard Miège argues that contemporary cultural labor is determined "by the place it occupies in the relations of production," and that whether a performance is "in an artisanal, a capitalist or a non-market form (amateurism)" it is all still within the capitalist relations of production (1989: 25). These are useful reminders that "separate spheres" is not necessarily the optimal metaphor for understanding relations of a playwright to her environment (or posterity). Working in nonmarket (amateur) circumstances does not necessarily constitute marginalization. Nancy Gutierrez argues this point with respect to Renaissance closet drama, making a case for the political content of women's dramatic output (1991: 233–52); the same idea is applicable, I think, to later playwrights' status as writers and workers in the theatre industry. If they do not sell their work to commercial theatres, if they write with profit for only an amateur, home, or school market, or even if they accrue no payment of any kind for their dramatic writing, they still exist in relation to others who do these things. They are not lesser, or necessarily even different, but are contiguous with others who pursue the same craft. Thinking otherwise would render Hannah More lesser than Elizabeth Inchbald, rather than focused in another direction with another purpose.

II

It is germane to ask if the dramatic output of women justifies positing their work as a coherent minor literature on its own terms, and if so, what those terms should be. Although Deleuze and Guattari use a psychoanalytic base to define a "minor literature," their basic criteria resonate suggestively for further historical scrutiny. Referring specifically to Franz Kafka, minor literature, they claim, is not necessarily the literature of a minority, and comes not from a minor language, but is constructed by a minority within a major language (their chief example being early twentieth-century Jewish literature from Warsaw and Prague written in German). Such

authors experience the "impossibility of not writing" because a
national consciousness exists through literature. When one's verna-
cular language is so localized and the minority elite's language is so
distinct from mass culture, a minor literature deterritorializes in
ways "appropriate for strange and minor usage" (1986: 16; see also
Bensmaia 1994), like African–American syntax in the urban USA, or
Ibsen's use of Danish to write plays of Norwegian life while exiled in
Germany and Italy.

In a minor literature, everything is political, so every individual
intrigue has political significance connecting, for example, familial
concerns immediately to environmental context. Major literatures
can luxuriate in an Oedipal triangle, but minor literatures necessarily have a "political program." This accords with feminist critics'
desire to find political valences in women's writing and to elevate
commentary to the level of allegory, as in Ntozake Shange's celebration of Frantz Fanon's "jungle breathing" (1984: 22; see also
Gutierrez 1991). Thus, in minor literatures, everything has a collective value: "Indeed, scarcity of talent is in fact beneficial and allows
the conception of something other than a literature of masters"
(Deleuze and Guattari 1986: 17). And while consensus amongst a
minor literature's writers is unnecessary, paradoxically each individual's statements constitute common action. This suits an image of
women playwrights as cultural guerrillas, battling gender bias on
stage and in rehearsal halls, or retreating to their boudoirs to nurse
tender scars, but always having to prove something beyond their
own individual worth. Deleuze and Guattari assert that "if the
writer is in the margins or completely outside his or her fragile
community, this situation allows the writer all the more possibility to
express another possible community and to forge the means for
another consciousness and another sensibility" (1986: 17). This is an
idea, of course, and not proof, but it is provocative to think of
nineteenth-century women playwrights as the revolutionary vanguard, akin to how Beckett and Joyce rank as Irish authors in the
history of Modernism. When using a language "not their own" –
French in Beckett's case or English in Joyce's, or 2,500 years of
Aristotelean dramatic theory as a possible corollary for women – the
minority is susceptible to accusations of unsuitability on the grounds
of undereducation and the impropriety of literary aspiration. But
this also explains what is at stake in persisting, and why authors did
so in many guises. The clear answer: "steal the baby from its crib,

walk the tightrope" (Deleuze and Guattari 1986: 19). In other words: appropriate what is already culturally half yours, take it to town, and summon every reservoir of strength, tact, and mental discipline to keep balanced.

Of course, minor figures are not the same thing as a minor literature. The distinction has to do with the security of one's claims to public air time, and the degree to which one strives to adopt without critique the standards of the major literature. On just these terms, Frances Kemble launches into Mrs. Norton's new play in 1831:

What a terrible piece! what atrocious situations and ferocious circumstances! – tinkering, starving, hanging – like a chapter out of the Newgate Calendar. But, after all, she's in the right; she has given the public what they desire, given them what they like. Of course it made one cry horribly; but then of course one cries when one hears of people reduced by sheer craving to eat nettles and cabbage-stalks. Destitution, absolute hunger, cold and nakedness, are no more subjects for artistic representation than sickness, disease, and the *real* details of idiocy, madness, and death. All art should be an idealized, elevated representation (not imitation) of nature; and when beggary and low vice are made the themes of the dramatist, as in this piece ... they seem to me to be clothing their inspirations in wood or lead, or some base material, instead of gold or ivory. (Kemble 1878: vol. III, 36–37)

This resonates with Neoclassical ideas preferring elevated dramatic incident, character, and setting, as if pitting Schiller against Zola. Kemble concedes that Norton knows the taste of the town and the fundamentals of theatrical dramaturgy, reserving her criticism as an expression of taste taking the form of a judgment upon dramatic theory. But it is also a political remark insofar as Kemble's preference to banish the destitute from dramatic address is a very loaded position to take in 1831, the year before the first Reform Act. Jane Moody's refutation of boundaries between the cultural fields of the theatre and politics, as a repudiation of the nonsensical "mental theatre" of Regency dramaturgy, might well be extended to such specific instances of dramatic opinion throughout the century, in line with Mary Waldron's work on Ann Yearsley's *Earl Goodwin* (Moody 1996: 223–44; Waldron 1996: 173–205). By Kemble's criteria, Mrs. Norton's play is a robust weed: too much like popular taste and too little like art. Whether it fulfills the criteria of a minor literature depends on longer historical trends represented in other women's

work, and the critique brought to bear on prevailing dramatic
theory and production values (the "languages" of "major" theatre).

III

So, in conclusion, the question is not were there women playwrights,
but where they were, and the consequences of this within the
associative public sphere. The conventions of theatre history send us
to look on the commercial stages, especially in London and specifically in the West End, giving even higher preference to the most
aesthetically prestigious houses. While many women had plays
produced in such venues, it takes more than mere presence (to
borrow a proverb) to make a house a home. In all likelihood,
women's plays remained an oddity on the commercial stage for
more reasons than just their numerical inferiority. The strictures on
women's sociability meant that they spent much of their lives at
home; supposedly, this was the saving grace for any woman with a
"room of her own" and literary ambition to write novels within the
comfort and sanctity of domestic privacy. Yet why should we suppose
that the custom of composing moral plays for school or home
production – a practice most famously credited to Hannah More – is
any less significant as a historical phenomenon than Macready's
championing of the plays of Lord Lytton or George Eliot's success as
a novelist? Or that because productions in schools and drawing
rooms are not reviewed in *The Times* they are of insignificant social
or political consequence for the students and parents or friends and
relations who gathered there to perform, watch, or even just listen to
a reading? Or that despite their prevalence in sociable contexts
other than the commercial stage, women's plays have no coherence
as a class of texts, and therefore cannot be regarded as "a literature"
(minor or otherwise).

We need to investigate women's lives *and* their work in a context
for interpretation that sets theatrical activity within the options for
sociability construed as politics by "discussion, debate, deliberation,
collective decision making, and action in concert" (Weintraub 1997:
11). Florence Bell wittily epitomises this in her instructions for *Fairy
Tale Plays and How to Act Them* (1899), addressed to children and their
parents:

Some people prefer to make the auditorium quite dark during the
performance. Personally, I find this depressing at an amateur play, which is

a social occasion as much as a dramatic one . . . The methods of Bayreuth or of the Lyceum, which I have heard invoked with great gravity in discussing this particular question, do not seem to me to bear upon it much. (xv)

Playwrights, thus, operate within their own (appropriate) communities of speech and action, while they themselves are poised between doing and silence, in the "impossibility of not writing" (Deleuze and Guattari 1986: 16). This is potentially revolutionary, and potentially not. Susan Carlson's observation "that comedy can be an instigator of social change as well as a blueprint for plurality" speaks to the circumstances by which a playwright presented her work as well as what is argued within a play (1991: 161). Social history needs to be closely investigated in tandem with dramatic theory to seek explanation for puzzling ambiguities and what some critics called blatant ineptitude. Consider Emma Robinson's *Richelieu in Love*, which was for at least eight years banned by the Lord Chamberlain. When produced at the Haymarket in 1852, a reviewer for a periodical addressed to architects and building contractors remarked that for a play by a lady it was "rather a bold one, and chiefly remarkable for terse and sparkling writing, but it is for the most part the sparkle of pounded ice, – there is a want of warmth and feeling. Still the piece amuses" (*Builder*, 6 November 1852: 709). The valences of the last sentence, "Still the piece amuses," speak volumes, for the play was billed as a drama. Women's writing can underpin political culture, just by virtue of existing in the wake of such barbed praise, but at the very least by investigating it we will undermine historiography and challenge the comfortable categories of activities and the genres that they contain.

As a sociable playwright and a representative citizen, the female dramatist entered into a contractual relationship every time she put pen to paper. She was still a daughter, wife, or mother, with the reciprocally unbalanced legal and caretaking obligations that entailed, negotiating her writing with these responsibilities. She was still a friend, neighbor, and parishioner, with the visitations, exchanges, and observations involved in fulfilling those roles. Though not a citizen of the state, enfranchised for her opinions, she nevertheless partook in the cultural life of the nation, reading about and performing in its rituals, and by writing also contributing to her class rituals' solidification or evolutionary change. And by writing she also staked her claim as a colleague of other writers and creative people, whether her colleagueship was enacted or symbolic, and

whether her coparticipants in the theatre were mutually known or
not. She was, in Jeremy Bentham's sense of the term, socially
engineered and yet she also exerted agency through writing, and a
particular kind of agency through *dramatic* writing in pursuing her
interests. She became an active participant, a member of many
communities, deliberately signaling the dialectic tensions between
household and marketplace, acting in concert with all other women
of her kind. The outcome of this varied amongst women: Jane Scott,
Melinda Young, and Sarah Lane achieved local celebrity whilst
Joanna Baillie, Catherine Gore, Emma Robinson, and Felicia
Hemans came to national prominence; Florence Bell, Constance
Beerbohm, Harriet Glazebrook, and Lillie Davis wrote dozens of
texts for amateurs whilst Elizabeth Maxwell (Braddon) and Fanny
Kemble were produced by professionals across the nation; and
Elizabeth Inchbald, Marie Saker, Teresa de Camp, and Isabel
Bateman were actresses who wrote plays, whilst Katharine Bradley
and Edith Cooper (as Michael Field), Isabella Harwood (as Ross
Neil), and Mary Russell Mitford were verse playwrights who also
wrote in other genres and forms. What is true across their ranks,
however, is an economy of exchange instrumentally connected in
multiply overlapped spheres, "assisting the equitable negotiation or
arbitration of competing interests through democratic processes"
(Curran 1991: 29–30). Women enjoyed different privileges than men,
just as women in different classes and regions experienced different
opportunities, but if they are classified as a counterpublic sphere – as
opposed to one integrated with but not necessarily visible to what is
historicized as the public and private – it sets them aside, oppositionally and marginally, rather than as minor voices within the dominant
culture and historiography. Because they are in no way unified,
either mythically or formally, they are not a counterpublic but rather
part of the public sphere struggling with the structures and settings
of sociability leading to representation.

　　Bruce Robbins writes that "to belong to the public sphere has
always meant to wield some share of the ruling power" (1993: xx).
While this kind of belonging is rarely within the grasp of women
playwrights, we see through their life histories and critical reception
what is at stake in reaching for their share. If, as Carpignano, *et al.*
assert, "the formation of public opinion becomes an act of govern-
ing" and "Public opinion becomes a matter of public relations"
(1993: 100), we start to understand the forces that strove to keep

playwriting a masculine occupation, that continually named men's plays as normative and women's plays as gender-marked, and that encourage forgetfulness – despite overwhelming evidence in standard sources – that there were nineteenth-century British women playwrights. What we are urgently pressed to explore, at this juncture, are the contours of their work in the context of their own and others' ruling power, relative to public opinion and public relations of more than just the official discourse and traditional categories of theatre and literary practice.

NOTES

I am grateful to Linda Fitzsimmons and Margaret Ezell, who both offered encouragement and critical responses to this work in its latter stages.

1   London music halls, on a one-a-night system, had five times this capacity.

2   As Clarke argues, "this, in its insidious ways, defines woman in relation to man every bit as much as heterosexual marriage might contain an identity as a writer within the public facade of a married woman. While the work and lives of women warrant complex modeling, we will do well to remember that it was women of all classes, but not men, who had to uphold "their fundamental entitlement to speak and write" (1990: 26).

3   Here I echo Dawn Keetley's sense of a "permeable border" between private and public, but in the context outlined by George Chittolini of the horizontal and vertical structures of "clans, kin groups, courtly circles, factions, and parties" which are "private in that they are not always formalized like public institutions" yet are "draped in institutional dignity" while outside official systems. The sociability of literary circles might easily be added to this group (Keetley 1996: 188; Chittolini 1995: S40; Kaplan 1992; Clarke 1990).

REFERENCES

Baillie, Joanna, MS Gen. 1835; letter 12 December, 542/7, University of Glasgow: Special Collections.
Bell, Mrs. Hugh [Florence] 1899, *Fairy Tale Plays and How to Act Them*, London: Longman, Green, and Co.
Benhabib, Seyla 1995, "The Pariah and her Shadow: Hannah Arendt's Biography of Rahel Varnhagen," *Political Theory*, 23.1: 5–24.
Bensmaia, Réda 1994, "On the Concept of Minor Literature: From Kafka to Kateb Yacine," *Gilles Deleuze and the Theatre of Philosophy*, ed. Constantine V. Boundas and Dorothea Olkowski, New York and London: Routledge, 213–28.

Builder 6 November 1852: 709.

Burke, Sally 1996, *American Feminist Playwrights: A Critical History*, New York: Twayne.

Burroughs, Catherine B. 1997, *Closet Stages: Joanna Baillie and the Theater Theory of British Romantic Women Writers*, Philadelphia: University of Pennsylvania Press.

Byron, Lord 1976, *Letters and Journals*, vol. v, ed. Leslie Marchand, Cambridge, MA: Harvard University Press.

Carlson, Susan 1991, *Women and Comedy: Rewriting the British Theatrical Tradition*, Ann Arbor: University of Michigan Press.

Carpignano, Paolo, Robin Andersen, Stanley Aronowitz, and William DiFazio 1993, "Chatter in the Age of Electronic Reproduction: Talk Television and the 'Public Mind,'" *The Phantom Public Sphere*, ed. Bruce Robbins, Minneapolis: University of Minnesota Press, 93–120.

Chittolini, George 1995, "The 'Private', the 'Public', the State," *Journal of Modern History* 67: S34–61.

Clarke, Norma 1990, *Ambitious Heights: Writing, Friendship, Love – The Jewsbury Sisters, Felicia Hemans, and Jane Walsh Carlyle*, London and New York: Routledge.

Curran, James 1991, "Rethinking the Media as Public Sphere," *Communication and Citizenship: Journalism and the Public Sphere in the New Media Age*, ed. Peter Dahlgren and Colin Sparks, London: Routledge, 27–57.

Davidoff, Leonore, and Catherine Hall 1987, *Family Fortunes: Men and Women of the English Middle Class, 1780–1850*, London: Hutchinson.

Davis, Gwenn, and Beverly A. Joyce 1992, *Drama by Women to 1900: A Bibliography of American and British Authors*, Toronto and Buffalo: University of Toronto Press.

Davis, Tracy C. 1994, "Private Women in the Public Realm," *Theatre Survey*, 35.1: 65–72.

Deem, Melissa D. 1996, "From Bobbitt to SCUM: Re-membernent, Scatological Rhetorics, and Feminist Strategies in the Contemporary United States," *Public Culture* 8: 511–39.

Deleuze, Gilles, and Felix Guattari 1986, *Kafka: Toward a Minor Literature*, Minneapolis: University of Minnesota Press.

Drury Lane Theatre *circa* 1814, account books, W.b. 393, Folger Shakespeare Library.

Ezell, Margaret 1993, *Writing Women's Literary History*, Baltimore: Johns Hopkins University Press.

Finney, Gail 1989, *Women in Modern Drama: Freud, Feminism, and European Theater at the Turn of the Century*, Ithaca, NY: Cornell University Press.

Frere, Benjamin 1813, *Adventures of a Dramatist on a Journey to the London Managers*, 2 vols., [London: William Lane].

Gutierrez, Nancy A. 1991, "Valuing *Mariam*: Genre Study and Feminist Analysis," *Tulsa Studies in Women's Literature*, 10.2: 233–52.

Huet, Marie-Hélène 1994, "The Revolutionary Sublime," *Eighteenth-Century Studies*, 28.1: 51–64.

Judd, Catherine A. 1995, "Male Pseudonyms and Female Authority in Victorian England," *Literature and the Marketplace: Nineteenth-Century British Publishing and Reading Practices*, ed. John O. Jordan and Robert L. Patten, Cambridge: Cambridge University Press, 250–68.

Kaplan, Deborah 1992, *Jane Austen Among Women*, Baltimore: Johns Hopkins University Press.

Keetley, Dawn 1996, "The Power of 'Personation': Actress Anna Cora Mowatt and the Literature of Women's Public Performance in Nine-teenth-Century America," *American Transcendental Quarterly*, n.s. 10.3: 187–200.

Kemble, Frances Ann 1878, *Record of a Girlhood*, 3 vols., London: Richard Bentley.

Klein, Lawrence E. 1995, "Gender and the Public/Private Distinction in the Eighteenth Century: Some Questions about Evidence and Ana-lytic Procedure," *Eighteenth-Century Studies*, 2.1: 97–109.

Lauretis, Teresa de (ed.) 1986, *Feminist Studies/Critical Studies*, Bloomington: Indiana University Press.

Marshall, David 1986, *The Figure of Theatre: Shaftesbury, Defoe, Adam Smith, and George Eliot*, New York: Columbia University Press.

Mellor, Anne K. 1994, "Joanna Baillie and the Counter-Public Sphere," *Studies in Romanticism*, 33.4: 559–67.

Mermin, Dorothy 1993, *Godiva's Ride: Women of Letters in England, 1830–1880*, Bloomington: Indiana University Press.

Miège, Bernard 1989, *The Capitalization of Cultural Production*, New York: International General.

Moody, Jane 1996, "'Fine Word, Legitimate!': Toward a Theatrical History of Romanticism," *Texas Studies in Literature and Language* 38:3/4: 223–44.

Nicoll, Allardyce 1955, *A History of English Drama, 1660–1900*, 3rd edn, vol. IV, Cambridge: Cambridge University Press.

Nicoll, Allardyce 1959, *A History of English Drama, 1660–1900*, 3rd edn, vol. V, Cambridge: Cambridge University Press.

Owen, Alex 1990, *The Darkened Room: Women, Power and Spiritualism in Late Victorian England*, Philadelphia: University of Pennsylvania Press.

Porter, Jane 1801, diary 27 January, 25 and 26 May, M.b.15, Folger Shakespeare Library.

Report from the Select Committee on Theatrical Licenses and Regulations; Together with the Proceedings of the Committee, Minutes of Evidence, and Appendix, 1866.

Robbins, Bruce 1993, "Introduction: the Public as Phantom," *The Phantom Public Sphere*, ed. Bruce Robbins, Minneapolis: University of Minnesota Press, vii–xxvi.

Ryan, Mary P. 1990, *Women in Public: Between Banners and Ballots, 1825–1880*, Baltimore: Johns Hopkins University Press.

Shange, Ntozake 1984, *See No Evil: Prefaces, Essays and Accounts 1976–1983*, San Francisco: Momo's Press.

Stephens, John Russell 1992, *The Profession of the Playwright: British Theatre 1800–1900*, Cambridge: Cambridge University Press.

Tuchman, Gaye, and Nina E. Fortin 1989, *Edging Women Out: Victorian Novelists, Publishers, and Social Change*, New Haven: Yale University Press.

Turner, Cheryl 1992, *Living by the Pen: Women Writers in the Eighteenth Century*, London: Routledge.

Ulrich, Laura Thatcher 1991, *A Midwife's Tale: the Life of Martha Ballard, Based on her Diary, 1785–1812*, New York: Vintage.

Wach, Howard M. 1996, "Civil Society, Moral Identity, and the Liberal Public Sphere: Manchester and Boston, 1810–40," *Social History*, 21.3: 281–303.

Waldron, Mary 1996, *Lactilla, Milkwoman of Clifton: The Life and Writings of Ann Yearsley, 1753–1806*, Athens, GA: University of Georgia Press.

Warner, Michael 1993, "The Mass Public and the Mass Subject," *The Phantom Public Sphere*, ed. Bruce Robbins, Minneapolis: University of Minnesota Press, 234–56.

Weintraub, Jeff 1997, "The Theory and Politics of the Public/Private Distinction," *Public and Private in Thought and Practice: Perspectives on a Grand Dichotomy*, ed. Jeff Weintraub and Krishan Kumar, Chicago: University of Chicago Press, 1–42.

Wolf, Alan 1997, "Public and Private in Theory and Practice: Some Implications of an Uncertain Boundary," *Public and Private in Thought and Practice: Perspectives on a Grand Dichotomy*, ed. Jeff Weintraub and Krishan Kumar, Chicago and London: University of Chicago Press, 182–203.

CHAPTER 2

"To be public as a genius and private as a woman"
The critical framing of nineteenth-century British women playwrights

Gay Gibson Cima

Playwrights typically thrive in the marketplace only if critics provide a supportive framework for their plays, and critics flourish only if dramatists provide interesting material for review. This symbiotic relationship develops most favorably for playwrights when both sets of writers move comfortably and equitably within the same social sphere and discourse, shaping public debates and policy through the process which Jeff Weintraub, as Tracy Davis explains, calls "sociability" (see Chapter 1 above). Nineteenth-century British women dramatists, however, rarely circulated within precisely the same social circumstances or spoke from the same situated discourse as their reviewers. Critics, typically male, often spent their days and evenings together in the halls of Parliament or in their clubs or taverns, formulating a sense of collectivity through their interactions. Their individual reviews reflected and, in fact, helped shape the very sphere of sociability that generated their commentaries in the first place. Indeed, critics sometimes even wrote interchangeably, pinch-hitting for each other without altering their bylines. Their individual voices held weight partly because they emerged from a particular public realm which, for all practical purposes, was off-limits for women critics as well as dramatists. Only within the public realms of the suffrage, socialist, and socialite press could women critics and playwrights more easily develop a symbiotic network.

Within the mainstream press, young male critics – often themselves dramatists or law students studying for the bar – were not necessarily favorably predisposed toward female playwrights. In fact, as Ellen Donkin has demonstrated, by 1800 male critics were anxious about the inroads that had been created by eighteenth-century women playwrights, and a backlash had begun. Critics started to represent playwriting as a gendered, manly activity

(Donkin 1995: 177–81). For many critics, this was an act of self-validation: at least *40 percent* of the men who reviewed Victorian plays were themselves dramatists (Kent 1980: 33). Already feeling socially marginalized, they were determined to forestall the feminization of their profession.

Even in the provinces, where by mid-century the sheer number of publications, the family owned status of the newspapers, and the lively world of amateur theatricals seemingly offered women critics easier access to the press, male critics nearly eclipsed women. Only one woman, Pearl Mary Theresa Craigie, appears in Christopher Kent and Tracy C. Davis's listings of 241 Victorian theatre critics (Davis 1984; Kent 1980: 38; Kent 1986). Men cornered easier access not only to the quarterly and monthly journals, but also to the daily newspapers, frequently writing for multiple papers and in some cases remaining on the same staff for decades.

Despite numerous challenges, eighteenth-century dramatists such as Elizabeth Inchbald (1753–1821) and Frances Moore Brooke (1724–89) managed to gain access to mainstream careers as playwright-critics. Brooke even launched her own weekly review with the defiantly redundant title *Old Maid, by Mary Singleton, Spinster* (1755–56) (Adburgham 1972: 116). By the 1820s, however, few women could provide the more substantial funding required to start a new paper. Usually that funding was provided by large syndicates, partnerships which historically avoided innovations and were much less likely to hire a woman critic (Asquith 1978: 103).

Nonetheless, a number of women did enter the public sphere as journalists in nineteenth-century England, establishing "early forms of political and feminist journalism" (Hunter 1992: 687). They wrote for a variety of venues, covering political events and advocating divorce reform like Harriet Martineau on the *Daily News* (1852–69) or championing women's voting rights like Lydia Becker on *Woman's Suffrage* (1870–90). They contributed to women's journals such as the *Englishwoman's Domestic Magazine* (1852) and the *Lady's Newspaper and Pictorial Times* (1847–63) (Hunter 1992: 686). Women also acted as joint editors, with their husbands. Anna Maria Hall of the *St. James's Magazine*, Mary Howitt of *Howitt's Journal*, and Mrs. Christian Isobel Johnstone of the *Inverness Courier* (1817–24) and *Tait's Edinburgh Magazine* (1834–36) all edited publications, and Johnstone in particular printed the work of women writers. Provincial women typically wrote for family newspapers: Catherine Young in the 1840s published in her father's *Sun,* Euphemia Margaret Tait in 1882 penned articles for her family's paper, and Emilie Marshall reported for her father's *Northern Echo.* While the Institute of Journalists listed only twelve London-based women reporters in 1885, within five years that number multiplied five times, and the Society of Women Journalists, launched in 1894, boasted sixty-nine members by 1900 (Hunter 1992: 689). Although most women journalists were not university graduates, Girton graduates Rachel Cook, Helena Swanwick, and Henrietta Moeller (H. B. Temple) built careers as editors and reporters (Hunter 1992: 690).

At least one male editor, W. T. Stead of the *Pall Mall Gazette* (1880–90), deemed women journalists more reliable than men, and paid them equal wages. Through the *Gazette,* journalists such as Hulda Friederichs, Flora Shaw, Susan Carpenter, and Lady Colin Campbell gained experience. Friederichs later parlayed her position into an editorship of the *Westminster Budget,* and Shaw wrote for *The Times* and *Guardian* as well as the *Gazette* (Hunter 1992: 687). Literary and art critics like Anna Brownell Jameson (1794–1860), who published her study of the Shakespearean *Characteristics of Women* in 1832, typically did not write journalistic theatrical criticism, but their critical acts deserve attention as well (Schlueter and Schlueter 1988: 248–49).

However, mid-century journalist Eliza Lynn Linton (1822–98) encapsulates the paradoxical positioning of these woman writers and the pressures they faced in public debates: while Linton advocated "female emancipation" in her writings for the radical *English Review,* she denounced it for Charles Dickens's *Household Words* (Griffiths 1992: 374). In 1898 Arnold Bennett, the editor of *Woman* and publisher of *Journalism for Women,* illustrated the typical nineteenth-century attitude toward critics like Linton who dared to enter public space: "in Fleet Street there are not two sexes, but two species – journalists and women journalists, and we treat the species differently ... femininity is an absolution, not an accident" (quoted in Adburgham 1972: 272). Male journalists simply could not envision women as a part of their "species" of cultural worker, even after the fact. They had grown so accustomed to completely different realms of sociability that the inclusion of women seemed like heresy. In July of 1889, a London journalist decried the way "journalistic damsels" had launched an "invasion of Fleet Street's sanctity ... hurrying up to the offices about midnight with their 'copy'" (quoted in Hunter

1992: 688). Many men felt that these new journalistic freaks sullied the inner sanctum of journalism itself.

Despite this resistance, the New Journalism of the 1880s prompted a rise in the number of British women journalists, though they did not, as their American counterparts did, customarily move into theatrical reviewing. New journalistic features such as "women's pages, gossip columns, sports coverage, parliamentary sketches and political commentaries, the extensive use of illustrations, sensational exposés, and the 'Occasional Notes' columns were quite common-place between 1850 and 1880," and editors like W. T. Stead added to that mix the concept of the newspaper as an instrument of the people's will to force government change (Baylen 1992: 37–38). As the New Journalism gained ground, writers like "Wilhelmina Wimble" justified the work of British women reporters by comparing them to the growing number of successful women novelists: "Their alert interest in the many sides of life, their quick perceptive qualities, their sense of character, their light if somewhat superficial handling of a theme, tend, with sufficient training, to adapt them for the New Journalism" (quoted in Hunter 1992: 689). The gradual inclusion of women critics in the realm of journalistic sociability was accommodated, then, by labeling women "narrators" rather than "reporters." Women were to write of things of the heart and senses rather than of the mind and reason.

A select group of nineteenth-century British women succeeded as theatre critics despite the multiple barriers they faced. Some found a place in the socialist press.[1] Unlike the mainstream newspapers increasingly driven by profit motives, radical labor papers were fueled by debates. Women could justify writing reviews for the socialist press because they were ostensibly aligning themselves with moral causes rather than robbing men of jobs. And labor papers, like the mainstream press, realized the importance of covering the arts.

That opened the door for Eleanor Marx, who in 1890 not only published her translation of Henrik Ibsen's *The Lady from the Sea* but also acted as an assistant editor and reviewer for the socialist monthly *Time*. Marx and her partner Edward Aveling (also known as Alec Nelson) each contributed "Dramatic Notes" to *Time* until its demise at the end of the year, when they continued in like fashion reviewing for *Tinsley's Magazine*, "a shilling monthly" (Kapp 1977: 362, 393, 442). In the March 1891 issue of *Time*, Marx collaborated with Israel Zangwill on "A Doll's House Repaired," a parody of the alternative ending to *A Doll's House* that debunked the "English sense of morality" (Kapp 1977: 517).

Sometimes a desire for knowledge about forbidden topics prompted women to become theatre critics. When Fabian socialist Annie Besant compared West and East End theatres and music halls for her journal *Our Corner* in August 1886, she asked George Bernard Shaw to escort her so that she could investigate the nearby public houses full of dancing and amusements (Peters 1980: 40). A similar curiosity drove socialite Violet Hunt, who acted as a theatre critic for *Black and White* in 1891. Her position was regarded as "a singular honor for a woman," but carried a certain risk for an unattached woman (Belford 1990: 102). Already embroiled in a flirtation with her editor, the diplomat Oswald Crawfurd, at the time of her appointment, Hunt impetuously arranged an assignation with another suitor, a British lawyer. They were to meet at the Aquarium, "an amusement park that displayed freaks," an assignation that she regarded as safer than attending the theatre with him. In her diary she reflected that "He did not treat me casually or any different ... as if I had lost ground by going alone with him. It was an awful thing to do but one must have a lark sometimes – and worse, I should dearly like to go [to] the theatre with him as he continually asks me to" (quoted in Belford 1990: 79).

Hunt's reviews drew attention because they were strong-minded and independent, sometimes even patronizing: Ibsen, for example, was "a dramatist of a nationality only just beginning to dare to think for itself" (quoted in Belford 1990: 82). Other editors voiced an interest in hiring Hunt, but Crawfurd, by then Hunt's lover as well as her editor, counseled her not to take on multiple jobs. He jealously advised that "by working in an office she might jeopardize her position in society," so she did not, as her male colleagues did, write for numerous dailies (quoted in Belford 1990: 92). There were curious gaps in Crawfurd's protective instincts, however. He felt free to sit at Hunt's feet in a box at the Tivoli while, disguised with the help of a feather boa, she enjoyed music hall entertainments. Of these theatrical evenings Hunt privately wrote: "Under these maddening influences I am a different woman or a woman revealed. I cry and laugh; anything but be the practical cynical woman I usually am" (quoted in Belford 1990: 92). Hunt's critical legacy threatens to disappear, as she is not mentioned in standard sources such as *An Encyclopedia of British Women Writers* (Schlueter and Schlueter 1988: 240–42).

Another socialite, American-born Pearl Craigie (1867–1906), wrote plays as well as criticism. Lady Randolph Spencer Churchill's *Anglo-Saxon Review* published her scripts as well as her reviews of contemporary French plays (Sullivan 1984: 18–19). Having settled in England as a child, Craigie moved comfortably in British social circles. From 1889–90, in the middle of her brief, disastrous marriage with the well-connected Reginald Walpole Craigie, she wrote criticism for the journal *Life*. She reviewed both theatre and art, launching a successful career as a novelist and playwright as well as a critic (Kent 1980: 38). Craigie's finesse at socializing in upper-crust circles advanced her career, but exhausted her when coupled with the "immense labour" of writing articles (quoted in Harding 1987: 36). She soon retreated with her young son to her parents' house, writing novels and plays under the pseudonym John Oliver Hobbes. By 1895, Craigie was elected President of the Society of Women Journalists (Harding 1987: 23).

Perhaps the success of these socialists and socialites is due to the broader definition of "female sociability" operating within these two social groups. Socialist women were, in fact, *expected* to judge mainstream cultural performances, and women socialites were *expected* to be able to comment intelligently on the arts. Furthermore, the definitive cultural boundaries of these two groups, their clearly demarcated social codes of behavior, served to reassure the other members of the group that the individual women who chose to write as critics from within their ranks would never, in fact, break ranks. And if they tried, they could, if necessary, be stopped, as is illustrated by Crawfurd's preventing Hunt from extending her critical output.

As Joel H. Kaplan and Sheila Stowell have demonstrated, fashion commentators in the 1890s frequently reviewed theatrical productions. Through the reviews of "Florence in *Sketch*, Virginia in *Black and White*, Miss Aria in the *Queen*, Thalia in the *Players*, Player Queen in the *Lady's Pictorial*, and Diana and Flower-o'-the-May in the *Illustrated Sporting and Dramatic News*," readers learned to question "dramatic types and moral expectations" (Kaplan and Stowell 1994: 8, 25).

In addition, some women built careers as reviewers by stressing their mastery of European languages. Fanny Holcroft, who translated German and Italian drama for publication in her father's short-lived *Theatrical Recorder* (1805), may have written some of the criticism in that monthly (Graham 1930: 349). From 1877 to 1915 Emily Crawford routinely included theatrical criticism in her weekly "Letter from Paris" for *Truth* (Sullivan 1984: 429; Hunter 1992: 687).

All these critics were uniquely positioned within British culture, as were female playwrights. The public aspect of a playwright's job was to entertain, or perhaps to reflect on a moral issue – and such work was occasionally deemed feasible for women, who, after all, were expected to complete such tasks in their own homes. As a playwright, a woman was often understood to be more artistic than her sisters, born with an exceptional but natural talent. As long as her play-scripts were the primary visible representations of her personage that left the domestic sphere, her reputation remained relatively safe from most, though not all, attacks. The anonymous author of *Public Characters of 1800–1801* bemoaned that gentlewomen writers such as Charlotte Smith were "arraigned, not merely as writers, but as *women*, their characters, their conduct, even their personal endowments become the subjects of severe inquisition" (quoted in Adburgham 1972: 178). Unable to "shield themselves from detraction, by the severest prudence, or the most entire seclusion," Smith and her colleagues were subject to "wanton malice, [which] in the failure of facts, amply supplies materials for defamation" (quoted in Adburgham 1972: 178). The empathetic tone of this commentary, the use of the strong language, and the direct reference to a woman's "personal endowments" may suggest that this critic was a fellow woman writer struggling to make visible the strictures within which both she and other writers labored. Outraged, this critic explains how playwright Hannah Cowley (1743–1809) fought the trap of her cultural positioning:

The general tenor of her life has been by no means *theatrical*; at the Playhouses she is very seldom seen; and her life has been so strictly domestic, with no intercourse with the Theatres beyond what was necessary for the production of her Plays; it has also prevented the accumulation of materials for a more busy biography; perhaps, however, the very circumstance of want of incident is the highest praise; for to be public as a GENIUS, and private as a WOMAN, is to wear laurels gracefully veiled. (Quoted in Adburgham 1972: 174)

The female playwright, like the supposedly anonymous critic commenting on her, had to try to be *invisibly* talented, and in a God-given, "natural" manner. She could be a genius, a kind of freak of nature, but there could be no public display of her training, virtuosity, or labor. Because women playwrights and critics were at least potentially more publicly exhibited and more closely associated with actresses than their literary counterparts in the novelistic trade, they faced unique challenges.

In several ways the critic's challenge exceeded that of the playwright. The critic was required not only to send her writing out into the public domain, but also routinely to appear, herself, as a woman-worker in public. She was not toiling behind the scenes, submitting copy, but rather was visibly public, dressed as other women in the theatre auditorium and masquerading as a woman, but actually engaged in a process of "manly" judgment and even caricature. The critic evaluated public debates, perhaps even guided them, correcting others' work: all processes that were regarded as manly perogatives. Tracy C. Davis has explained how Victorian actresses "defied ideas of passive middle-class femininity and personified active self-sufficiency" (Davis 1991: xiv). But Victorian women critics went beyond self-sufficiency to judgment. They intervened in the process of representation.

At mid-century, feminist journalist Harriet Martineau (1802–76) explained that many young male critics preemptively set themselves up as indisputable authorities, a difficult pose for women to assume publicly. She described the critics as "a small established corps of men undertaking to pronounce on works in regard to each one of which the reviewer is, probably, less competent than the author," and concluded that "the failure to perceive this, and the virulence of tone natural to young men who felt themselves under a political and social ban, made the great Review a receptacle of unjust judgments and indefensible tempers" (quoted in Salmon [1923] 1976: 295). Only a very well-established newswriter such as Martineau could risk publishing such a statement. She herself wrote carefully modulated articles from her home, anonymously.

The theatre critic, however, could not remain invisible as she worked, nor could she disguise that fact that her judgmental labor was a *nightly* one. In direct contrast to the early eighteenth-century schedule of afternoon performances, nineteenth-century theatrical productions typically began at night, usually at 6 p.m. though later after the mid Victorian period. Productions that began at the end of the business day accommodated the growing interest of the workforce in the theatre. To satisfy the interests of this more diverse audience, the playbill was lengthened, often extending until 11 p.m. Consequently, nineteenth-century reviewers composed their columns between 11 p.m. and 1 or 2 a.m., when proper women were sleeping. Critics were regarded as sleep-deprived, dangerously overworked, and especially susceptible to illness. The early nineteenth-century critic James Henry Leigh Hunt (1784–1859) explained that "it was the necessity of going to the theatre night after night, and of writing the criticism before I went to bed, that broke me down" (quoted in Sullivan 1983: 410). Hunt's description of the sheer labor involved in reviewing for his *Tatler* in 1832 is revealing:

I did it all myself, except when too ill; and illness seldom hindered me either from supplying the review of a book, going every night to the play, or writing the notice of the play the same night at the printing office. The consequence was, that the work, slight as it looked, nearly killed me ... I was sensible of becoming weaker and poorer every day. When I came home at night, often at morning, I used to feel as if I could hardly speak. (Quoted in Sullivan 1983: 405)

Women critics, of course, faced the added burden of trying to accomplish all of this work without drawing censure.

Critics necessarily circulated at night, and in gatherings populated by spectators from all social classes. The large East End theatres which drew mixed audiences were regarded by many from the British uppercrust as especially equivocal terrain for respectable women. Even the West End theatres were sometimes rowdy, as is signaled by Charles Lamb's 1807 satire on "Hissing at the Theatre," and more serious disturbances, such as the 1809 Covent Garden riots, also occurred (Sullivan 1983: 373). A female critic could not risk being as peripatetic as the ambitious editor of the 1819 *Inspector*, who promised "to visit every theatre every night" (quoted in Graham 1930: 350). Even when she only reviewed a single production, she had to leave the theatre early to meet her press deadline, thereby losing the minimal protection offered by leaving at the same time as other spectators. A mark of impropriety was attached to unescorted women attending the theatre, and neither newspaper editors nor theatrical managers wanted to sanction their appearance.

Furthermore, journalism, like the theatre, gradually became associated in the public mind with loose morals, and only men of a certain stature could move into those worlds without being tainted by them. For women it was virtually impossible. Charles Lambs's 30

January 1801 letter to William Wordsworth romanticizes the purported tawdriness of Fleet Street's news offices and the neighboring
theatre district:

The lighted shops of the Strand and Fleet Street: the innumerable
tradesmen and customers, coaches, wagons, playhouses: all the bustle and
wickedness round about Covent Garden: the very women of the town, the
watchmen, drunken scenes, rattles: life awake if you awake[n], at all hours
of the night: the impossibility of being dull in Fleet Street: the crowds, the
very dirt and mud ... the print shops, the old bookstalls, parsons
cheapening books; coffee houses, steams of soups from kitchens, the
pantomimes! (Quoted in Gibbs 1952: 14)

Women who nightly traversed this market-driven landscape risked
the possibility that they would be perceived as prostitutes.

As late as 1952, the journalist and novelist Philip Hamilton Gibbs
still sustained this myth in his description of Fleet Street. He quoted
Sir Walter Scott to marginalize women within the neighborhood:
"'That the full character of the place might be evident, several
faded, tinselled, and painted females looked boldly at the strangers
from their open lattices'" (Gibbs 1952: 7). Then he represented
himself as a dangerous bohemian critic within the masculine terrain:

Reporters were regarded with suspicion and superciliousness by the nobility
and gentry ... "A journalist? Good God! Better be careful" ... careful of
saying anything indiscreet or confidential which by Jove! might be
published in next day's paper ... we knew that in the long run we were the
critics, the caricaturists, and the judges of social and political life. (9–10)

Paradoxically, this mythic figure of the vagabond critic was expected
to monitor the morals of the stage. While the reading public
managed to absorb this paradox when it was applied to the male
critic, it was more difficult to do so with a female critic. She had
positioned herself as a public woman, accepting theatre tickets,
daring to look at strangers, allowing them to view her, and she had
therefore given up the right to guide others on to the moral high
ground.

Male critics, in contrast, could actually move freely back and forth
from Fleet Street's news district to the nearby theatre district,
combining business with pleasure and playwriting with criticism as
they built up a network of influence and sociability. Perhaps George
Bernard Shaw (1856–1950) was the most successful of the playwright-critics, launching his career from the *Dramatic Review*, the *Pall*

Mall Gazette, the *World*, and the *Saturday Review*. But there were many prominent playwright-critics who wrote in various genres and for a variety of theatres. For forty years Edward Blanchard (1820–89), the popular writer of pantomimes, reviewed for seven newspapers, including the *Sunday Times* (Griffiths 1992: 115). Blanchard's successor, Clement Scott (1841–1904), was also a playwright, as was John Oxenford (1812–77), the prolific dramatist-critic for *The Times* (Stedman 1994: 165). The *Leader's* G. H. Lewes (1817–78) wrote criticism as well as plays in the 1850s, and in the provinces dramatist-critics such as William Bestow of the *Theatrical Journal* (1837) promoted their own work (Sullivan 1984: 186; Stedman 1994: 170).

While theatrical reviewing in the United States was often combined with arts and social reporting and allotted to unpracticed women critics, in Britain a common assignment for drama critics throughout the century was to cover the law and parliamentary reports as well as the theatre. Perhaps more than any other barrier, this coupling of assignments deterred women critics. Typically, by mid-century, the London morning dailies "had twelve to sixteen parliamentary reporters, about six law reporters, a foreign correspondent in every major European capital, leader writers, and a number of provincial correspondents and 'penny-a-liners'" (Asquith 1978: 109). The parliamentary reporter-critic's pay was customarily a respectable 5 to 7 guineas a week, eventually reaching £8 to £10 for a top critic in the 1890s (Kent 1984: 32). However, Davis reports that "by 1885, a leading comedy actress could earn between £20 and £40 a week, and a popular prima donna in opera-bouffe could make from £40 to £50 a week" (1991: 25), so without the networking opportunities to garner multiple jobs, women could make more money as performers than as critics.

Often journalists worked as law reporters by day and as theatre critics by night. For example, in 1813 William Hazlitt (1778–1830) covered Parliament and theatres for the *Morning Chronicle*, moving on to the *Champion*, the *Examiner* and finally *The Times* (*History* 1935: 164–65). Later in the century, in 1883, both William Archer (1856–1924) and William Amstrong (1856–1924), a critic for six different London publications, were called to the Bar of the Middle Temple, though neither ever practiced (Griffiths 1992: 76–77). Even Oxford graduate Herbert Henry Asquith (1852–1928), 1st Earl of Oxford and Asquith and eventually prime minister, supplemented his lawyer's income in the 1870s through journalism (Griffiths 1992:

80). Many prominent Victorian critics attended British public (i.e., highly select, tuition-driven) schools, with 42 Oxford men and 29 Cambridge men represented (Kent 1986: 99). Max Beerbohm (1872–1956), for example, used his Oxford network to establish himself as a critic.

At least 21 nineteenth-century Victorian critics were barristers (Kent 1986: 99). Like Barron Field (at *The Times* 1806–9), many supported their law studies by writing theatre criticism. These law student-cum-reporters took notes at court, covering the King's Bench during the day and the theatre at night (*History* 1935: 95).

Gibbs shows how newsmen in the gallery or the reporters' room of the House of Commons worked on public display and in close, sociable quarters under lamps that gleamed like spotlights (1952: 41). These critics were visibly public evaluators, not just of the representative field of the drama but also of the representative process of the parliamentary system. In 1810 Barron Fields's successor, Thomas Barnes (1785–1841) quite typically "combine[d] occasional reporting of law cases, theatres and political meetings with his legal studies and his West End amusements" (*History* 1935: 190). Fellow journalist Leigh Hunt praised Barnes's "Parliamentary Criticism" as well as his theatrical criticism, explicitly linking the two. Both in court and onstage, speakers deliver speeches, and the journalist evaluates the process of representation. Hunt explains:

It is of importance to the readers of these [parliamentary] speeches to know at what rate to estimate those who deliver them, either from the extent of their views or the soundness of their principles. This is the Writer's object; and after the attention [Barnes's] criticisms have excited, both on Senators and Actors, for the extent of their views, the soundness of their principles, and that keen insight into the causes of character and manners, for which they are more particularly remarkable, the addition of our praise can be of little worth to him, except to show how sensible we are of his help. (*History* 1935: 191)

Hunt's linking of Senators and Actors, of legislative and theatrical discourse, reveals the cultural positioning of English theatre critics. One can even imagine the critics returning to the warm, well-lit reporters' room in the House of Commons at midnight, to write up the theatre review for the night.

While Victorian actresses might be read within the context of pornography, as Davis has demonstrated (1991: 105–36), Victorian women critics were more likely to be read within the context of the legislative and judicial systems. An editor of the *Daily Telegraph* described the qualifications necessary for these cultural critics: "A paper of high authority should always have at command such men as can write with correctness, certainty, distinct force and authority on military, on naval affairs, on law" (quoted in Burnham 1955: 8). Parliamentary reporting was linked to vital national security issues, and could be trusted only to men of the "highest order." Since theatre reviewing was customarily handled by these legal reporters, it, too, became off-limits for women.

Certainly women were not welcomed into the other common journalistic slot for those who wanted to write about theatre: the sports-cum-theatre critic position. The *Illustrated Sporting and Dramatic News: A High-Class Weekly Journal of Sports, Art, Literature, Music, and the Drama* and less pretentious journals such as *Sporting Times, Pictorial Sporting and Theatrical Guide*, and the radical *Referee* all hired newsmen to cover the full gamut of entertainment, from the wrestling match to the pantomime. But British women critics evidently did not participate, as a handful of American critics did, in this type of theatrical criticism.

As the century progressed, British journalistic power became centralized in the hands of a few owners, editors, and critics, all male. Many men held interest in more than one newspaper, and at mid-century as few as fifteen men ran the Fourth Estate in London (Asquith 1978: 104). London news agencies further centralized journalism in the 1870s, robbing potential critics of jobs (Baylen 1992: 34). Furthermore, critics frequently reviewed for weeklies and dailies simultaneously, and therefore "were able ... to reinforce their own viewpoints" (Stedman 1994: 165). Michael D. Ryan, for example, covered both music and theatre for three London dailies (Kent 1980: 32). Critics sometimes stayed at the same paper for decades, as John Oxenford did at *The Times*, making it difficult for women critics and playwrights to wedge their way into the news columns (Kent 1980: 33). Finally, editors themselves were sometimes playwright-critics, as was the case with *Punch*'s Tom Taylor, who penned *Our American Cousin*; F. C. Burnand, an "indefatigable burlesque writer"; and H. J. Byron, a dramatist and editor of *Fun* (Stedman 1994: 165). All of these critics had a "direct impact on the immediate success (specifically, financial) of the artists ... through their influence over mass tastes" (Kent 1980: 31).

Theatrical press notices and commentaries flourished during the nineteenth century, as newspapers themselves proliferated, prompted by government subsidies and rising profits.[2] The Libel Act of 1792 also offered editors new protections, emboldening journalistic efforts. The number of British papers grew impressively, especially among periodicals, which tripled from 1833 to 1860 (Mott 1962: 216).

Newspaper taxes were the primary impediment to growing press profits. British news agencies had to pay "a stamp tax on each sheet of paper used as newsprint, [and] a duty charged on each advertisement – at a flat rate, irrespective of the size of the advertisement or the circulation of the newspaper" (Brown 1992: 24). However, journals devoted solely to the arts, supposedly apolitical, escaped stamp taxes, and partly because of this loophole, arts publications proliferated. By mid-century there were more theatrical periodicals than ever before in British history (Stedman 1994: 162). Furthermore, because of frequent theatrical changes of bill, there were more than twice as many Victorian drama critics as music or art critics, which makes the paucity of women theatre critics even more striking (Kent 1986: 99–100).

By the 1830s, radicals attacked the newspaper duties that had generated this explosion of arts publications, arguing that knowledge disseminated through newspapers should be free from taxes. The stamp and advertisement duties were consequently abolished in 1853 and 1855 respectively (Brown 1992: 25). Advertising revenues jumped immediately, and from the 1850s onwards newspapers increasingly depended on advertising rather than sales to make a profit (Asquith 1978: 110). By 1886, "60–[6]6% of the columnage of the *Daily Telegraph*, [and] 49% of that of *The Times* ... was devoted to advertisements" (Lee 1978: 119).

Instead of depending on individual men and women to buy newspapers, editors in this increasingly profit-driven atmosphere found themselves dependent upon advertisers. Editors encouraged critics to praise productions whose managers paid for handsome advertisements. By mid-century, many critics routinely puffed theatrical endeavors to appease advertisers and secure their own salaries, as the history of *The Times* acknowledges: "the criticisms may be properly regarded as of commercial inspiration, designed to support the advertisements" (*History* 1935: 47). Plays were routinely applauded even before they were produced. Thomas Dutton of the *Dramatic Censor, or Weekly Theatrical Report* (1800–1), for instance, ridiculed the *Morning Herald*'s puffing of a pantomime scene that appeared in the press kit but never reached the stage (Graham 1930: 348). This custom of matching the theatrical coverage to the size of the advertisement abated by the end of the century, but managers still treated critics to drinks and dinner in a covert effort to garner a positive review. This tradition impeded women's access to the profession of critic by jeopardizing their social reputations (Davis 1984: 159).

As newspapers began to be figured in the national consciousness as a means of profit rather than as a noble means of shaping public debate, they were further defined as male territory. Many viewed the new dailies as reflective of the desires of an increasingly broad-based and ill-educated public. This shift in perception meant that the critic was often figured as the hired hand of an unprincipled profit-mongering institution, which again threw the critic's morals into question. This cultural positioning of the critic created another hurdle for women, whose social mobility depended partly on a spotless reputation.

Critics initially tried to use anonymity to shield themselves from accusations of governmental intervention and advertisers' influence. Anonymity supposedly allowed "a full and free discussion without any mixture of that egotism and self-intrusion which are almost inseparable from the compositions of any individual writer in his own personal character" (quoted in *History* 1935: xiii). This anonymity would grant journalists power as they became "the foundation of the whole, the first necessary condition" of independent thinking in the larger populace (quoted in *History* 1935: xiv). Independent journalists would secure an independent nation.

Until the end of the century reviewing was seemingly anonymous. In most cases reviews carried no byline, or only a corporate byline that masked several writers under one label. *Fun*'s 1860s theatre column, for example, "might in any given issue contain reviews by [Tom] Robertson, [Henry S.] Leigh, and [W. S.] Gilbert, with no indication that more than one writer was involved" (Stedman 1994: 166). Critics also often filled in for each other, or asked stringers to cover for them, without changing the byline. However, as H. R. Fox Bourne explained in 1887, the critic "may be anonymous to the public, but he cannot be anonymous to his neighbours and those about whom it is his business to write. He may eschew the society of actors and actresses, but he cannot avoid intercourse with their friends" (Bourne 1887: 383). Citing Blanchard's diaries, Kent ex-

ploded the myth of anonymity among critics by explaining that they
"regularly dined together before setting off for the theatre, where
they would often sit together as well" (1980: 32). Kent describes the
"bonhomie (of a bibulous, bohemian kind)" that male critics
enjoyed, identifying the Strand's Edinburgh Castle pub and the
Albion Tavern just off Drury Lane as "popular late night haunts of
music and theatre critics," where everyone knew everyone (Kent
1986: 101). By 1867, John Hollingshed made it impossible for critics
to remain anonymous, by publishing the names of London critics
and their employers. Soon thereafter critics began to advocate
signing reviews as a means of professionalizing their work (Davis
1984: 158).

Nineteenth-century critics eager to maintain their independence
from commercial interests faced a difficult task, largely because "the
entertainment industry was too fruitful a source of advertising
revenue and dramatic news to be alienated" (*History* 1935: 48).
Shortly after Leigh Hunt began to publish his independent criticism
in 1805, Barron Field followed suit, but "The fresh note sounded by
Field in *The Times*, and Leigh Hunt in the *News*, was unwelcome to
actors and managers alike" (*History* 1935: 90). The business of the
theatre was still assumed to be based on "friendly intercourse"
among gentlemen, which counted women out. Sheridan's response
to Field's independent reviews illustrates the private manner in
which male theatre professionals of the period handled not-so-
private business. Anxious about the monetary losses he might suffer
as a result of the new independent reviews, Sheridan wrote a
personal letter to *The Times* editor, John Walter, calling on their
friendship more than the threat of legal action: "addressing you, not
as an Editor, but, on the footing of the fair and friendly intercourse,
wh[ic]h, *as a private man*, I have always met you and your Father, I
must regret, that you could have permitted the publications of such
Libels – A proper answer will be sent – tho' not from me – And, I
hope, I shall have the pleasure of finding you at home between three
and four to morrow" (quoted in *History* 1935: 93). The continuing
references to Walter as a friend and the plan to meet in his home, as
well as the emphasis on meeting privately to settle public matters,
would carry sexual overtones if the writer were a woman.

Independent theatrical reviewing placed several other barriers in
a woman critic's way. First, with the dissolution of the "family
compact" between the press and the theatre, she was no longer

working for two powerful men with a common goal. She was no longer indebted to the editor for a job and to the theatre manager for a ticket, nor could she potentially fashion a positive review to satisfy both. Instead, she was working for two powerful men with conflicting goals. The newspaper editor handed her a theatre ticket so that she could write trenchant criticism certain to alienate the theatre manager, who expected her to puff his show because of his cash outlay for advertising. Another barrier was that the new independence championed by Hunt and Field was characterized by very direct attacks on plays and players: words like "contemptible," "damned," "mediocrity," "senseless," and "nauseous" abounded. Those targeted by these epithets fought back in kind. Managers castigated the independent theatre critics in the magazines, casting aspersions on the critics themselves. Many women may have had apprehensions about publicly defending themselves from such sallies. And while managers protested the male critics' attacks, such assaults launched by women critics would have been intolerable.

Moral objections to women as theatre critics typically cloaked other apprehensions, such as the financial anxieties Sheridan voiced. As England emerged from the Napoleonic Wars, "scarcely a theatrical management escaped bankruptcy between 1817 and 1843," and Drury Lane receipts dropped precipitously (Brockett 1977: 393). Within this anxiety-ridden atmosphere, theatrical managers and the editors who derived income from their advertising opposed any change that might affect profits. Hiring a female critic surely qualified as a change.

Nineteenth-century women playwrights most likely sensed at the very moment that they launched their careers, that their work would typically be judged not by those from within their own sphere of sociability, not by critics who shared their cultural positioning and who took risks similar to their own, but probably by critics who moved comfortably from the halls of Parliament to the aisles of the theatre. Furthermore, they understood that many of their reviewers doubled as direct competitors, that the critics who were to evaluate their work might very well be opening their own shows at rival theatres, or covering their dining companions' productions at houses nearby. They also anticipated that the printed responses to their work would not be couched in genteel eighteenth-century prose but in the scrappier style of the new century. Consequently, they entered into their work as we perhaps should, with an effort to reach beyond the critics to connect with the ever-widening assemblage of Victorian spectators.

NOTES

1   I am deeply grateful to Margaret Debelius of Georgetown University for calling my attention to the work of Eleanor Marx, Annie Besant, and Violet Hunt.
2   During the mid-century population boom, people moved into the cities, where newspapers were more easily produced and distributed. The railroad, Koenig steam press, and telegraph contributed to the growth of the press, as did the 1792 practice of free delivery. In 1781 there were 76 newspapers in England and Wales, in 1821 the number jumped to 267, and by 1851 the total numbered 563. The number of provincial papers followed suit: "about 50 in 1782, to 150 by 1830, and to over 230 by 1851" (Asquith 1978: 98–102).

REFERENCES

Adburgham, Alison 1972, *Women in Print: Writing Women and Women's Magazines from the Restoration to the Accession of Victoria*, London: Allen and Unwin.
Asquith, Ivon 1978, "The Structure, Ownership and Control of the Press, 1780–1855," in Boyce *et al.* 1978, 98–116.
Baylen, J. O. 1992, "The British Press, 1861–1918," in Griffiths 1992, 33–46.
Belford, Barbara 1990, *Violet: The Story of the Irrepressible Violet Hunt and Her Circle of Lovers and Friends*, New York: Simon and Schuster.
Bourne, H. R. Fox 1887, *English Newspapers: Chapters in the History of Journalism*, vol. II, London: Chatto and Windus.
Boyce, George, James Curran, and Pauline Wingate (eds.) 1978, *Newspaper History from the Seventeenth Century to the Present Day*, London: Constable.
Brockett, Oscar 1977, *History of the Theatre*, 3rd edn, Boston: Allyn and Bacon.
Brown, Lucy 1992, "The British Press, 1800–1860," in Griffiths 1992, 24–32.
Burnham, Lord [Edward Frederick Lawson, Baron] 1955, *Peterborough Court: The Story of The Daily Telegraph*, London: Cassell.
Davis, Tracy C. 1984, "Theatre Critics in Late Victorian and Edwardian Periodicals: A Supplementary List," *Victorian Periodicals Review*, 17.4: 158–64.
Davis, Tracy C. 1991, *Actresses as Working Women: Their Social Identity in Victorian Culture*, London: Routledge.
Donkin, Ellen 1995, *Getting into the Act: Women Playwrights in London 1776–1829*, London and New York: Routledge.

Gibbs, Philip 1952, *The Journalist's London*, London: Allan Wingate.

Graham, Walter 1930, *English Literary Periodicals*, New York: Thomas Nelson.

Griffiths, Dennis (ed.) 1992, *The Encyclopedia of the British Press 1422–1992*, New York: St. Martin's Press.

Harding, Mildred 1987, "Pearl Craigie ('John Oliver Hobbes') in India: Lord Curzon's Durbar (1903)," *Turn-of-the-Century Women*, 4.2: 23–41.

The History of "The Times": "The Thunderer" in the Making 1785–1841 1935, London: The Times.

The History of "The Times": The Tradition Established, 1841–1884 1939, London: The Times.

Hunter, Fred 1992, "Women in British Journalism," in Griffiths 1992, 686–90.

Kaplan, Joel H., and Sheila Stowell 1994, *Theatre and Fashion: Oscar Wilde to the Suffragettes*, Cambridge: Cambridge University Press.

Kapp, Yvonne 1977, *Eleanor Marx*, vol.II, New York: Pantheon.

Kent, Christopher 1980, "Periodical Critics of Drama, Music, and Art, 1830–1914: A Preliminary List," *Victorian Periodicals Review*, 13.1/2: 31–54.

Kent, Christopher 1986, "More Critics of Drama, Music, and Art," *Victorian Periodicals Review*, 19.3: 99–105.

Lee, Alan 1978, "The Structure, Ownership and Control of the Press, 1855–1914," in Boyce *et al.* 1978, 117–29.

Mott, Frank Luther 1962, *American Journalism, A History: 1690–1960*, 3rd edn, New York: Macmillan.

Peters, Margot 1980, *Bernard Shaw and the Actresses*, Garden City: Doubleday.

Salmon, Lucy Maynard [1923] 1976, *The Newspaper and the Historian*, New York: Octagon.

Schlueter, Paul, and June Schlueter (eds.) 1988, *An Encyclopedia of British Women Writers*, New York: Garland.

Stedman, Jane W. 1994, "Theatre," *Victorian Periodicals and Victorian Society*, ed. J. Don Vann and Rosemary T. VanArsdel, Toronto: University of Toronto Press, 162–76.

Sullivan, Alvin (ed.) 1983, *British Literary Magazines: The Romantic Age, 1789–1836*, Westport, CT: Greenwood Press.

Sullivan, Alvin (ed.) 1984, *British Literary Magazines: The Victorian and Edwardian Age, 1837–1913*, Westport, CT: Greenwood Press.

CHAPTER 3

Mrs. Gore gives tit for tat

Ellen Donkin

On 21 October 1843, just after the parliamentary debates on theatre regulations brought to a formal end legalized monopoly by the majors, the following squib appeared in a weekly arts journal called the *Critic*:

A meeting for the advancement of the National Drama was held at Covent Garden Theatre on Wednesday evening, the 11th instant ... Mr. Bunn [manager of Drury Lane] was unanimously called to the chair ... Mr. Bunn could not exactly define what the national drama was ... Mr. T. P. Cooke here hitched up his trousers, and observed, His dear eyes! He looked upon the national drama as a woman – ... and the man who would not assist an unprotected female in distress was unworthy to sail beneath the flag that had braved a thousand years. (*Critic*, 3: 34–35)

Indeed, what was the national drama? In this commentary, it emerges as a gendered metaphor, "an unprotected female in distress." Those who would rescue her are male (playwrights and managers), and project a virility that invokes chivalry, patriotism, nostalgia, nationalism and masculine narratives of heroism. In an age of pressure for free trade and social reform, one wonders if the very idea of a "national drama," rather like the monopoly system itself, was not itself an anachronism harking back to an earlier social order.

The August 1843 parliamentary debates included a last-ditch effort by the majors to maintain control at least over the performance of Shakespeare (an effort which was hotly contested) as if to suggest that Shakespeare was the national drama, and as such should be kept inviolate from the audiences and managements of the minors. But no one at this juncture seemed able to agree on what else might be counted as national drama. Was it nautical drama? (T. P. Cooke thought so). Mr. Bunn thought it was that which drew the largest audience. Everyone, including Mr. Wallack and Mr. Serle (likely the dramatist T. J. Serle) who was standing in for Mr. Macready, agreed that it was *not* French plays in translation. "The British drama," wrote the *Critic*,

> should be the boasted organ of noble, manly, and moral sentiment, and, to a certain extent, of liberal principles; for sentiments expressing the most tempered and general condemnation of tyranny and oppression should never be considered as calculated to make a people discontented or dissatisfied against just authority. (*Critic* 14: 162)

Or, as someone had pointedly commented in December 1843, "We want a Garrick's theatre, and, as nearly as may be, Garrick's means of filling it" (*Critic* 40: 123).

Running parallel to all of this animated discussion was a well-publicized initiative in the direction of actually discovering what a new national drama might be. In the June 1843 playbills at the Haymarket, and subsequently in the *Dramatic and Musical Review* (of Saturday 10 June 1843) a contest was announced. Benjamin Webster, "the spirited lessee" of the Haymarket, offered "a prize of £500 with contingent advantages, for the best modern comedy illustrative of British manners." A committee was appointed. On 3 February 1844, Webster delivered to them the anonymous manuscripts, and the process of narrowing them down to a single winning entry began in earnest. The committee included at its helm Charles Kemble, formerly the Lord Chamberlain's Examiner of Plays (from 1836 to 1840), as if to underscore publicly the need for this new drama, whatever it was, and to demonstrate its compliance with official sanctions. Also on the committee were Charles Young, a retired actor; E. R. Moran and Henry Ottley, both critics; J. Charles Searle (or Serle); G. P. R. James, the novelist; and the Reverend Alexander Dyce, an editor of Shakespeare's works.

On 26 May 1844, the news was official. Of ninety-seven anonymous submissions (even Charles Dickens had threatened to join the fray), only one had met with the committee's unanimous approval. On their twentieth meeting, the committee chose *Quid Pro Quo; or, The Day of Dupes*. The *Era* said coyly, "Of the authorship of this production, we do not know that we are at liberty to say more at present than that it is by a lady, and one who is by no means unknown to literary fame" (26 May 1844: 6). The *Era* went on to report in great detail the means by which the committee had narrowed the ninety-seven (or ninety-eight – reports vary) submissions down to seventeen, and thence to five or six. Then, with the excitement of a newscaster saying "And now, this just in," the paper revealed its trump card in the final paragraph: "We are now authorized to state that the comedy is from the charming pen of Mrs. Gore."

It was an awkward moment. It was one thing for a group of distinguished male playwrights and managers to imagine collectively the national drama as a woman in distress, in need of rescue by their manly efforts. It was quite another to countenance a scenario in which the rescuer was herself a woman. It was not that Mrs. Gore had not won fair and square, if the *Era*'s elaborate reportage is to be believed. Nor was it that the lady was a theatrical *parvenu*. She had by this time an established reputation as a minor but successful playwright, with a decade of productions to her credit: four at the Haymarket, three at Covent Garden, two at Drury Lane, and one at the Strand (in fact, one of these plays, *The Maid of Croissey*, had earned Ben Webster himself some very high praise as an actor).

The entire notion of a "National Drama" was now thrown open to question at the very moment when all theatres, major and minor, finally had an equal right to produce spoken drama.[1] The numbers of officially approved venues for playwrights had enormously increased meaning that demand could potentially far outstrip existing supply. There must have been considerable anxiety, particularly among the men running Drury Lane, Covent Garden and the Haymarket (including Webster) about how their traditional control of the "legitimate" market was going to be maintained. It was as if the end of the privileges accorded to the majors had resulted in the loss of England's national theatres, and that consequently it was more urgent than ever that England at least restore or reinvent a national drama.[2]

On a larger scale, the bitter struggles for enfranchisement in the 1830s and 1840s, and the slow but important gains consequent to the Reform Act of 1832, had also destabilized whatever assumptions had underpinned what a "national" drama might be. No one, even in that select meeting of managers and playwrights in 1843, could any longer imagine with confidence a single kind of drama that would represent the nation. The whole notion of a "national drama" was by definition monolithic, invoking a certain nostalgia for Garrick and the eighteenth century, and resting uneasily on the assumption that the multiple voices and classes of the nation could be subsumed, which was precisely what the Chartists and others were challenging. Under the circumstances, one could have predicted that any contest for "the best new comedy" was likely to be a target for competing interests, especially when the play was billed as being representative of "English manners as they are." The question was "whose manners?"

Whatever it was that Mrs. Gore had written, it apparently was not a "national drama." In the ensuing onslaught of reviews, it becomes possible to piece together just what the reviewers thought a representative comedy ought to be. The show opened on Tuesday evening, 18 June 1844. The *Morning Chronicle* subsequently reported on Wednesday, 19 June:

> it makes no attempt at the higher objects of dramatic writing: it points no moral, it asserts no lofty correcting principle; it involves no single conflict between virtue and vice, between high sentiment and grovelling impulses; it contents itself with bringing together all the frivolities and absurdities which are exhibited in the everyday conduct of the most shallow portion of the world; playing them off one another with some skill . . .

The reviewer reflects a set of disappointed expectations which appear to be based on what great comedy should be. He refers repeatedly to the idea of a "single conflict," or a single moral, and is made uneasy by something multivalent in this playwright's sensibility that resists categorization. The play *does not seem to favor anybody*, this writer seems to be saying. The *Morning Chronicle* also reported that the show began well "in spite of a very determinately critical audience. The fourth and fifth [acts] hung fire considerably, and the dissentients, who had been gathering their strength, now showed in such force that they frequently succeeded in interrupting the progress of the piece." By the end, the audience was in uproar. "Every opportunity which the dialogue afforded . . . was seized upon to launch a shout of derision against the performers, mingled with observations which proved that a strong feeling of disappointment (from whatever cause arising) existed in the minds of a great portion of the audience as to the result of this literary competition."

The second night afforded some surprises. The writer for the *Chronicle* still did not like the play, but he was forced to admit that by comparison the second night was a sparkling success. The script had been "judiciously curtailed," but also the audience was there to see the play rather than damn it. Incidents and lines which had been obliterated by the uproar on opening night now played to laughter and applause: "Such was the result, as far as last night was

Plate 1. Playbill for *Quid Pro Quo*, opening night, 18 June 1844.

concerned, of this second division; a reaction only equalled by the recent counter-marching of the ministerial ranks in the House of Commons" (20 June 1844: 5). The reviewer believed that this was a compensatory audience of sympathizers, "having had their attention awakened to the suspicion of unfair bias in the clamour of Tuesday night, many have rallied strongly on behalf of its authoress with a view of seeing justice done her."

The review in the *Illustrated London News* (Sunday 23 June 1844) was more ruthlessly critical, and made a point of the playwright's gender: "The piece is incoherent and plotless," the reviewer wrote;

it is a chance-medley-meeting of characters, and it is distinguished throughout by the lowest and most witless dialogue that was ever spoken on a stage. Occasionally it is indecent – witness that speech of Bridget in the garden ... One word at parting: if ladies will write such things, and ladies play such *smoking* parts [Mrs. Nisbett played young Lord Rivers with a cigarette] as the Etonian Gamin, if vulgarity rudely turn out politeness, and coarse thoughts garbed in bad grammar take precedence of refined idea – why then, indeed, farewell to comedy.[3]

Also on June 23, the *Weekly Dispatch* noted "the unsuccessful candidates ... formed a little section of the audience on Tuesday night, and vented their anger in a determined manner as the piece proceeded." The *Era* (23 June 1844) ventured a further critique based on gender: "From Mrs. Gore's previous dramatic efforts, we were prepared for something far better; in the illustration of the manners of the day the female has been eminently weak; it may be assignable to the fact, that although Hercules could wield a distaff, Juno was incompetent to the thunderbolts."

Nevertheless, by 26 June the tide had shifted. The *Morning Chronicle* reported that "*Quid Pro Quo* increases nightly in attraction, and has been drawing crowded audiences." The *Morning Chronicle* lists among those who attended a number of peers, including the Duke of Devonshire, a personal friend of Mrs. Gore's and himself a former Lord Chamberlain. The show ran for twenty-six nights altogether. Notices of its impending closure appear in periodicals of the week of 20 July; the final performance was on 27 July.[4] In early July, well before the run of *Quid Pro Quo* had come to an end, *Punch* reported that the judges of the committee were so distressed by their own bad judgment that they took up a subscription to replace Webster's prize money. The story is probably apocryphal since its alleged source is Douglas Jerrold, but it was a nasty swipe at Mrs. Gore.[5]

At the close of this production, Mrs. Gore quit playwriting altogether. She evidently had qualms about the contest well before the announcement of the winner. The *Dramatic and Musical Review* (20 July 1844) reported that she had tried early on to withdraw her play from the contest, saying in a letter to Webster that it was "more an *acting* than a *readable* play." Her language suggests that she anticipates trouble with this script from the literary quarter, or from the expectations connected to writing "a high-life comedy." She allegedly went on to say she now preferred to take her chances by submitting the play through regular channels to Webster. If she had, and if Webster had complied by withdrawing her script from the competition, this footnote in theatre history might never have come into being. It is a certainty that Mrs. Gore's play, had it been produced through normal channels and not as "the prize comedy," would probably have slipped by without undue comment, as her first ten plays had done.

Mrs. Gore, however, seems to have felt persecuted primarily for reasons of gender, rather than for reasons connected to national drama *per se*, although both issues emerge in her own commentary. Her preface to the 1844 printed edition is a remarkable one, because rather than making a demonstration of public gratitude (or angry frustration) to a male manager, as women playwrights of the eighteenth century were wont to do, she identifies herself instead as a member of a select cohort of *other women playwrights*: Joanna Baillie (whose first big production was in 1798 and who continued to be a very important figure for women of letters up to her death in 1851), Lady Emmeline Wortley (whose play *Moonshine* had been damned at the Haymarket in August 1843), and Lady Dacre (Barbarina Wilmot, whose play *Ina* failed at Drury Lane in 1815). It is the first instance to my knowledge of a woman playwright identifying in a collective sense with other women playwrights. She does not identify Ben Webster as a mentor or defender; in fact, she makes no mention at all of his generous support as manager.

The importance of this change cannot be overstated. It marks the infinitesimally small beginning of a new kind of entitlement in the profession. Mrs. Gore's prose reflects not the gratitude and anxiety one might have expected from someone whose position in the profession is embattled, but a certain degree of cool authority that invokes a constituency of other women, and by extension, their support based on gender: "For the animosity on the part of the pit and the press (the dramatic critics of the press being, almost without an exception, rival dramatists) which succeeded in condemning the very superior plays of Joanna Baillie, Lady Dacre, and Lady Emmeline Wortley, could scarcely fail to crush any attempt of mine" (Gore 1844: v). It is a constituency of the imagination in the sense that she is having to borrow from disparate decades in order to make up her cohort. There is perhaps some resonance here between Mrs. Gore's stated identity as a woman playwright and the political strategies that had been used by certain working-class women during the Reform era, women who organized themselves into Female Friendly Societies for the purposes of mutual support and survival, in direct contradiction to the increasing pressures being leveraged on women all over England to retreat from public life altogether (Clark 1995: 37–41). In the history of women in playwriting, the collective identity of working women playwrights emerges *as an idea* for the first time in Mrs. Gore's career.

In her preface, Mrs. Gore makes a strategic effort to distance herself from any claims to national drama, at least of the kind that is being prescribed by her detractors. She states that she had no intention of writing a "high-life comedy, a style of piece which the experience of the last twenty years proves to be wholly ineffective on the modern stage. No such object was suggested by the manager [Ben Webster]; and a bustling play of the Farquhar, or George Colman school, appeared far more available to the resources of the theatre, and *the taste of the play-going classes*" (my emphasis). She goes on to say that much as she wishes the boxes to be filled on a nightly basis by "those aristocratic and literary classes of the community who have absolutely withdrawn their patronage from the English Stage," those people in fact *do not* attend the theatre on any regular basis. She continues: "no one familiar with the nightly aspect of our theatres will deny that they are supported by a class requiring a very different species of entertainment; for whose diversion, exaggeration in writing and acting is as essential, as daubing to the art of the scene-painter" (Gore 1844: v).

Mrs. Gore's claim is that she has been criticized unjustly for writing a play that addressed the requirements of the Haymarket's *actual* audience, rather than its *putative* audience. In other words, she was being held responsible for not having written for a kind of

Plate 2. Portrait of Mrs. Catherine Grace Gore, engraved by S. Freeman from an original drawing by J. Slater.

theatre that no longer existed. According to contemporary commentary, some of Mrs. Gore's key colleagues in playwriting (some of whom were also managers) favored an explicit and nostalgic return to Garrick and to monolithic claims to quality and standards. Some of the criticism directed at Mrs. Gore's play (not only by contemporary reviewers, but also later by Dutton Cook and others), even went so far as to suggest that her play was guilty of "vulgarity" and "indecency" (I am quoting the *Illustrated London News* critic here), thereby leveling – which is to say, destroying – the old theatre (which I take to be a reference to Garrick's management and repertoire). So not only was she not cooperating with expectations connected to national drama; she was now revealed to have undermined basic standards.

The fact of Mrs. Gore's being a woman left her open to charges related to vulgarity that would not likely have had any currency had she been male. Because she was a woman playwright and had failed to abide by some separate unwritten code of decency, she was contributing to the way the theatre was being leveled by playing to the lowest "common" (as in "vulgar") denominator. The words *level* and *leveling* in connection with a "fusion of classes" occur in both the play and the preface. Mrs. Gore comments in her preface that "the fusion of the educated classes [presumably by virtue of the 1832 Reform Act] has smoothed the surface of society to a railroad level." In *Quid Pro Quo*, this smoothing of the surface plays out in real terms: characters from the merchant class fall in love with upper-class members of the landed gentry while working together to mount a home theatrical production, thus throwing class distinctions into complete disarray, in effect, leveling them.

The bivalence of the term *level*, meaning to destroy on the one hand and to even out a surface on the other, is further complicated by the fact that young Lord Bellamont (the Etonian Gamin) was played in breeches by Mrs. Nisbett, suggesting that this fundamental distinction between genders was also fluid in the context of theatrical practice. Breeches roles were common in this period, but there seems to be some animus attached to a *woman* writing a breeches role, as if this demonstration of gender mobility took on a different meaning in the context of female authorship. If breeches roles written by men were for the primary purpose of legitimizing looking at women's legs, one wonders if breeches roles written by women resonated quite differently, perhaps with political debates around allowing women a fuller public and political presence. In point of fact, during this period efforts to gain equality for women were called "the struggle for the breeches" (Clark 1995: 64).

In a long retrospective piece written in the 1880s, Dutton Cook archly observed that Mrs. Gore was writing "down" to her audience (Cook 1882: 70 ff), but his comment only makes sense if the presumption is that she should have been writing a "high life" comedy in the first place, a play that presumably confirmed the appropriateness of class distinctions. Instead, she wrote a comedy in which theatre itself is the great leveler: in the course of getting ready for the home theatricals, upper-class characters (one of whom is a boy being played by a woman) paint scenery side by side with laborers hammering the set together, and in the chaos and excitement of getting the show up it is difficult to distinguish a character of

one class from a character of another. Her play offers a stark contrast
to Jane Austen's earlier rendition of the same scenario in *Mansfield
Park* (1814), in which the daughters of the middle class are seen to be
at grave risk to their social standing by merely performing in home
theatricals (never mind painting scenery). Mrs. Gore, by contrast,
keeps the radical possibilities of social mobility alive in her play by
allowing the unions that have been forged during rehearsals for
home theatricals to mature into marriage. The contrast is startling,
and points to a very different social milieu, one that is in the process
of experimentation and self-analysis.

The possibility of theatre functioning as a laboratory for social
experimentation and change rather than as a sanctified homage to
historic privilege was at the heart of the matter.[6] Mrs. Gore's
situation may have been exacerbated by the fact that the Haymarket
(even though – unlike Drury Lane and Covent Garden – it was
functioning on a year-to-year license) had the cachet of having been
one of the old triad of legitimate London houses. Now, because of
new rulings, it was allowed to run all year, not just as a summer
theatre. Webster was in the peculiar position of being in pressing
need of more scripts because of the extended season, but simultaneously wanting to capitalize on the fact of the Haymarket's historical
position as a keeper of the national drama.[7] The contest was no
doubt an attempt to address both issues, but the winning play
seemed to be facing in the direction of a new day, rather than
looking back nostalgically to an earlier time. This failure to pay
homage to an old order was a public relations problem for Webster,
but for Mrs. Gore it was the end of a playwriting career.

We come at last to the play itself, both as a script and as a
production. There lingers always in these discussions of women's
drama some anxiety that the play – for all our careful contextua-
lizing – is actually just a bad piece of work which deserves its fate
after all. I saw a fully mounted production of *Quid Pro Quo* in
February 1997, probably the first production in 153 years.[8] The show
deftly drove home Mrs. Gore's observations about the essential
fluidity of class, and created delicious possibilities for performative
invention. One particularly telling moment involved young Henry
Grigson, a lieutenant in the Royal Navy, who has been mistaken for
a wealthy and powerful young lord named Fitz-Urse. Henry decides
not to confess his real identity, but instead to "perform" Fitz-Urse to
the hilt, to see where the charade takes him. In a sustained moment

reminiscent of Steve Martin, the actor playing Grigson stood on stage in his new "costume" and rehearsed being Fitz-Urse. He isolated and rotated the wrist, practiced the graceful line of the leg and the inclination of the head, until he had them all working in concert with one another. The message was clear: if Grigson can pull it off (and he does), then class, like gender, is performative.

At the end of the play, Henry, still disguised as Fitz-Urse, has won the love of the aristocratic Lady Mary Rivers. He gleefully announces to her mother, the Countess, his real identity, and that their mutual passion developed during rehearsals for the very theatricals that the Countess herself had been sponsoring: "It means that the charming Duchess of Segovia [Lady Mary's role] has pledged her heart and hand to the fortunate stage manager of your ladyship's theatricals!" The Countess snorts with rage. "Lady Mary GRIGSON? – I shall expire." Lady Mary's father, the Earl, is about to impose himself violently when Sir George Mordent, a kinsman to the Earl who has functioned throughout as a voice of moderation and reason, intercedes on behalf of the young lovers, and proceeds to "perform" the Earl, by quoting him to his face:

EARL [*to* HENRY]: Sir! I desire you will instantly quit the castle!
MORDENT: Come, come, come! – [*assuming the manner of the Earl*] – Let *me* reconcile matters! As you were saying just now, "the times are past for resenting such disproportions! – In these days of social enlightenment, education makes the man! – The philosophy of the age we live in recognizes no pragmatical distinctions. – We are more *generous* – we are more *just*! Come! – give your blessing to the young people!"
EARL: But, a Grigson engrafted on our family tree!
MORDENT: What then? – The tree is in a sad decaying state, and will be all the better for a healthy graft or two. (Gore 1844: 78)

The play, in defiance of comic convention, does not end on this note of marriage and reconciliation. At the last moment, Cogit, the Earl's agent, instead of putting the Earl up for the local election as he had been instructed to do, reveals that he has put himself up for the same seat. He returns to the castle and announces with relish to the Earl that he, Cogit, has been elected to Parliament as the Member for Oldfields. The Earl is aghast at this treason, and the Countess wails "The borough gone too!," referring not only to the Earl's being replaced but also to the Reform Act of 1832 which had reallocated parliamentary representation from certain rural boroughs depopulated by the Industrial Revolution to heavily populated urban centers. The power of landlords like the Earl to control the lives of local people declined significantly as a result of Reform, a decline that Mrs. Gore dramatizes with Cogit's opportunistic seizure of political office. To add insult to injury, Cogit not only has the Earl's seat; he now *represents* the Earl. Mrs. Gore was a shrewd observer of her own period. Rather than invoke a class system of privilege for the sake of reifying it, she scrutinizes the way that class system is undergoing destabilization and change with refreshing circumspection and wit.

There is a peculiar epilogue to the script which underscores the play's contemporary political currency (Gore 1844: 81–82). Young Lord Bellamont comes downstage to announce that he is on holiday from Eton, and plans to spend his free time betting on horses and drinking liquor on a yacht. Once he has spent all his money and is in need of a place to sober up respectably, he plans to wander into Parliament and hold forth:

My empty head with streaming locks supplied –
Locks – *et praeterea nihil* [and nothing else], – Young England's pride!
On sugar-duties show my vote invincible,
And *stun* them with the "voluntary principle?"
Or should it chance –

At this moment, Bridget Prim enters and interrupts, hissing at him, and reminding us suddenly that the "he" in this case is a "she," as if to check the flow:

Hist, Mrs. Nisbett! – Pray!
Less of yourself, and something of the play!

One wonders if Mrs. Gore was invoking here the debates of 1830–32 when it seemed briefly possible that women might even become enfranchized. That hope dashed, working-class women resolutely put their efforts into salvaging the vote for working-class men. Certainly the reference to "Young England" and the streaming locks would not have been lost on this audience. Mrs. Gore was satirizing Benjamin Disraeli, who in 1843–44 had been instrumental in creating a small dissenting party within the ranks of the Tories who called themselves "Young England." This group sought a nostalgic return to a kind of benevolent stewardship of the working classes by the artistocracy, harkening back to the days before industrialization. Disraeli's group was short-lived, but it stood in direct opposition to free trade and to repeal of the Corn Laws; Disraeli himself published his novel *Coningsby* in 1844, the year *Quid Pro Quo* was produced, and would have been very much in the public eye. I read this epilogue as a strategic thrust at the forces opposing change, because Mrs. Gore puts the speech about Young England in the mouth of a lazy, cheerfully unprincipled upper-class male adolescent (played by a woman), who is then publicly shut up by a female character who is explicitly working-class and Irish. It is all the more disconcerting to discover that Mrs. Gore was a personal friend of Disraeli and his wife Mary Anne. Their surviving correspondence goes back at least as far as 1842, and there are affectionate references to "Dizzy" as a "misguided protectionist," suggesting that her own views favored free trade (Hughenden Dep. 190/1). Whatever the personal subtext, Mrs. Gore's epilogue for this play (and by extension for her play-writing career) was remarkable for the way it placed contemporary gender, class, and political issues at the center.

Quid Pro Quo is universally described in theatre histories as having been damned, but it sustained a remarkably long run for a show that was virtually shouted down on opening night. Without some systematic follow-up, it would appear to anyone reading Allardyce Nicoll, the *Dictionary of National Biography*, or most recently Richard Altick (Altick 1995: 724) that the play was just an embarrassing failure. But the facts do not bear this out. Her 1831 production at the Haymarket of *The School for Coquettes* had a run of thirty nights (as compared to *Quid Pro Quo*'s twenty-six), and was deemed a note-worthy success. The intense negative publicity of that opening night in 1844 undoubtedly contributed to the length of the run because it turned the play into a *cause célèbre*. But those same reviews have had the long-term effect of consigning the play to historical oblivion by historians who have never troubled either to read the play or to check the length of the run.

Sometime during the summer or fall of 1844 *Punch* published a little volume entitled *Scenes from the Rejected Comedies*. It included at the front a thinly disguised list of names of the disappointed contribu-tors: James Sheridan Knowles, Douglas Jerrold, Sir Thomas Tal-fourd, James Robinson Planché, Edward Fitzball, Dion Boucicault, Leigh Hunt, Gilbert à Beckett, Mark Lemon, and Edward Bulwer-Lytton. It is likely, given that the publisher was *Punch*, that à Beckett, perhaps with the collaboration of Lemon, not only assembled the pieces, but also wrote them: each scene is a deliberate send-up of an existing play by the given author.[9] The book refers to "B_____t"

(Boucicault) as "one of that almost extinct species – the writer of a successful Five Act Comedy." A Beckett comments tongue-in-cheek about his own rejected comedy (*The School for Sentiment*) as follows:

The extreme conciseness of this gentleman's style enables us to print his comedy entire, and when we see the wide range of subjects it embraces; the rough honesty of the tar; the recklessness of the libertine lord; the abiding endurance of the patient girl; the affectionate bluffness of the admiral her father; the merry promptness of the coxswain to indulge in one of those hornpipes which constitute the distinctive character of the British seaman; – when we see so much genuine nature, such pathos, such a wholesome enthusiasm for English commerce, such a nice feeling for the peerage, which makes the libertine lord repent in the fourth act; – when we see all this, we are only surprised that the comedy is in this collection instead of being acted on the boards of the Haymarket. (A Beckett 1844: 35)

A Beckett's satirical commentary about his five-page play suggests that in the absence of any clear sense of what comedy ought to be, there was a frenzied effort by this playwright to throw every available stereotype into the pot, in the desperate hope that *something* would please the audience. One is vividly reminded of that meeting in October 1843, when some of the same playwrights and managers struggled to define national drama. A Beckett reflects the chaos in which contemporary playwrights found themselves, faced with demands for a still indeterminate national drama, a demographically shifting audience, and an immovably cautious and conservative tradition of censorship. In fact, it would appear that *Scenes from the Rejected Comedies* had as its primary object the task of reflecting on the chaotic situation confronting playwrights in general, and to make fun of this undignified scramble to create and define genres, rather than what we might have expected from the title, that is, a satirical treatment of Mrs. Gore and her prize-winning comedy.

This surmise is borne out by other evidence. *Punch* had been diligently tracking the development of the Prize Comedy competition, and had published à Beckett's parody, *The School for Sentiment* (without the narrative introduction) sometime in 1843, long before it ever appeared in the *Rejected Comedies* and well before the committee had made its final selection. It is in fact possible that all the "rejected comedies" were written for this collection before Mrs. Gore's name became known, which would account for her complete absence from the book, either by name or by implication. Nothing in the book makes use – satirically or otherwise – of *Quid Pro Quo*'s plot devices, or of Mrs. Gore's gender. If my speculation is correct, then in a peculiar way the book gives us a glimpse of what a response to the Prize Comedy competition might have been if gender had been removed from the equation. The playwright, as a species, is assumed to be male. *Punch* does not indulge in any overt malice toward women playwrights; they simply seem not to exist. Even after the names of the winning play and playwright were announced, it referred to *Quid Pro Quo* without a single reference anywhere, negative or positive, to the fact that Mrs. Gore was a woman.[10] It was as if Mrs. Gore's gender had been completely erased.

There is a peculiar footnote to the history of *Quid Pro Quo* which takes us back full circle to the issue of national drama. In 1839 and again in 1840, Mrs. Gore wrote to her publisher Richard Bentley about something she wanted him to consider: not a novel, this time, but a five-act historical verse tragedy called *Dacre of the South*, based on the reign of Henry VIII (Franceschina 1997; Gore 1840). She contradicts herself by writing in one letter that "it is not intended for the stage," and in another that she "cannot get it acted to my satisfaction" (Bentley letters: fos. L9 and L11). So far as I have been able to discover, *Dacre* was never acted on the stage, undoubtedly because it would not have passed the censorship. Any play during this period which showed an English monarch to be cruel, devious and opportunistic with regard to his subjects' property was certain to be refused by the Examiner of Plays.[11] It did not matter how meticulously the play followed recorded history (Mrs. Gore's printed text cited *Holinshed's Chronicles* and a number of other historical sources, in a vain effort to underscore the documentary aspect of her play). If a parallel could be drawn between the historical monarch and the contemporary one, no matter how remote the resemblance, the play would never be licensed for production, although it might very well be published.

If we consider *Dacre* and *Quid Pro Quo* (which was her next and final play) in tandem, some interesting possibilities emerge. Mrs. Gore seems to have reasoned that if she was going to write on subjects that were topical and political, she was going to have to work in a different genre, namely comedy. Politically sensitive tragedy, as she implies to Bentley, was likely to be a publishing venture rather than a producing one. Her letters even state that she did not expect money for this play, although she reassures Bentley that the sales will cover the cost of publication. But what is most striking about these letters is the urgency and insistence of her tone, as if to suggest that regardless of the financial issues this script must go to press. She seems bent on staking out some territory in the drama, and because this play cannot be produced on the public stage, she needs his cooperation to get it into circulation. Bentley in fact did cooperate, and *Dacre* was published in 1840.

The significance of pairing *Dacre* with *Quid Pro Quo* is that it situates Mrs. Gore not as an unfortunate victim of historical circumstance, but as a canny player in a large and treacherous game. She wanted to be counted as a serious contender in this quest for a national drama, and she was looking for a way to position herself. *Dacre* was her own proof that a tragedy which reflected on English history might never see production. Then came Webster's contest and a chance to try her skills in another genre. Her play evidently made a strong impression with that committee; the vote was not a compromised one, but marked a firm consensus that this play had hit the mark. But initially no one on the committee knew that the play they chose had been written by a woman, and that this contest, falling as it did in the midst of the national drama controversy, would place Mrs. Gore squarely in the middle of a battlefield in which gender was to become a critical issue.

Was Mrs. Gore right? Was her play unfairly judged, with judgments based on gender discrimination? If her name had been kept secret as she was promised it would (instead of being leaked to the press three weeks before the show opened, giving her detractors time to organize),[12] would it have made a difference to the play's reception? I think it would have. This same play, written by a man, and more particularly written by one of the men in the inner circle, so to speak, might have come in for its share of criticism, but it would never have had to justify its existence in the way *Quid Pro Quo* did, or to defend itself against accusations of indecency. Mrs. Gore's detractors were asserting their claim to a shifting field. But her being a woman had symbolic importance far beyond what she herself claimed in her 1844 preface.

The legislation of 1843, even though it was functionally symbolic, intensified a sense of "what's next?" for those already involved in the national drama debate. This, combined with the publicity connected to Webster's competition, contributed to a situation in which the stakes of winning the contest began to assume disproportionate significance. The timing of the announcement set up the winning play to be part of a new and undefined chapter in which theatre reform and the quest for national drama were linked to the demands of an expanding market for new plays and the loss of the majors as a cultural focal point. Underpinning all of these expectations was Reform itself, which played out not only as Mrs. Gore's subject matter, but also as the resonating social theme of the 1830s and 1840s. It is certain that no play, however well crafted, could have satisfied all the diverse anxieties and expectations that were circulating at that moment.

But when a woman won the contest, something shifted. Suddenly the main issue, if I have interpreted the *Rejected Comedies* correctly, was no longer which kind of drama was going to be the national drama, but who was going to write it. Genre, which had been at the center of the debate, was now complicated by gender. Mrs. Gore's triumph threw the profession into an undignified scramble to distance itself from her winning play. It had to be discredited, either as literature, or as production, or both.

What was it about Mrs. Gore's gender that could not be digested? Her public presence, not only as a playwright but also as a nationally known novelist, must have suggested that in addition to occupying public space, women were poised and ready to redefine that space and to set its terms. The prospect of a woman taking a leadership position in the profession at this psychologically loaded moment, especially when the authors of the *Rejected Comedies* were at a complete loss as to how to proceed, was simply untenable. Mrs. Gore's colleagues were prepared to let her work, but they were not prepared for her to become the poster girl for the national theatre debate.[13]

No matter that the publicity around *Quid Pro Quo* was negative, or even that Mrs. Gore never wrote for the stage again. A marker had been placed at mid-century. It was by no means the first time a woman playwright had worked professionally, but it was the first time a woman had *represented* the profession. Mrs. Gore's experience with *Quid Pro Quo* has something to teach us about the history of women playwrights, but only if we consciously resist the army of journalists and historians who have worked so industriously to minimize her presence in the records that remain. She stands squarely at the center of nineteenth-century theatre history, blocking traffic, a signal reminder that, as Cogit himself reminds us, a new order was already in the making.

NOTES

1 In 1840, Frederick Guest Tomlins published a book about the damage
   the monopoly had done to playwriting and to the life of British drama.
   His book, entitled *A Brief View of the English Drama*, may have contributed
   to the pressure to review the legislation to reform the monopoly system
   three years later.

2 My thanks to Tracy C. Davis for suggesting this formulation.

3 I have been unable to detect who this reviewer might be; he has the
   embittered sound of someone whose play did not get picked, but an
   examination of Christopher Kent's lists of reviewers for the period did
   not produce a name that could be successfully checked against Nicoll's
   handlists. See Kent 1980: 41 ff.

4 The playbills for the run are held by the Harvard Theatre Collection,
   Cambridge, MA (see plate 1).

5 In Richard Altick's recent treatment, for example, this incident is
   unfortunately reported as if it actually happened, even though Altick's
   source is Jerrold's report in *Punch* (vol. 7, no. 3). Matters are further
   muddied by the fact that Altick cites a transmittal letter written by
   "Charles Kean, the chair of the committee," when in fact the chair was
   Charles Kemble (Altick 1997: 724).

6 There is a small blurb in the *Critic*, dated Saturday 13 January 1844 (15:
   172) in which it is reported: "Talking – or rather writing of letting
   [Covent Garden] reminds us that you have let your theatre to the 'Anti-
   Corn-Law League.' This is wrong; a patent theatre is not the proper
   arena for political meetings of any party." This commentator is
   offended by the presence of a political group in one of the patent
   theatres, as if there were some aura of respectability connected to the
   patents that precluded activities overtly connected with politics.

7 The Harvard Theatre Collection holds a license for the Haymarket that
   reads as follows: "Act of the 6th and 7th of Victoria, Cap. 68 for
   regulating theatre: License for 1844–45, Little Theatre in the Haymarket, in the Parish of St. Martin in the Fields" which states that the
   licensee may stage plays performed on all days of the year except Ash
   Wednesday and Passion Week. This theatre, although housed in a new
   building as of 1821, would have been associated in the mind of the
   public with Foote and both the Colmans, father and son.

8 This production was directed by Denise Walen at Vassar College's
   Powerhouse Theater, 27 February to 1 March 1997. Professor Walen
   found that the original script needed cutting. Her one major change to
   the text was to cast Sir George Mordent as Lady Mordent, which to
   some extent redeemed what many have felt is a failure to give the
   wonderfully outspoken character of Mrs. Grigson her due at the end of
   the play.

9 The *Rejected Comedies*, also appears in an anthology of *Punch* materials

edited by Gilbert à Beckett entitled *The Quizziology of the British Drama* (1846).

10 For example, there is an open letter published in *Punch* (7.3) in 1844 in which Charles Kemble says "*Quid Pro Quo* has deceived us all" and offers to give Webster back his £500, with the apologies of the committee, but nowhere is there any mention either of Mrs. Gore or her gender, and that holds true all the way through this period.

11 Stephens (1980) is particularly helpful about the patterns of censorship during this period. He cites the cases of Mary Russell Mitford's *Charles the First* (1825) and Emma Robinson's *Richelieu in Love, or the Youth of Charles I* (1844) as important cases in point.

12 The story, as Mrs. Gore tells it in her 1844 preface, is that someone on the committee recognized her handwriting and leaked her name to the press. It might have been Charles Kemble, since it was he who had been Examiner of Plays from November 1836 through to 1840, and his initials to allow licensing are on her copy of *A Tale of Tub* (1837).

13 There is another extraordinary incident of this kind: Kerry Powell has documented a contest won by Netta Syrrett in the 1890s, in which the same kind of protest and defamation took place (1997: 143–46).

REFERENCES

A Beckett, Gilbert Abbott 1844, *Scenes from the Rejected Comedies*, London: Punch.

A Beckett, Gilbert Abbott 1846, *The Quizziology of the British Drama*, London: Punch.

Altick, Richard 1997, *Punch: The Lively Youth of a British Institution, 1841–1851*, Columbus: Ohio State University Press.

Bentley letters 1839 to 1840, Richard Bentley to Catherine Gore, Bentley Collection, L9 and L11, Special Collections, University of Illinois at Champaign-Urbana.

Clark, Anna 1995, *The Struggle for the Breeches: Gender and the Making of the British Working Class*, Berkeley: University of California Press.

Cook, Dutton 1882, 'The Prize Comedy,' *Theatre*, 1 August: 65–74.

Critic, 12 October 1843, 13 January 1844.

Disraeli correspondence 1842, Hughenden Dep. 190/1 Bodleian Library, Oxford University.

Dramatic and Musical Review, 20 July 1844.

Era, 26 May and 23 June 1844.

Franceschina, John (ed.) 1997, *Sisters of Gore: Seven Gothic Melodramas by British Women, 1790–1843*, New York: Garland.

Gore, Catherine Grace 1840, *Dacre of the South, or, The Olden Time*, London: Richard Bentley.

Gore, Catherine Grace 1844, *Quid Pro Quo: or, The Day of Dupes*, 3rd edn,

London: Richard Bentley; also facsimile edition CD-ROM *Nineteenth Century Theatre* 26.2 (Winter 1998).

Illustrated London News, 23 June 1844.

Jones, Gareth Stedman 1983, *Languages of Class: Studies in English Working Class History*, Cambridge: Cambridge University Press.

Kent, Christopher 1980 'Periodical Critics of Drama, Music and Art, 1830–1914: A Preliminary List,' *Victorian Periodicals Review*, 13.1/2: 41 ff.

Morning Chronicle, 19, 20 and 26 June 1844.

Nicoll, Allardyce 1955, *A History of English Drama, 1660–1900*, 3rd edn, vol. IV, Cambridge: Cambridge University Press.

Powell, Kerry 1997, *Women and Victorian Theatre*, Cambridge: Cambridge University Press.

Punch, 1843–44, 4–7.

Stephens, John Russell 1980, *The Censorship of English Drama, 1824–1901*, Cambridge: Cambridge University Press.

Tomlins, Frederick Guest 1840, *A Brief View of the English Drama*, London: C. Mitchell.

Weekly Dispatch, 23 June 1844.

PART 2

Wrighting the play

CHAPTER 4

Jane Scott the writer-manager

Jacky Bratton

Jane Moody's chapter in this volume offers the idea that powerful women in the theatre, as performers and managers, are co-creators of plays made for their use, in "a kind of performative intertextuality." My term for this vital process is *intertheatricality*; and it can be exemplified even more strongly by those exceptional cases where the pen was in fact held by a woman, but one whose writing practice was part and parcel of her own performances and managerial activity. Whoever wields the pen, such a creative process is by no means a second-best form of authorship. I would suggest that in such nineteenth-century work we may see a distinctive quality that is still recognizable in feminist theatre practice today. Such a reconceptualization of the categories of creative work is, however, a challenge to hegemonic notions. Collaborative writing is just about acceptable, though it tends to be categorized as "good entertainment" only, from Beaumont and Fletcher to Rogers and Hart; but when a solitary or bipartite compositional process does not dominate, and the creative collaboration includes the work of actor, scene painter and manager, the resulting work has been devalued and erased from the record of significant writing.

My example of this is Jane Margaret Scott (1779–1839),[1] performer, writer, manager, founder of the Adelphi theatre in London. During her working life, "Miss Scott" was generally known to be the moving force behind the successful new theatre, as well as its principal writer and performer. She retired from the stage in 1822, and died in 1839; after the passage of the Theatres Regulation Act of 1843 her removal from history began. The *Theatrical Observer* of 11 December 1844, for example, tells us that

Miss Scott developed strong symptoms of dramatic disease and though her extraordinary talent was undoubted by her father and friends, it was delicately hinted that the greedy public not only expected intrinsic merit

for their money, but also that it must be hallowed o'er with beauty to secure
the first impression. Now Miss Scott, in addition to some natural defects
had the smallpox and the rickets unfavourably, but as genius comes in all
disguises, she really had great talent, both as an actress and a writer ...
(quoted in Nelson and Cross, 1990: 1)

Such "diseased" ambition was soon eliminated from history. In 1889
she was still sufficiently visible to be included in Barton Baker's
History of the London Stage as an actress who appeared for thirteen
years at the Adelphi. By the time she appears in Harold Scott's *The
Early Doors* in 1946 she is not indexed: he includes her father's name
only. She figures in Richard Klepac's *Mr. Mathews at Home* (1979)
among the people who paved the way for Charles Mathews; Klepac
has not had the curiosity to do more than quote Baker. Allardyce
Nicoll, in the master play index of the British stage, lists her has
having written only two plays (Nicoll, 1952: vol. II, 387). It is only in
the exhaustive archival work of the London Stage Project that she is
at last credited with most of her works, at least in the summary form
of the listings in the *Adelphi Theatre Calendar* (Nelson and Cross 1990);
and here her first name is finally revealed to posterity.[2] Modern
theatre history remains complicit in obscuring Scott's achievements;
they are of interest only to the calendar makers, whose objective is
simply completeness.

Yet Jane Scott's work was an important foundation of popular
theatre, both commercial and "alternative," pioneering Victorian
burlesque and music hall. Her theatre, first called the Sans Pareil,
gained its Lord Chamberlain's license in the flurry of permissions to
perform in Westminster that were granted by Lord Dartmouth, the
antipatent Lord Chamberlain (Nicholson 1906: 164–67). Not all
applicants were so successful: there is a long list in the *Morning
Chronicle* of 16 November 1807, many of whom are not heard of
again. Why Scott's theatre was amongst those chosen can only be
conjectured. Its location was, I think, important: it was newly built
in 1806, next door to John Scott's paint and dye shop at 417 the
Strand, in a space created by knocking down twelve dwellings in a
side alley, Bayley's Court (*Rate Books* 1780–1820). It was thus very
near to the old theatres and to several other successful new ventures
like the Olympic Pavilion, built in 1802 by Philip Astley the circus
manager to be his foothold in Westminster. The Sans Pareil and the
Olympic (which was bought up by John Scott and bequeathed to his
daughter when he died in 1838, and is mentioned in her own will –

so John Scott was proprietor during Vestris's management) were both regarded as serious threats by the patent managements. But others in the *Morning Chronicle*'s list also stood within the profitable ambit of the major theatres. The Minor, in Catherine Street, for example, between the Sans Pareil and Drury Lane, never obtained a license and remained a private theatre, in the half-light of disreputable quasi-professionalism. There were all sorts of houses of entertainment in the area; the Strand was at the heart of London nightlife. The Sans Pareil may have been thought worthy of a license by association with the Sans Souci, a tiny theatre in Leicester Square run by Charles Dibdin Sen. for his own one-man shows: Jane Scott did similar solo entertainments. She was trained as a musician, and gave professional singing lessons until she began performing her solo act and showing off her pupils to a subscription audience of friends. The shows were illuminated by her father's own optical inventions (part of his trade was in magic lanterns). The licensing of the entertainments for public admission was gradual. In 1806 they obtained permission for "dancing, song, recitation and optical and mechanical exhibitions"; then the theatrical license, for pantomime, in 1807, expanded to include burletta in 1809. By this time they were already offering a full evening's entertainment including two plays with full scenery as well as all forms of music and spectacle (Nicholson 1906: 283). On the triumphant defeat of the patentees' attempt to suppress the minors in 1818, the Scotts sold a fully fledged theatre to James Rodwell and Willis Jones.

Jane Scott's theatre was therefore essentially illegitimate. One might even say that it came into existence as a kind of institutionally endorsed oppositional voice, deliberately allowed to exist in order to challenge elements within the hegemonic mainstream, specifically the grip of self-serving aristocrats and their lackeys – "Old Corruption" – upon the patent theatres. There were modernizing forces, especially the literate middle-class movement toward reform, that wished to see the patent holders discredited to make room for themselves. This did not mean, however, that such forces wished to see Jane Scott's work replace the legitimate theatre. That was to be the role for the champions of the Drama, who would move in upon the tottering patent managements as they fell, and triumphantly recapture the national stages for the expression of a new dominant voice. Hence the rhetoric of "the Decline of the Drama" that pervaded cultural polemics and theorizing during the first three

decades of the nineteenth century.[3] Houses of entertainment, like
the Adelphi, and female managements, *de facto* ones like that of Jane
Scott or actual like those of Eliza Vestris, Harriet Waylett and a
number of women who were temporarily able to manage for
themselves during this period of upheaval, were useful sticks with
which to beat the patent managements via the press.[4] But they were
also themselves a sign of the shockingly bad state of theatrical
culture, where audiences had come to prefer shows got up by
illiterate actors and women in breeches to Shakespeare at Covent
Garden; and their work was by definition of little real or permanent
value, since they were forbidden to stage the Drama.

Antitheatrical prejudice linked public performance and immor-
ality. For the (male) hegemonic voice to achieve the "freedom of the
stage," women – along with wild beasts, mindless music and
lascivious spectacle – had at all costs to be kept from polluting the
philosophical and literary genius of the Drama. If this distinction
failed, there would be no stopping place on the slippery slope
between high art, the vehicle of great thoughts, the influential voice
shaping national and personal identities – our Shakespearian heritage – and the debilitating exploitation that is popular entertainment: music, dancing, the singer, the stripper, pornography and
prostitution. Plato, Jeremy Collier, and the politicians of the Com-
monwealth who closed the theatres would be proved right.

As theatre and literary historians, we have still not completely rid
ourselves of this mindset: most writers still seek to discriminate, even
in these postmodern times where high and low art merge, between,
on the one hand, drama (which may make use of modern techniques
such as solo performance, devising, or multimedia, and old devices
such as songs or spectacles, but is in itself something written, by an
author or, at most, authors, for the sake of expressing something
important), and on the other hand, mass entertainment created for
money. How these lines can be drawn is an important debate still,
and it intersects with feminist questions about spectatorship, ownership, and the performer. I am interested in producing a reconceptua-
lized history of the stage and its arts that will not need a literary
hierarchy or the binary that underpins the dramatic canon, and so
will give due weight to the contribution made by the work of
practitioners like Jane Scott, and will enable us to recognize her and
the very many other entertainers who foreshadow modern feminist
ideas about the making of new work.

For the decade or so of its formation, Jane Scott's work created and dominated the institution which was to become the Adelphi. She was aware of this and wanted others to be so too: in a period where authors' names are given little publicity, the Sans Pareil bills normally flag her writing, and often proudly announce "the whole of the evening's entertainments written by Miss Scott." It is interesting that conventional theatre history and bibliography has nevertheless, despite this unusual help from the publicly available playbills, contrived to lose all but two of her plays until 1990. I have so far retrieved forty-nine titles from the bills, with the help of the *Adelphi Theatre Calendar*, and twenty-two scripts from the Larpent Collection of plays submitted for licensing. These are direct if sketchy transcriptions of her working texts, valuable for reconstituting the life of her theatre.[5] She was providing materials for use by a company and an audience well known to her, materials one might call site-specific: plays that were part of the bill for a small, new theatre in a West End in which, then as now, hugely prestigious centres of culture were mingled with places for drinking, gambling, and prostitution. So her plays cannot be read alone as literary productions; the "whole of the evening's entertainments" needs to be considered when attempting to understand her writing. The plays are created to be part of a good night out. In John McGrath's terms (1984), of course, they merely constitute the kind of popular entertainment that purposeful, socially responsible playmakers must appropriate so as to speak to the people; but it is the historian's task first to understand what such material was saying of itself. The values carried and developed by Scott's work as writer, manager, and performer may be very different from ours in the late twentieth century, but the integration of all the theatrical arts that she deployed in setting up an evening at the Adelphi is oddly like the holistic ideals of some modern theatre work, especially women's companies. And like more ideologically self-conscious modern community theatres, her work poses a threat to the formative individualistic paradigm of high art.

I therefore propose to hang my analysis of her writing on an ordinary Sans Pareil bill, that for 24 February 1817 (plate 3). I would read this as an intentionally planned mixed bill of entertainments that includes plays and ballets, variety turns, music and songs both within and outside the plays. The editors of the *Adelphi Theatre Calendar* stress that the Sans Pareil always offered such mixed entertainment, even when the turns are not registered on the bills

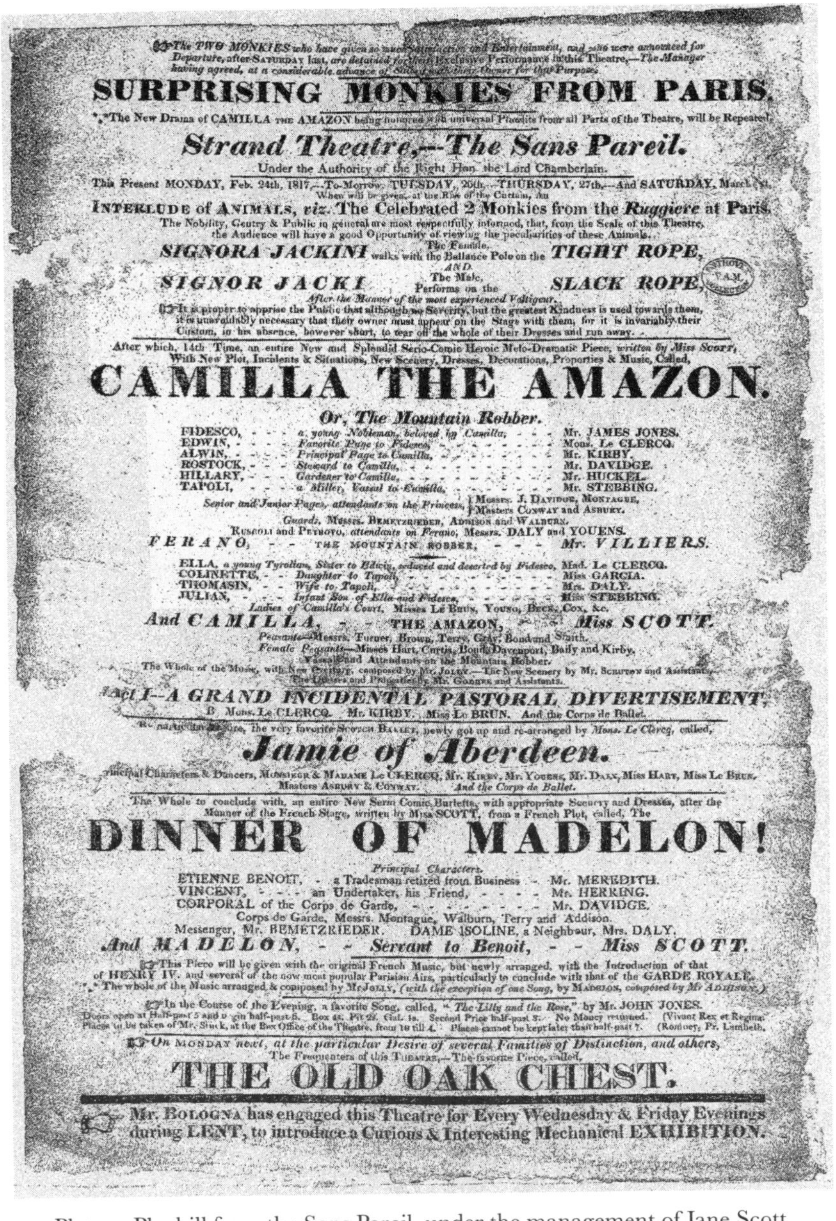

The TWO MONKIES who have given so much Satisfaction and Entertainment, and who were announced for Departure, after SATURDAY last, are detained for their Exclusive Performance in this Theatre,—The Manager having agreed, at a considerable advance of Salary with their Owner for that Purpose.

SURPRISING MONKIES FROM PARIS.

, The New Drama of CAMILLA THE AMAZON being honored with universal Plaudits from all Parts of the Theatre, will be Repeated.

Strand Theatre,—The Sans Pareil.

Under the Authority of the Right Hon. the Lord Chamberlain.

This Present MONDAY, Feb. 24th, 1817,—To-Morrow, TUESDAY, 25th,—THURSDAY, 27th,—And SATURDAY, March 1st,
When will be given, at the Rise of the Curtain, An

INTERLUDE of ANIMALS, viz. The Celebrated 2 Monkies from the Ruggiere at Paris.

The Nobility, Gentry & Public in general are most respectfully informed, that, from the Scale of this Theatre, the Audience will have a good Opportunity of viewing the peculiarities of these Animals.

SIGNORA JACKINI — The Female, walks with the Ballance Pole on the TIGHT ROPE,
AND
SIGNOR JACKI — The Male, Performs on the SLACK ROPE,
After the Manner of the most experienced Voltigeur.

It is proper to apprise the Public that although no Severity, but the greatest Kindness is used towards them, it is unavoidably necessary that their owner must appear on the Stage with them, for it is invariably their Custom, in his absence, however short, to tear off the whole of their Dresses and run away.

After which, 14th Time, an entire New and Splendid Serio-Comic Heroic Melo-Dramatic Piece, written by Miss Scott, With New Plot, Incidents & Situations, New Scenery, Dresses, Decorations, Properties & Music, Called,

CAMILLA THE AMAZON.

Or, The Mountain Robber.

FIDESCO, - - - a young Nobleman, beloved by Camilla, - - - Mr. JAMES JONES.
EDWIN, - - - Favorite Page to Fidesco, - - - Mons. Le CLERCQ.
ALWIN, - - - Principal Page to Camilla, - - - Mr. KIRBY.
ROSTOCK, - - - Steward to Camilla, - - - Mr. DAVIDGE.
HILLARY, - - - Gardener to Camilla, - - - Mr. HUCKEL.
TAPOLI, - - - a Miller, Vassal to Camilla, - - - Mr. STEBBING.
Senior and Junior Pages, attendants on the Princess, Messrs. J. Davidge, Montague, Masters Conway and Asbury.
Guards, Messrs. Bemetzrieder, Addison and Walburn.
Ruscoli and Petrovo, attendants on Ferano, Messrs. DALY and YOUENS.
FERANO, - - - THE MOUNTAIN ROBBER, - - - Mr. VILLIERS.

ELLA, a young Tyrolian, Sister to Edwin, seduced and deserted by Fidesco, Mad. Le CLERCQ.
COLINETTE, - - Daughter to Tapoli, - - - Miss GARCIA.
THOMASIN, - - Wife to Tapoli, - - - Mrs. DALY.
JULIAN, - - Infant Son of Ella and Fidesco, - - - Miss STEBBING.
Ladies of Camilla's Court, Misses Le Brun, Young, Beck, Cox, &c.
And CAMILLA, - - THE AMAZON, - - Miss SCOTT.
Peasants—Messrs. Turner, Brown, Terry, Gray, Bond and Smith.
Female Peasants—Misses Hart, Curtis, Bond, Davenport, Baily and Kirby.
Vassals and Attendants on the Mountain Robber.

The Whole of the Music, with New Overture, composed by Mr. Jolly.—The New Scenery by Mr. Scruton and Assistants.—The Dresses and Properties by Mr. Gonner and Assistants.

Act I.—A GRAND INCIDENTAL PASTORAL DIVERTISEMENT,
By Mons. Le CLERCQ. Mr. KIRBY. Miss Le BRUN. And the Corps de Ballet.

[illegible], the very favorite Scotch Ballet, newly got up and re-arranged by Mons. Le Clercq, called,

Jamie of Aberdeen.

Principal Characters & Dancers, Monsieur & Madame Le CLERCQ, Mr. Kirby, Mr. Youens, Mr. Daly, Miss Hart, Miss Le Brun, Masters Asbury & Conway. And the Corps de Ballet.

The Whole to conclude with, an entire New Serio Comic Burletta, with appropriate Scenery and Dresses, after the Manner of the French Stage, written by Miss SCOTT, from a French Plot, called, The

DINNER OF MADELON!

Principal Characters.
ETIENNE BENOIT, - a Tradesman retired from Business - Mr. MEREDITH.
VINCENT, - - - an Undertaker, his Friend, - - - Mr. HERRING.
CORPORAL of the Corps de Garde, - - - Mr. DAVIDGE.
Corps de Garde, Messrs. Montague, Walburn, Terry and Addison.
Messenger, Mr. BEMETZRIEDER. DAME ISOLINE, a Neighbour, Mrs. DALY.
And MADELON, - - Servant to Benoit, - - Miss SCOTT.

This Piece will be given with the original French Music, but newly arranged, with the Introduction of that of HENRY IV. and several of the now most popular Parisian Airs, particularly to conclude with that of the GARDE ROYALE.
, The whole of the Music arranged & composed by Mr Jolly, (with the exception of one Song, by Madelon, composed by Mr Addison.)

In the Course of the Evening, a favorite Song, called, "The Lilly and the Rose," by Mr. JOHN JONES.

Doors open at Half-past 5 and begin half-past 6. Box 4s. Pit 2s. Gal. 1s. Second Price half-past 8. No Money returned. (Vivant Rex et Regina.
Places to be taken of Mr. Stack, at the Box Office of the Theatre, from 10 till 4. Places cannot be kept later than half-past 7. (Romney, Pr. Lambeth.

On MONDAY next, at the particular Desire of several Families of Distinction, and others, The Frequenters of this Theatre,—The favorite Piece, called,

THE OLD OAK CHEST.

Mr. BOLOGNA has engaged this Theatre for Every Wednesday & Friday Evenings during LENT, to introduce a Curious & Interesting Mechanical EXHIBITION.

Plate 3. Playbill from the Sans Pareil, under the management of Jane Scott, dated 24 February 1817.

(Nelson and Cross 1990: 12). On this quite ordinary night two turns are separately billed. These are the sorts of things that will later form part of the segregated offerings of the music halls: the monkeys, hired for at least a week, and the song by John Jones. Jones is probably a filler, worth advertising because he has a following, but not scheduled for any particular moment and so useful to cover gaps and set-ups. I would suggest that the monkeys are rather different: they are being brought in to attract an audience at the early opening time, 6.00 p.m. There is a press cutting in Winston's *Scrapbook* (Winston n.d.) advertising them as specially for children, who would then presumably go home. I also see them as enticing in the curious rather than the deliberate playgoer, appealing to the unsophisticated who might not like to go to the expensive and intimidating legitimate theatres; possibly these would be the tourists, up to London to see the sights, of which this is one. Hence the note on the bill, telling those who are not acquainted with this theatre that they will get a good view.

Then comes a full-scale melodrama, no expense spared, new in all its aspects (it premiered eighteen days earlier), starring Jane Scott. It is notable that this, the main dramatic offering, integrates "entertainments." It contains several songs, as indeed the terms of the license required. But it also incorporates the group of dancers who were part of the season's company: the "Grand incidental pastoral divertisement" is a large-scale dance interlude, with principals and *corps de ballet*. It is led by Le Clerq, the principal dancer and choreographer of the house, who has a full role in the play as Edwin. He and his wife appear again in the second ballet, billed in its own right.

The last scheduled piece is a "French" farce, whose cast includes, again, Jane Scott herself. She plays two very different roles on this evening, the near-tragic princess Camilla in the melodrama and the comic and no doubt singing servant in the farce. She wrote both these pieces, as she is at pains to point out. The farce, she wishes to make clear, is new, and her own, but based on a French model, which is a selling point; but it is a point of pride, it seems, that the melodrama is not based on a preexisting plot, incidents, or situations, but is entirely original.

By the time the farce comes on, the bill has mutated to the taste of the half-price audience, coming in after 9 p.m., making the theatre merely a part of their night on the town. If they are City workers, of course, they would not be free from shop and office until around 8 p.m. So this is the late-night piece, calculated to attract the fashionable strollers: it is laced with Parisian songs, turning the play into a cabaret, so that the young bloods who come can display their knowledge of the newest French shows, and their acquisition of the latest tunes, next day in shop, office, or drawing room. These men were an important part of the West End audience, whose taste continued to shape Adelphi bills, in particular, beyond the mid-century (Yates 1884: vol. i, 200). At the bottom of the bill there is a note that suggests the existence of an audience of *habitués*: *The Old Oak Chest* is requested by "the frequenters of this theatre."

This is the immediate setting, then, in which one must read the texts of Jane Scott's plays. There are two more dimensions: the contemporary situation in London, involving great unrest as postwar economic distress expressed itself in extreme radicalism, riots and the suspension of *habeas corpus*:[6] and, in the case of *Camilla the Amazon*, the play's location in a powerful literary and dramatic tradition. It is a Gothic melodrama, of which she wrote three during this period: *The Old Oak Chest* (February 1816), *Camilla the Amazon* (February 1817), and *The Lord of the Castle* (November 1817). She had had an interest in the genre since the theatre opened, composing *Asgard the Demon Hunter* in 1812 and other Gothic or Oriental Gothic pieces in 1808, 1813 and 1814. The definition of "the Gothic" in modern criticism was, for a long time, a matter of listing certain characteristic settings and objects as its "stage properties," but analysis of Gothic drama *per se* has been the last and slowest to materialize. Recently, however, Jeffrey Cox, identifying Joanna Baillie as "the most important playwright in England" between 1798 and 1851 (Cox, 1992: 50), has suggested that the strongly Gothic elements in her work are linked to the performances of Sarah Siddons, "the perfect actress for the Gothic drama, for she was at her best in the two stances the Gothic demanded of women: women were either terrorized and mad or stoic and indomitable, but they were always passive" (53). Cox argues for Baillie's conscious challenging of this requirement, while still drawing upon the inspiration of Siddons's performances in writing such a play as *De Monfort* with her in mind. I would offer Scott's Gothic plays as being far less deliberately theorized – she wrote nothing remotely resembling Baillie's analytical introduction to her *Series of Plays*[7] – but far more clearly challenging the assumptions of the genre, especially about women and morality. She did this simply by virtue of the symbiosis of her writing with her theatre practice. She writes the plays for the Sans Pareil audience, which determines their tone; for her coworkers, which influences their form; and for herself as performer, which gives her creative freedom in conceiving the leading female character.

In the early work *Asgard the Demon Hunter*, the demands of writing for the dance company as well as the actors obviously shape the piece. The licenser's manuscript in the Larpent Collection is a scenario of action, its plot revolving around the interventions of the demonic Asgard, played by dancer Rivolta, while the choreographer Gabriel Giroux played the hero. The Giroux daughters also appeared, Peggy Giroux playing a runaway nun married to the evil Baron Wildgrave. They are supported by singing huntsmen, dancing demons and demonic hounds who eventually carry the Baron off to Hell. The women are by no means passive in this piece, and what small amount of dialogue it was felt necessary to submit to the licenser, containing the decisions and necessary verbalizations of the action, belongs almost exclusively to them, chiefly to the ex-nun Adele. At one point she enters with clothes to disguise herself as the ghost of a hermit murdered by the Baron, announcing "I'll save the helpless Lilla or I'll die / This dress – this dagger – shall strike his soul with Dread" – in the manner of the famous female ghost in Lewis's *The Castle Spectre*.

Baillie sought to distinguish her writing as tragedy, rather than melodrama, but it is the pervasive presence of the comic perspective, melodramatically intercut with the serious scenes, that marks Scott's Gothic. Even in the first flowering of Gothic writing in the 1790s some leading practitioners, like Monk Lewis, were inclined to alternate between terror and laughter, sometimes approaching the horrors they described with an ambiguous tongue in cheek. Before many years had passed this became a near-universal tendency. Robert Miles calls the writing of the generation of Mary Shelley and Byron "belated Gothic," "texts which, in their self-consciousness, bespeak both an awareness of the 'discursive' subtext of the Gothic and an attitude towards it" (Miles 1993: 14). Scott is part of this later generation of Gothicists with attitude, writing for an audience long used to the trappings of the form and comfortable about enjoying them, and her plays give a central place to self-reflexive humor. It is sometimes hard to avoid the conclusion that her Gothic is deliberately trashy – that it is, in fact, high camp. The dancer Le Clerq, playing Edwin, is not only integrated into the action, heroically rescuing the child at the end of the play, but also becomes a subject for jokes around effeminacy – he is disguised as a peasant girl – and is mocked for belonging to the ballet, a high art form. In *Asgard* Scott resorts to comic rhythms and rhymes, with a chorus of singing Inquisitors who enter singing "Tremble proud baron by heaven accursed / Thy castle's high turrets shall soon meet the dirt" and seem to foreshadow the Gilbertian chorus, especially since their menace is topsy-turvy – they embody the threat that has kept Adele from denouncing the Baron's cruelty since he carried her off, but now announce "we bring her peace and pardon."

Genre self-consciousness is most obvious in her last Gothic play *The Lord of the Castle*, which the *British Stage* (November 1817) called "a melodrama ... in which serious and ludicrous incidents are very happily blended." In it Robert Stebbing, a comic performer in the company from 1809 to 1818, played Fabin, manservant to Loredan, the nephew of Lord Alberti, played by J. Jones – a straight man. These two enter in Act 1 with a song, and fall immediately to discussing their sinister situation: they have turned out in the dusk from an inn at the edge of a forest because they were afraid of its fierce-looking clientele, and now they are lost. "Did you ever see a right good piece at the playhouse that did not warn you of such abodes as a woodman's hut – a fisherman's hovel, a small inn and an old castle is always the abode of rogues," Fabin demands. Their fears are continually confirmed, especially when they are let into the castle and immediately wish themselves out again, while the servants deliberately scare them by describing the place: "it was formerly an old monastery which getting out of repair the monks deserted it. O, there are such grand corridors – only you daren't step in them, for fear of popping down unexpected caves; then there's such beautiful apartments only the ivy has grown so over the windows that you can't see, such a fine library only there's no books, and such dismal curious subterrainans [*sic*]." This is all before the evils of the action actually take place; even when they do, the servant who so gloomily relishes his Gothic situation – which he would leave, but it pays so well – comments on the unfolding plot: "the devil every hour presents something new – a man in a mask, an unknown child." Fabin anticipates death knells, and bells do dolorously ring; the master of the castle stalks in ferociously on cue, "his hat ... drawn over his eyes ... and his figure wrapped in a cloak," scattering all before him, sighing tempestuously over a miniature portrait, demanding pistols and poignards.

Before Act 1 is over, however, Lord Alberti has informed us in agonized soliloquy that he has had his wife locked up for five years in "a cavern damp and drear" because she will not tell the name of a man who saved her from bandits but then detained her from home; and we know from an earlier off-hand conversation between Loredan and Fabin that this violator of the first patriarchal law (the absolute imperative of the preservation of impeccable lineage) is none other than Loredan, his nephew and dependent, who cannot resist having fun with a pretty face. Act 2 begins with a slapstick sequence in which Loredan and Fabin are driven back to the hall in search of a place to sleep, terrified out of rooms containing one-year-old corpses and holes for the entry of gypsies, and so are in a position to witness Alberti raising the trapdoor and vowing to end it all by killing his long-suffering wife. Then they suddenly realize that where the gypsies came in they can get out, and decamp, leaving the stage clear for the emotional confrontations between agonized husband and wife and the weeping child through whom Lord Alberti tries to force her surrender. The comics return, of course, at the last moment; Loredan confesses he was the thoughtless sinner, so that the supernaturally honorable Theodosia is not compelled to betray him to the Lord – and the gloomy servant revives her with a draught from his brandy flask. Her curtain speech prays for release from "Destructive Jealousy," but rescue from the overpowering machinery of the Gothic castle would be a more appropriate petition. Modern critics have seen the castle as a malign projection of domestic ideology, the oppressive force that prevents women from getting out of the house (Delamotte 1990); and Jane Scott and her audiences would probably have appreciated the burlesque humor of that idea.

The Old Oak Chest, Scott's most performed Gothic melodrama, the only one of her plays to have been printed, also makes ample room for the comedians of the company and deploys the cultural knowledge of the audience. The published version affords the chance to check the manuscript as a document relating directly to its theatre of origin. In the licensing copy there is both more and less material than saw print: it begins with a subsequently deleted scene in which Miss Le Brun, a dancer dressed as a boy, helps with a piece of plot exposition by conversing with the messenger (currently lost in the forest) who will eventually arrive with the pardon for the discredited General Almanza. She then shows us the precariousness of fate by running across a broken plank bridge suspended over a chasm – so much a standard Gothic prop that its superfluous presence here is arguably a playhouse joke as well as a setting for the display of agile legs.[8] This cut scene is followed by another, in which a chorus of huntsmen sing and tell smutty jokes as they further the exposition. These cuts are both a tightening up and a removal of material specifically created for the Sans Pareil company. The printed version has further cuts to expository material which are damaging to the play, making it appear that events, for example the rescue of Almanza's child, happen without explanation or preparation.

The gap in the manuscript comes where the leading comic – Stebbing again, playing the smuggler's son Tinoco – has an opportunity for a piece of stand-up comedy, dressed up in the character of an old woman. The script has a heading "Tinoco solo" and a blank page and a half. The licenser does not seem to have objected to this oversight, which perhaps was the result of a gap left for consultation with the actor and never filled in; the printed copy has no extended passage here, and indeed cuts various other speeches of Tinoco's, especially his interaction with the heroine Roda (played by Jane Scott), to tone down their sexual and political outspokenness. So the comparison between printed text and manuscript shows Jane Scott accommodating the talents she had to hand, and satisfying the expectations of their audience for a full measure of physical and verbal humor, and a fully-understandable story line.

This play's popularity beyond the Sans Pareil needs an explanation. Other Scott plays were performed at the Coburg, for example, in 1824 and 1825; when John Scott bought the Olympic in 1826 his manager Le Clerq staged a season of Jane Scott's work. But only *The Old Oak Chest* was pirated and later published. Perhaps reference to the larger world beyond the theatres might be illuminating. Another modern critical approach to the understanding of the Gothic vogue has been to see its motifs as symbolic, whether of the fragmented subject (Sedgwick 1980; Miles 1993), the situation of women under patriarchy, or, deriving clues from Michel Foucault's pinpointing of "the moment of history" (Miles 1993: 18) and from Peter Brooks's exposition of the meanings of melodrama (Brooks 1976), of the politics of the revolutionary and Napoleonic period. *The Old Oak Chest*, the first of Scott's three full-scale Gothic melodramas, premiered in February 1816. It played solidly every night while, from the beginning of March, "ultra-Jacobin agitation" broke out in London. An autumn of starvation and unemployment followed, and large-scale protests were organized. The government was alarmed; informers reported that the Hampden Clubs were set upon revolution, stones were thrown at the Prince Regent, and in spring 1817 *habeas corpus* was suspended and the "gagging laws" against seditious meetings and literature were rushed through Parliament (Thompson 1968: 691). There can be, of course, no possibility that the authorities would have overlooked any overtly political play staged in London at this time; but it is interesting that instances of *The Old Oak Chest* being performed beyond the Sans Pareil come from the reports of informers set on by the patent houses to prosecute illegal theatrical venues. It was popular with the most illegitimate reaches of the stage, beyond the law.[9] Political meanings can in fact be adduced from the play.

The plot revolves around Almanza and his wife Adriana – at first called De Lamora and Antoinette in the manuscript. Almanza is on the run because, after great service to his country (Spain), he has been denounced as a traitor on being defeated in a single battle; his castle has been burned and looted. His enemy Lanfranco is the governor of the nearby town, and is in league with a gang of robbers who plunder and terrorize the forest, keeping people away by dressing up as spectres and skeletons: thus the civic power is in the hands of an enemy to virtue who protects theft and terrorism. Over against them are the smuggler Nicolo, his sons Tinoco and Paulo, and their band, who rob only the excise – taxes generally agreed in England at this time to be unjust – and are stout supporters of Almanza, having rescued his goods and, we eventually learn, his infant son from the burning of his castle. Their caves communicate conveniently for rescuing purposes with the dungeons of Lanfranco. The oak chest stands in a cottage inhabited by one of the robbers, a terrifying figure of drunken violence clad in skins, who is barely kept under control by his daughter (played by Jane Scott). It conceals the entrance to an underground passage leading to the castle, and inevitably ruffians surge out of it, dressed as skeletons, to capture Roda and carry her off. She eventually escapes with the aid of Tinoco, leaving the deer brought in for dinner dressed up as herself on a sofa, where her infuriated father stabs it, thinking to kill her to preserve her from dishonor.

Aside from the wry comment on patriarchal images suggested by Roda's relations with her father (Macready was to build one of his most successful roles on the story of Virginius' stabbing of his daughter to keep her from the rapacious ruler of Rome), some more generally political aspects of this seem to me to be clear. The opposition between honest smugglers and dishonest state-supported robbers is consonant with the discontents of the Hampden Clubs and the popular voice they represented, full of grievances about rapacious misgovernment and heartless aristocracy in league with farmers to rob the people of bread. The suggestion for the plight of Almanza could come either from the uncertain treatment of Wellington, victor at Waterloo but in a war whose expenses were unpopular, or, as the suppressed names suggest, from France, where Louis XVIII had returned and begun the White Terror, purging the generals and others who had served Napoleon. It is interesting that in the manuscript, but not in the printed version, General Almanza on coming into his own at the final curtain gives Tinoco a place as an exciseman and makes the robber patriarch a policeman, taking all the smuggler band into some unspecified "state service." Jeffrey Cox maintains that by this date the Gothic dramatists had turned to introspection, and their plays no longer figure popular protest and mass movements triumphant; I would refute this from all of Scott's Gothic work, which appeals to a mob of liberators, sometimes singing songs of liberty, always popular and often comic, to storm the castle, suppress the villain and reinstate justice at the end of the play.

The role of Roda gave her a chance as a writer for covert comment on disruptive fathers and as a performer considerable opportunity for activity and decision, as well as a seriocomic scene full of innuendo with Stebbing as Tinoco. It may have suggested to Jane Scott the possibilities of the Gothic for herself. She wrote *Camilla the Amazon* for her own benefit night. It was not as successful as her other Gothic plays, and did not run beyond eight nights; and while it shares many of the effective aspects of the genre, it does make use of them in a way that the Sans Pareil audiences might not have found very comfortable. Certainly it is less determinedly unserious, less camp than her other Gothic pieces: its humor serves, rather than undercuts, the tensions of its main plot.

Camilla the Amazon rules in some unspecified European locale in a castle surrounded by mountains. As the comics tell us, she was once "mild as a midsummer's morning," but when her husband was lost in battle "she lost her senses – as some think – and became – a perfect Hurricane – why bless you she don't dress like other women but wears a kind of armour and means to defend her castle in person in case of any attack from the desperate Robbers." When this onslaught inevitably materializes, at the end of the play, she does indeed wield a sword but is defeated, and is about to commit suicide rather than be the robber's bride when he reveals himself to be her lost husband. He bids her "lay aside helmet and the Shield – Believe me love the brightest ornament to grace a woman's brow is meekness – her best defence and shield – the arms of an affectionate husband" and the curtain falls.

Before this comfortable conclusion, however, she experiences all the trials of being a woman in charge of a large concern. She is rightly suspicious of the motives of her steward Rostock; the peasantry do not understand what she is doing for them; and most of all she is beset with the problems of finding an emotional life of her own, in her exalted position. Count Fidesco, "a kindhearted young Nobleman who came here" as the bluff old miller tells us ironically, "with the humane purpose of comforting the widow and the afflicted," has persuaded her to marry him, and she has just set up the festivities at the opening of the play when his deserted mistress Ella and his child show up. Camilla tries to be nice: she gives the wedding to Fidesco and Ella, despite Fidesco's less than enthusiastic welcome of his family. But when the robber chief is captured she weakens, seeing an opportunity to have her wedding after all, and employs him to carry off the girl and the child. One foot on this dangerous path is enough, and she has locked the parents up in separate towers, ordered the child to be slowly crushed to death, and generally lost her grip on everything before her husband rides in to her rescue.

Critics were complimentary about the scenery, and the power of the writing, but insisted that Jane Scott "wields the pen, however, with more becoming grace than the sword."[10] Perhaps they did not like her exhibiting herself overtly as a ruling power. The complexity of the character of Camilla is quite striking, though it is normally expressed by her commanding physical presence rather than in words, and therefore is difficult to deduce from the script; but she is clearly neither heroine nor villain, more tragic than evil, and potentially a heroic figure. Certainly she explores the difficulties not of the passive female victim but of a woman determined to be active and independent. The issues raised by the character are repeated and replayed in other keys in the rest of the action. The comics' commentary on the rulers extends throughout, making use, perhaps, of a two-level set to intercut and ironize the action via juxtaposition. The question of "maistrie," of women in charge, is burlesqued in the relationship between the miller and his wife, via an interminable argument about which way they should walk to the castle – by the forest or by the fields – and the issue of financial gain from marriage is parodied by the wife's shameless pocketing of delicacies at the wedding banquet.

These ironies are not confined within the play. The effect of the mixed bill is that the performers in the Gothic melodrama then drop character, sing incidental songs, dance in a ballet, or, in the case of Jane Scott herself, change costume and romp on stage as a singing maid in the French farce – also a role she wrote for herself. Unfortunately, the text of *The Dinner of Madelon* is not available; but her writing of comedy can be seen in other examples. It is interesting for its frequent cruelty and violence, its social and sexual explicitness, and for the occasional game she plays with what one imagines was her own situation. In *The Animated Effigy* (1811), which is a slapstick farce full of knockabout, she played a braying fashionable lady who is put in her place by the "effigy," an old maiden aunt whose fortune the various worthless society types hope to inherit. The old lady has feigned death and pretends to be her own statue, which her relatives all come round to view; she hopes to hear what they really think of her. The story was perhaps suggested by Scott's own experiences of flattery from people with an eye to her money. Her position of unmarried power and wealth was, as Camilla suggests, one of which she was keenly aware. She eventually did marry, in 1822, but with a secure settlement which ensured her continued enjoyment of her own income. She left substantial bequests to fellow theatre workers and to the women's cancer ward of a London hospital, where perhaps she was treated for the breast cancer of which she died in 1839.

Jane Scott's husband was a half-pay naval officer twelve years her junior. Her contemporaries would certainly have supposed that her wealth added to her attractions for him; we have no evidence about her personal appearance beyond the brutal sneers of the *Theatrical Observer* quoted above. But she was sufficiently self-confident – and sufficiently conscious of wealth and beauty as issues in marriage – to write an extraordinary burlesque about beauty and the male gaze, *The Vizier's Son and the Merchant's Daughter, or the Ugly Woman of Baghdad* (1811). In this she played the merchant's daughter, Delta, who has rejected the marriage offer of the ruling judge of the city, the Cali; in revenge he has passed off a poor traveler on her father as a rich man, and reveals this on the day the young man marries Delta. She is faithful to her husband, whom she declares she likes, to her father's annoyance. She sets about a vengeful plot, whereby she will dupe the Cali into marriage with a hideous girl, "The greatest fright that nature ever made / Wide mouth'd – gapped tooth'd – has but one eye / Red haired – lame footed – and awry." This is possible because none of these men, including her husband, has seen her unveiled, but "by mere report according to our Turkish fashion / . . . fell in love." She pretends she is the famed ugly woman, and lures the Cali (Stebbing again), who is very old and fat and vain, into inspecting her beauty in order to refute, she says, the slanders her father has published about her hideousness. In a protracted scene – one of several between her and Stebbing that deploy explicit sexual comedy – she winds him round her little finger by a lascivious physical display, humiliates him by dancing him round till he is dizzy, extracts a proposal of marriage and proceeds smartly to banish his elder wife's embroidery frames and to change the curtains. In the denouement the poor traveler is revealed to be the Vizier's son, the Cali's senior wife takes her revenge (at one point she calls him a "superannuated shambling antiquated goose"), Delta laughs at them all and invites the audience's approbation. The scene is remarkable for its exposure of the titular "ugly woman" carried on in a litter and revealing herself as "a most hideous ludicrous burlesque figure of a female" (played by a man, C. H. Simpson) who overwhelms the Cali in her embrace; his wife laughs and exclaims, "'twill employ a barber day and night / To keep the lovely angel's muzzle white," and he howls "keep off you baggage / You variegated misshapen lump of pilfered cabbage." In this cruel knockabout burlesque, Jane Scott strikingly presents for all to see the ruthless competition over marriageability, female beauty, love, and financial worth that her contemporary Jane Austen was exploring so very delicately elsewhere.

Interplay with the established company for whom Scott wrote was vitally important, and her use of it in creating the evening's entertainments was not confined within any single fiction. The leading comic performers appeared for several seasons at the Sans Pareil and were intimately known to the *habitués*, from their previous roles and as entertainers independent of the plays; their personae, and their relationships in the house, are built into Jane Scott's writing. Huckel for example, who played Hillary, the skeptical common man gardener in *Camilla*, a year later was playing Hodge, a farm servant seeking a job with the eponymous Fortunate Youth (played by Jane Scott) in a play of 1818. Huckel had a song recounting his trip to London, which includes the verse

> I went to the play that they call Sans Pareil
> And I relish'd the fun that I saw mighty well
> There was some mut to laugh at and sommut to cry
> And I laught at one Hodge till I thought I shou'd Die.

The London audience is invited to laugh because they are in the Sans Pareil; because they are amused by the country bumpkin character – who is amusing because he does not recognize his comic self; and they enjoy Huckel separating himself from both the Hodge who sings and the Hodge whom he sings of being and of seeing, to achieve a joke about identity. Scott's comic writing abounds in such jokes, playing upon consciousness of fictionality, of the frame of the play and the reality of the situation. Her most famous comic piece is *Whackham and Windham*, first performed in 1814 but frequently revived. She rarely achieved critical acclaim, but this play was an exception: the *Theatrical Inquisitor* for February 1814 opined that if it had been put on at one of the major theatres it would have placed Miss Scott "in the first class of our modern dramatic authors" (128). It is stressed in the bills that this is an original comedy, "founded upon an incident in the author's own family." It has a dimension of realism, especially in the still-comic dissection of the impatient, affectionate relationship between father and daughter (whom Scott played) in her own modern, middle-class world. The play evokes a strong sense of the personal, and of the London household in Scott's own time. These are excellencies of writing; but the success of the play also rests on its accommodation of things brought by other people. A performer with a talent for mimicry, Andrew Campbell, played Maria's lover Henry and scenes were written in for him to do his act. The audience did their part too, bringing into the fictional world their consciousness of being in the theatre: there is a rapid, casual joke in Act 1 where

Henry gets rid of the servant so he can be alone with Maria by giving her money for ribbons and saying "Don't hurry yourself Mrs. Becky, I entreat – / if you can't suit yourself in the Strand there is great variety in Oxford Street." No location has been specified for the drawing room in which they sit; the Sans Pareil, of course, stood in the Strand, and we laugh at the idea that fictional Becky will go out into the real street to do her shopping.

To return, then, to intertheatricality. I intend the term to apply both to the creation of performance events such as the evening described, and to our reading of them, as an aid to our understanding of the integration, coherence and variety of such theatrical experiences. What Jane Scott offered was exactly the sort of evening's entertainment that led, and leads, the champions of the Drama to cast up their hands in horror – plays framed by monkeys on tightropes and suggestive French songs, invaded by dancing and posturing and singing, puffed for their scenery and decorations, losing all pretence of integrity and literary worth. To change the valuation without denying the difference, and to reveal the root of the rejection with which this sort of theatre met, I wish finally to draw upon feminist theory to substantiate my reading strategy. Jane Scott's work has provided here and in her whole managerial writing career a developing, fully articulated instance of the female aesthetic – as defined by Jane Marcus "in terms of repetition, dailiness and process" (Marcus 1988: 287). If this is accepted, the intertheatrical can be read in a theoretical context, and Scott's contribution to nineteenth-century theatre will be given due weight.

Scott's playwriting, like that of her fellow writer-managers, men such as the Dibdin brothers, takes place in a context of the daily provision of scripts for the theatre she was running. Her performance can no doubt include self-expression – I would argue that the role of Camilla could be an instance among many of something she wrote for her own satisfaction – but the primary determinants are use and process. It is repetitious, the daily weaving of variations upon the successful pattern, attempting to reproduce the elements that succeeded in her previous shows spiced with new ideas, and all the while making use of the talents available, the company she established and reengaged each season for over a decade, plus this year's dancing troupe, and this week's monkeys. Her work exemplifies the aesthetic Marcus defines. For our part we need to read and understand her making of meaning intertheatrically, not valuing the word over the spectacle or the rational and unified over the multiple pattern existing in several dimensions of real and theatrical time. Thus theatrical satisfaction can be reread, and may be understood much more broadly, if we attend to work like Jane Scott's, which is *not* the Drama, and is not structured according to the dramatic rules that are metaphors of the masculine.

NOTES

1 These dates are derived from first sources, since no one has previously sought them out. Jane Margaret Scott's baptism on 6 June 1779 is recorded in the appropriate parish register (*Register* 1779) and her date of death, 9 December 1839, appears on the tomb she shares with her parents (but not her husband) in the churchyard of St. Mary with St. James, Walton on Thames.

2 A version of this account appeared in my article on Jane Scott and Elizabeth Macauley (Bratton 1996).

3 William Archer, the prophet of Modernism in the theatre, dubbed 1810–35 "the winter solstice of English drama" (1923: 246). The long tradition of its denegration began with the angry voices of disappointed contemporary poets – Coleridge, Wordsworth, Byron – complaining of the rejection or destruction of their work by the theatrical establishment, and came to its first crescendo in the campaign against the patentees in 1831–32. This protest was taken out of the hands of the theatre managers and became a political weapon in the Reform campaigns, wielded by the radical leader Burdett and, especially, the aspiring dramatist Bulwer Lytton.

4 For contemporary confirmation of Jane Scott's managerial role, see Oxberry 1827: 154 and her own will, in which she left £50 to "Godby property man to the Sans Pareil now called the Adelphi for his fidelity and attention to me during my conducting of the business of Theatre" (Scott 1839). Harriet Waylett managed the unlicensed Strand Theatre in the summer of 1832 – see the *Morning Chronicle*, 28 May.

5 The sketchiness of these transcripts has precluded the usual more precise citations to act and scene. All subsequent quotations have therefore been given without detailed references.

6 4 March 1817, after the Spa Fields riots in London in December 1816. Violent local uprisings took place across England and Wales, and a seriously alarmed government outlawed the democratic reform groups ("Hampden Clubs") as revolutionary; the radical leader Cobbett fled to America (Thompson 1968: 691–703).

7 Baillie 1798; Scott wrote an address to the audience when the theatre was refurbished in 1814 in which she outlined recent theatre history and ended on a remarkable couplet attributing the Adelphi's success to its

poorest patrons, when in 1809 "A Gallery was added, and the merry hive, / from that bless'd moment set the house alive" (unattributed cutting dated 27 December 1814, Winston, n.d.).

8 The precarious bridge is traced from *Pizarro* to *Indiana Jones and the Temple of Doom* by Allan S. Jackson (Jackson 1997).

9 See for example the *Morning Chronicle* 2 January 1832, reporting the prosecution of Edward Meyrick, proprietor of the Orange Coffeehouse in Pimlico, who had a theatre in his gardens where the informer had seen *The Old Oak Chest*.

10 Cutting dated 18 January 1817 (Winston n.d.).

REFERENCES

Archer, William 1923, *The Old Drama and the New: An Essay in Re-valuation* London: William Heinemann.

Baker, H. Barton 1889, *History of the London Stage 1576–1903*, London: Routledge.

Bratton, J. S. 1996, "Miss Scott and Miss Macauley: 'Genius Comes in All Disguises,'" *Theatre Survey*, 37: 59–73.

British Stage November 1817.

Brooks, Peter 1976, *The Melodramatic Imagination*, New Haven: Yale University Press.

Cox, Jeffrey N. 1992, *Seven Gothic Dramas 1789–1825*, Athens, OH: Ohio University Press.

Delamotte, Eugenia C. 1990, *Perils of the Night*, Oxford and New York: Oxford University Press.

Jackson, Allan S. 1997, "*Pizarro*, Bridges and the Gothic Scene," *Theatre Notebook*, 51. 2: 81–91.

Klepac, Richard L. 1979, *Mr. Mathews at Home*, London: Society for Theatre Research.

McGrath, John 1984, *A Good Night Out*, rev. edn, London: Methuen.

Marcus, Jane 1988, "Daughters of Anger / Material Girls: Con/textualizing Feminist Criticism," *Last Laughs: Perspectives on Women and Comedy*, ed. Regina Barraca, *Women's Studies*, xv, New York: Gordon and Breach, 281–308.

Miles, Robert 1993, *Gothic Writing 1570–1820 A Genealogy*, London: Routledge.

Nelson, Alfred L., and Gilbert B. Cross (eds.) 1990, *The Adelphi Theatre Calendar*, part 1, *The London Stage 1800–1900: A Documentary Record and Calendar of Performances*, New York: Greenwood Press.

Morning Chronicle, 16 November 1807, 2 January and 28 May 1832.

Nicholson, Watson [1906] 1966, *The Struggle for a Free Stage in London*, New York: Benjamin Blom.

Nicoll, Allardyce 1955, *A History of English Drama 1660–1900*, 3rd edn, vol. IV, Cambridge: Cambridge University Press.

Oxberry, Catherine (ed.) 1827, *Dramatic Biography and Histrionic Anecdotes*, n.s. 2, London: G. Virtue.

Rate Books for the Parish of St. Martin's in the Fields 1780–1820, Westminster Archive, London.

Register of Births for the Parish of St. Martin's in the Fields 1779, Westminster Archive, London.

Scott, Harold 1946, *The Early Doors*, London: Nicholson and Watson.

Scott, Jane 1811a, *The Animated Effigy*, Larpent Collection 1660, Huntington Library, San Marino, CA.

Scott, Jane 1811b, *The Vizier's Son and the Merchant's Daughter, or The Ugly Woman of Baghdad*, Larpent Collection 1697, Huntington Library, San Marino, CA.

Scott, Jane 1812, *Asgard the Demon Hunter*, Larpent Collection 1741, Huntington Library, San Marino, CA.

Scott, Jane 1814, *Broad Grins; or, Whackham and Windham*, Larpent Collection 1798, Huntington Library, San Marino, CA. [Also available at http://www-sol.stanford.edu/mirrors/romnet/wp1800]

Scott, Jane 1816, *The Old Oak Chest; or, the Smuggler's Son and the Robber's Daughter*, Larpent Collection 1908, Huntington Library, San Marino, CA.

Scott, Jane n.d., *The Old Oak Chest; or, the Smuggler's Son and the Robber's Daughter*, London: Thomas Hailes Lacy.

Scott, Jane 1817a, *Camilla the Amazon; or, the Mountain Robbers*, Larpent Collection 1954, Huntington Library, San Marino, CA.

Scott, Jane 1817b, *The Lord of the Castle*, Larpent Collection 1989, Huntington Library, San Marino, CA.

Scott (Middleton) Jane 1839, will (limited probate) prob. 11/1923, f86rh–f93rh, Family Records Centre, Public Record Office, London.

Sedgwick, Eve Kosofsky 1980, *The Coherence of Gothic Conventions*, New York: Methuen.

Theatrical Inquisitor, February 1814.

Thompson, E. P. 1968, *The Making of the English Working Class*, rev. edn, Harmondsworth: Penguin.

Winston, James n.d., *Adelphi Scrapbook*, London: Theatre Museum.

Yates, Edmund 1884, *Recollections and Experiences*, 2 vols., London: Richard Bentley.

CHAPTER 5

Illusions of authorship

Jane Moody

INVENTING DRAMATIC AUTHORSHIP

On 4 December 1831, a group of male playwrights met at the Albion Tavern, opposite the stage door of Drury Lane Theatre. Inspired by Thomas Thackeray's pamphlet, "On Theatrical Emancipation, and the Rights of Dramatic Authors," infuriated by their powerlessness in the face of unauthorized performances of their plays, and haunted by the sounds of publishers' copyists surreptitiously transcribing plays from the stage into print, the playwrights decided to petition for a change in the laws concerning dramatic authorship (Thackeray, 1832).[1] Two years later the Dramatic Copyright Act (3 & 4 Will. IV c. 15) became law, giving a dramatic author sole property in an unpublished composition, and exclusive rights to benefit from its stage representation, as well as copyright protection for printed dramatic texts.[2]

One of the leading figures in the campaign was James Robinson Planché, whose own play, *Charles XII*, had recently been performed without his permission in Edinburgh. Such was Planché's elegance and dramatic respectability, Moncrieff would joke, that "he wrote in white kid gloves"; recalling this observation in his memoirs, Edward Fitzball revealed his own suspicion that Planché "lived on honey and nectar" (Fitzball 1859, vol. II: 28). Fitzball's aside is full of gentle irony, wryly alluding to the social distance between himself – a printer's apprentice turned hack dramatist – and Planché, antiquarian and heraldic scholar, costume designer, playwright and Victorian gentleman. Planché, it would appear, exemplified the new profession of dramatic authorship.

The Albion Tavern playwrights quickly recognized that legislation alone would not be sufficient to protect dramatic copyright, and in particular to ensure the payment of fees to dramatic authors for stage representation. By 1833, the informal group of tavern play-wrights had evolved into the Dramatic Authors' Society – the first society whose membership (in contrast to the notorious Beef-Steak Club at Covent Garden, or the Garrick Club) distinguished dramatic authors from other theatrical groups such as performers and managers. The society established a table of fees for the performance of specific dramatic genres, and appointed the publisher John Miller as its agent. Soon, most of the working male playwrights in London, including Charles Dance, Sheridan Knowles, John Buckstone, and Edward Fitzball, had joined the society; the title pages of their published plays featured the proud announcement (and solemn warning to scheming managers), "Member of the Dramatic Authors' Society."

So where were the women playwrights? Elizabeth Inchbald, of course, was dead; Joanna Baillie, whose third volume of plays on the passions had been published in 1812, was no longer writing for the stage. Other female playwrights, like Elizabeth Polack or Mrs. Denvil, whose plays were performed at the Pavilion in White-chapel, and the Victoria on the South Bank, seem to have existed on the geographical and institutional periphery of theatrical authorship. But the list of society members, as published in Leman Rede's *Road to the Stage* (Rede 1836: 71), does include female honorary members such as Eliza Planché, Caroline Boaden, Felicia Hemans, and Mary Mitford. Honorary membership for women, we may surmise, entailed a distinction between the provision of the society's protection in matters of performance copyright, without the benefits of its professional sociability. Female honorary members might extract fees from provincial managers, as did their male counterparts, but were probably excluded from the society's meetings. Though legally acknowledged as dramatic authors, the Dramatic Authors' Society confined women dramatists to the institutional margins of authorship.

Why might this equivocal recognition of women dramatists be significant? The Dramatic Copyright Act inaugurated a new defini-tion of dramatic authorship. For the first time in theatrical history, a play now became regarded as the exclusive property of an individual author. Implicit in these legal definitions was a conception of dramatic authorship based on the presumed identity between an author and the dramatic text which bore his name. Above all, dramatic authorship now became vested in a written text.

Just as masculinity seemed to be a precondition for full society membership, so writing had become the implicit precondition for dramatic authorship. Plays, wrested from the grasping, predatory hands of managers and performers, were now perceived to belong not to a particular theatre (under a gentlemen's agreement, Covent Garden and Drury Lane had formerly regarded stock plays as the unofficial property of one or other theatre), but to individual dramatic authors.

The Dramatic Copyright Act represents the triumph of dramatic authors over the collaborative practices of playwrighting. Modern critics, too (as if approving of this triumph), privilege the authority of the dramatist whilst quietly ignoring those theatrical practices which might call into question an exclusive, proprietorial dramatic authorship. Yet, as Stephen Orgel has shown in relation to Renaissance drama, the role of theatrical companies in the commissioning of plays and the extensive revision of those plays by the company (revisions over which the author could rarely exercise jurisdiction) all qualify the authority conventionally attributed to an individual dramatic author. On the contrary, the authority represented by the text "is that of the company, the owners, not that of the playwright, the author" (Orgel 1981: 3).

Orgel's argument establishes an overarching dichotomy between, on the one hand, a theatrical company, and, on the other, an individual whom he describes as a "playwright" or "author." To categorize these authors as "playwrights," however, is a cultural anachronism, for the concept of playwrighting was scarcely formulated in language until the Restoration.[3] Interestingly, the emergence of the playwright as a maker of plays is broadly coterminous with the rise of female dramatists such as Aphra Behn, Mary Pix, and Delarivière Manley. The job of a playwright seems to have been coined via a process of linguistic back-formation from those ancient medieval trades of the shipwright, cartwright, and wheelwright (all of which existed in Middle English). How arresting that the etymology of playmaking should evoke neither the authority of writing, nor the permanence of print. On the contrary, making plays seems to have been imagined as a trade arising from the bodily labor of producing tangible, physical objects. For "wrighting," in the context of these medieval trades, took the form of making goods, perhaps from materials made or prepared by others, which would then be sold, assembled, or incorporated into larger objects, the identity of their craftsmen silently disappearing, without written trace, into history. The linguistic archaeology of playwrighting, then, suggests a delightful insouciance about authorship, property, and authority.

Just as the etymology of playwrighting encodes a form of dramatic creativity that might exist outside a written text, so this chapter, written against the grain of the Dramatic Copyright Act, explores the hypothesis that, in the nineteenth-century British theatre, a form of feminine dramatic authorship existed beyond writing. In this argument, my subjects – Eliza Vestris (1797–1856) and Céline Céleste (c. 1810–82) – represent two women "playwrights" who have never previously been recognized as dramatic authors. My chapter attempts to explore playwrighting in a particular institutional context, defined here by Vestris's and Céleste's commercial and theatrical authority as pioneering women managers in the nineteenth-century London theatre. More broadly, my argument also suggests that the concept of playwrighting may help to explain (and more properly to attribute agency to) two important moments of change in the period's stage history. The first of these is Eliza Vestris's management of the Olympic Theatre in the early 1830s – a management which soon became famous for its visual elegance, comic incongruities, and the stardom of Vestris herself. My discussion will focus on the Christmas extravaganzas performed at the theatre between 1831 and 1834, written jointly by James Robinson Planché and Charles Dance. The second moment of transformation occurs at the Adelphi in the mid-1840s, then managed by Céleste and Ben Webster. Here, in the passionate, almost demonic roles of Miami in *The Green Bushes* and Cynthia in *The Flowers of the Forest* – both played by Céline Céleste – a new feminine theatrical character was coming into being. Both transformations, I shall argue, were characterized by an idiosyncratic collision of theatrical circumstances: mutations of genre, the figure of the transvestite performer, the institutional authority (and, in Vestris's case, the sensation) of a female actor-manager, together with their buried stage histories, and, especially in the case of the Adelphi, the repertoire and stock roles of a particular company. The agency for these moments of change, then, will be located in intricate, often uncertain relationships between performance, management, and authorship. Above all, the invention of a proprietorial definition of dramatic authorship – and J. R. Planché's leading role in the playwrights' campaign – turns out to be a cunning historiographic decoy, or at least a picturesque theatrical illusion.

Neither Céleste nor Vestris claimed the identity of a dramatic author. Indeed, apart from their possible roles in the composition of playbills and other theatrical advertising, neither woman wrote a word for public consumption. Interpreting their playwrighting is a task rendered more difficult, too, by the extant traces of their professional lives as perceived through the eyes of male playwrights such as Planché and Boucicault; reviewers friendly, hostile, or rhapsodic and, in the case of Vestris, through the voyeuristic shadows cast by scandalous memoirs of her "public and private adventures." Can we interpret Vestris and Céleste as collaborators in a form of institutional playwrighting? To what extent did Vestris and Céleste "ventriloquize" a form of dramatic authorship through men such as Planché, Bernard, and Buckstone? My chapter questions the confidence with which scholars have claimed to distinguish male and female authorship.

The exploration of Vestris as an Olympic playwright entails in particular a challenge to a chivalric, masculine historiographic tradition which has portrayed Vestris's management either by reference to the magical and ethereal (Sir Lumley Skeffington published a poem in *The Times* on 14 February 1831, celebrating Vestris as the tenth muse and praising her theatre as a "fanciful dome"; critics also described Vestris as the "witch of Wych Street") or as a model of leisured domesticity. In this second tradition, reviewers and biographers celebrated Vestris's lesseeship as that of an ideal housekeeper who finally took domestic control of the disorderly, masculine theatrical house. Charles Kean's biographer, for example, declared the Olympic to be "a perfect theatrical boudoir" (Cole 1859: vol. I, 182), whilst journalists frequently praised Vestris for translating the laws of the drawing room to those of the stage: "Trifles and ices, champagne and rout-cakes, were the perpetual fare" (Tomlins 1840: 63).

The Olympic pleasures, in this historiographical tradition, are the pleasures of looking and feeding. Vestris becomes the proprietor of a confectioner's shop where theatrical spectators delightedly consume cakes, jellies, and "maids of honour" served on cups "of the most delicate china" ("Play-Houses and their Prospects" 1836: 175). Even E. B. Watson, the first theatre historian to draw attention to Vestris's pioneering management, seems to have been overwhelmed by her charisma:

Suddenly the little Pavilion in Wych Street, that since the departure of Elliston had failed under at least four managers, was touched, as it were, by a fairy's wand, and from a scrap heap of theatricalities was transformed into a palace of fairyland ... Furthermore, by this same stroke, a legion of subtle spirits were released to work greater wonders in the realm of dramatic art. The fairy was Vestris, and her wand the pen of Planché. (Watson 1926: 191)

For all its whimsicalities, the confusion of authorship and management here is revealing, for where do the roles of Vestris-as-fairy end and Planché-as-wand begin? How can we characterize the institutional relationships between Vestris and her authorial "legion of subtle spirits?" Watson's imagery unwittingly reveals the dramaturgical complexity of Vestris's Olympic, and the problems of distinguishing authorship from playwrighting amidst the champagne and rout-cakes.

THE RENUNCIATION OF PERSEUS

SCENE: *The Olympic Theatre, Newcastle Street. "By Permission of the Lord Chamberlain. Madame VESTRIS' Royal Olympic Theatre, Newcastle Street, Strand. Madame VESTRIS begs leave most respectfully to announce to the Nobility, and Public in general, that having become SOLE LESSEE of the above Establishment, it will open for the Season ON MONDAY, JANUARY 3rd, 1831, WHEN AN OCCASIONAL ADDRESS Will be spoken by Madame VESTRIS." (Olympic playbill)*

The Olympic Theatre opened with performances of W. H. Murray's play, *Mary, Queen of Scots*, starring Maria Foote, followed by a mythological entertainment entitled *Olympic Revels; or, Prometheus and Pandora* written by Charles Dance and J. R. Planché. Over the first week, London's aristocracy and the *beau monde* – including the Duke of Richmond, Lord Bolingbroke, Lady Agnes Byng, Lord and Lady Edward Thynne (Vestris would later have a disastrous affair with Lord Thynne) and Lord Adolphus Fitzclarence (the illegitimate son of William IV, from his relationship with the actress Dorothy Jordan) – bowled through the West End in their carriages to see Vestris's Olympic Theatre for themselves. "Female management for ever!" would soon become a fashionable clarion call amongst enthusiastic reviewers and spectators.

For the first time, a woman was commissioning drama in London.

Barred by the terms of the Olympic's license from the production of legitimate drama, and determined in any case to attract the public by the dramatic novelty of her repertoire, Vestris suddenly found herself in need of dramatic authors prepared to take part in the transformation of the Olympic, and indeed the metamorphosis of Vestris herself. In his *Recollections*, Planché remembered how he became involved in Olympic playwrighting. "Passing through Long Acre one day," he recalled, "I met her in her carriage." Having informed Planché about her recent acquisition of the Olympic, Vestris asked the playwright "if I had anything ready for immediate production" and also if Planché might be prepared to assist her "in any way by my advice or interest" (Planché 1872: vol. 1, 178–79). Planché agreed to help (the financial terms of this agreement are not known), and immediately became the Olympic's most important stock writer as well as Vestris's adviser, especially on matters of costume and visual design. Such was her trust in him that, when she departed for a tour of America with her second husband, Charles Mathews, in 1837, Planché was left in charge as her deputy manager. Their careers would remain inextricably linked until Vestris's retirement in 1855.

In response to Vestris's request, Planché decided to revive a classical burlesque, written some years earlier in the wake of her success in the role of Midas, but then refused by various managers. Long before Vestris had the financial power to commission *Olympic Revels*, her stage character had shaped Planché's mythological dramatization. Planché then persuaded Charles Dance "to try his hand at this style of composition"; together, *Olympic Revels* was accordingly "brushed up" in "two or three evenings" in time for the Olympic's opening night (Planché 1872: vol. 1, 179).

The emergence of Olympic extravaganza – one of the most innovative theatrical forms of its time – would seem to represent a triumph of theatrical contingency: two authors, touching up a discarded manuscript in a hurry, a motley collection of performers, many of whom were available only because they had failed to secure engagements elsewhere for the winter season, and a manager – formerly a scandalous icon of Regency London – who had never dressed or mounted a production in her life. Indeed, many of the Olympic's innovations, including shorter programs and burlesques in which absurd dialogue humorously clashed against picturesque costumes, did evolve in haphazard fashion whether in the wake of a chance idea, or as a result of conversations amongst Olympic spectators overheard in the street. Yet what these anecdotes reveal, of course, is the theatrical innovation which came about through Vestris's collaborative management.

Who were the authors of Olympic extravaganza? Did Vestris commission or substantially revise the plots, characters, and visual effects of extravaganza? More intangibly, to what extent might the *authority* for these plays be traced to an institutional dramaturgy of Olympic playwrighting, with Vestris at its centre, rather than attributed to the dramatic authorship of Planché and Dance alone? Whilst the questions I explore here might usefully be asked of the Olympic repertoire in general, the nature of theatrical authority at the Olympic would seem to emerge with particular force and complexity in the comic self-referentiality of the early extravaganzas.

To whom should we attribute authorship, for example, in the denouement of *The Deep, Deep Sea* (Christmas 1833)? Here, Olympic audiences were introduced to the submarine villa of the curmudgeonly Captain Neptune (played by James Bland), a henpecked husband who speaks a pseudonautical language; the Great American Sea Serpent (so long he needs to be measured for a new ocean) now employed on behalf of the slighted Amphitrite to eat up all creation, and a burlesque marriage dilemma. The romantic hero in this classical game is of course Vestris, in the role of Perseus (a commercially astute, pragmatic Perseus who regularly visits the pawnbroker, and is ready to pay interest in order to secure Andromeda). Having stabbed the serpent, released Andromeda from the rock, and disburdened himself of Medusa's head, however, Perseus renounces the clothes, the weapon, and the gender of the warrior hero in the concluding tag:

> For, ah! your suppliant away has thrown
> Her manly courage with *her* manly part,
> And comes with all the woman in her heart.   (Scene 4: 168)

Here, the conventional plea for clemency and favor from the audience seems to have been reinvented so as to allow the audience retrospectively to license Vestris's transvestite role as Perseus. Conflating the genders of life and extravaganza, Vestris's speech represents female performance/management as the social order of which her male part was but a temporary transgression.

In her shrewd readings of Renaissance plays, Jean Howard notes how the dramaturgy of cross-dressing releases a woman from the prison of her masculine clothes in order to return her "to her proper and natural position" as wife (Howard 1993: 33). Yet although Vestris's resignation of her male attire notionally follows this structural pattern, it is by no means clear that the "subversive resonances" of female cross-dressing are thereby abandoned. On the contrary, the sheer self-consciousness of Vestris's maneuver seems to draw ironic attention to her own authority as the Olympic's actress-manager to license the mutability and ambivalence of theatrical genders and identities.

The presence of these theatrical tags, or other autobiographical allusions, is not in itself proof of collaborative playwrighting. What is noticeable about these extravaganzas, nonetheless, is that their language and iconography are clearly inseparable from the figure, reputation, and theatrical identity of Vestris herself. Take, for example, the moment in *The Paphian Bower; or, Venus and Adonis* (1832), when Venus – responding to Adonis's anxiety about her marital status – acknowledges "a proper deed of separation" from Vulcan and "a flirtation with a chap named Mars" (101), references which many well-informed spectators would have been quick to interpret in relation to Vestris's own scandalous history, including liaisons with Thomas Duncombe, Horatio Clagett, and Montague Gore. Is it possible to distinguish authorship from production in these extravaganzas? What role did Vestris play in the making of Venus? The transvestite casting of *Telemachus*, as discussed below, offers another example of playwrighting beyond dramatic authorship.

Very little information survives about the day-to-day management of the Olympic. Vestris's insistence on meticulous rehearsal and her attention to the finest details of scenery, choice of props, and costume have been extensively chronicled, and indeed made possible the transformation of extravaganza from episodic collage to an elegant, incongruous genre of ostensible refinement and topical joke, founded on ensemble performance. In addition, Vestris must have been reading and selecting plays for performance (perhaps with Planché's advice) as well as casting and dressing her productions. Nor did her close supervision of production end when performances began. By spectating from her private box, Vestris was able to suggest improvements and alterations, whether in scenery, characterization, or perhaps even plot, throughout a play's run.

The making of Olympic extravaganza, I believe, involved a

collaborative playwrighting project. Vestris's authority as an actress-manager transformed her from a theatrical star into an Olympic playwright. This playwrighting, I would argue, took the form of making, adapting, and revising the materials of dramatists such as Planché and Dance. By the same token, Vestris's own reputation and theatrical history offered an unprecedented dramatic text for Planché and Dance – a much more intangible process of authorship which I shall call *ventriloquism*. The result of these two intricately connected forms of authorship was the generic transformation of extravaganza. Extravaganza's comic preoccupation with the meanings of sexual definitions, and the boundaries of gender, its curious mixture of luscious fantasy and verbal ingenuity: all these are attributable not to Planché and Dance alone, but rather to Vestris's evolution of Olympic playwrighting.

Concepts such as ventriloquism and collaboration, however, raise difficult issues of attribution and intentionality. I have suggested that Planché and Dance might be described as writerly participants with Vestris in a form of authorial ventriloquism. According to this model, the two playwrights were producing an Olympic mythology around and in the interstices of Vestris's own autobiographical "text" or history. We might imagine a process of composition, occurring in the green room and/or in Planché's study at Brompton Crescent, through which these playwrights created a dramaturgy for Vestris's self-representation. The concept of ventriloquism helps to conjure up a form of vicarious playwrighting which evolves in some inchoate theatrical region between authorship and performance. In addition, ventriloquism evocatively suggests an authorship which is inextricable from the performer's own body.

The model of collaboration, by contrast, as explored by Orgel in relation to Renaissance drama, is underpinned by the existence of shared financial ownership (i.e. the system of "sharers" and "half-sharers" within a theatrical company), and – inseparably linked to that financial system – by collective participation in the production of a theatrical script. By the early nineteenth century, however, theatres had become the objects of entrepreneurial speculation by a particular individual (the lessee) who risked his or her own capital in theatrical management. Eliza Vestris was therefore responsible not only for selecting the Olympic's repertoire, and supervising its dramatic productions, but also for the theatre's financial survival. Her management combined an unusual authority over her company

– an authority often evoked by her theatrical addresses, in which she compared herself to Cleopatra, Julius Caesar, Mrs. Nelson (a London omnibus manager) and the Prime Minister[4] – with a collaborative form of theatrical production.

The concepts of ventriloquism and collaboration help to explain the theatrical practices and institutional relationships at work in Olympic playwrighting. Both, however, imply a form of participation or relationship which is conscious and intentional. The image of the ventriloquist, too, assumes a performing body incapable of speech, or indeed of movement or gesture, except through the agency of the omnipotent dramatist. In some ways, however, surely the evolution of Pandora's new-made sexuality, or the production of the sexually voracious Calypso, involved a form of collaborative playwrighting taking place at an unconscious level?

A good example of playwrighting in practice – as well as the most audacious of the Olympic's mythological plots – is *Telemachus; or, The Island of Calypso* (Christmas 1834). The extravaganza takes the form of a comic epilogue to that episode in *The Odyssey* in which Ulysses is washed up on the island of Oggia, and held captive there by its absolute queen, Calypso (played by Vestris). In the play, Ulysses has left the island, leaving behind a suicidal Calypso. Then, having been washed ashore in a storm, Telemachus and his tutor Mentor (or so it seems) appear. Calypso, unaware that the boy is Ulysses's son, is enchanted by Telemachus. Finally, however, Telemachus succeeds in extracting himself from the clutches of both Calypso and Eucharis (her maid and amorous rival), builds a boat, and escapes from the island.

Reading Dance and Planché's text, we can easily discern how *Telemachus* made comic theatrical capital out of the figure of woman as sexual monster. Yet such a characterization is a dramatic innovation which becomes representable only when Vestris acquires the commercial and institutional power to burlesque her own scandalous reputation. What the visual and verbal subconscious of this play allows the audience to imagine, too, is a semi-incestuous union in which Calypso would couple with both father and son, Ulysses and Telemachus. At the same time, Calypso's island, with its beds aired and cold collations prepared, seems a curiously self-referential environment, as if the play were burlesquing the (questionable) domesticity so glowingly attributed to the Olympic by reviewers and spectators.

Planché and Dance, of course, may have invented Calypso and her island home without consulting Vestris about plot or character-ization. Alternatively, informal conversation and green-room experi-ment may have produced radical changes. What is certain, however, is that the figure of Calypso is inseparable from that of Vestris herself. What brings Calypso into being is the ironic and often contradictory Olympic project of Vestris's own authorial self-repre-sentation. Indeed, the identity of Vestris and Olympic extravaganza would tend to be confirmed by the fact that, despite their popularity at the Olympic, these plays do not appear to have been performed beyond their original home, or in the absence of their managerial "author."

With the exception of Mentor (played by James Bland), and various spirits, the cast of *Telemachus* is female: masculinity seems to become both marginal and precarious in Olympic mythology. Vestris herself, in the role of Calypso, played in her own sex; the cross-dressing role has been displaced to the character of Telema-chus, played by Mary Glover. Calypso/Vestris's obsessive pursuit of Telemachus thus acquires a peculiarly illicit (and comically doomed) character. When Telemachus rejects Calypso's love, claiming to be consumed by the loss of his father, for example, Calypso briskly dismisses this bereavement, and promptly transforms it into inces-tuous farce:

> CALYPSO: I'll be your father, mother, sister, wife.
> TELEMACHUS: Your Majesty's too gracious, on my life. (Scene 3: 195)

Beneath the play's glittering visual surface lurks Telemachus' archetypal terror of female sexuality, as well as a disturbing confla-tion of the sexual potency and erotic cult of his mother, Calypso, and Vestris herself. In dramatic language, as well as through the agency of transsexual casting, the play teases its audience with comic yet unsettling sexual taboos. Casting, here, has the effect of highlighting the plot's sexual uncertainty. Charles Dance and James Robinson Planché may have possessed the performance copyright for *Tele-machus* – though, since the mythological extravaganzas were never played beyond the Olympic, the ownership of that copyright remained a purely theoretical question – but were these men the sole authors of Olympic extravaganza? In these plays, definitions of authorship, like definitions of sexual identity, begin to collapse and become mutable.

Many Olympic plays, including those written by Eliza Planché, exploited the seductiveness of Eliza Vestris, often in soubrette roles, so as to create fantasies about illicit relationships. In her vaudeville, *The Welsh Girl* (Olympic, December 1833), Sir Owen Griffiths falls in love with Julia (played by Vestris, and disguised for her meeting with Sir Owen as a poor Welsh girl with a delightful singing voice). Unknown to Sir Owen, however, Julia has just married his nephew Alfred. At one level, Eliza Planché's piece simply provides a light, skillfully crafted vehicle for Vestris's singing voice; at another, however, this plot of mistaken identities creates the threat of an incestuous union between Sir Owen and his nephew's wife, a union very similar to that dramatized by J. R. Planché and Dance in *Telemachus*, performed the following Christmas. In 1838, Eliza Planché returned to a similar theme in her Olympic burletta, *A Hasty Conclusion* (adapted from the vaudeville *L'Aumônier du Régiment*). In this play, the Abbé serving a French regiment is to be billeted in the house where Maria (in love with Carl, a farrier) and Martelle (her injured father) are staying. Martelle, however, is bitterly opposed to the priesthood, for a priest (the Abbé's brother, as it turns out) has deprived Maria of her inheritance. In order to circumvent this hostility, the Abbé disguises himself as a soldier.

The tension between Vestris's stage roles and private life was essential to the play's success. For playing opposite each other as Maria and the Abbé were Vestris and Mathews (the Olympic's foremost light comedian), married the previous year, and recently returned from their stormy American tour. The audience's knowledge of that relationship licensed the otherwise forbidden sexual attraction which develops between Maria and the Abbé in the play, culminating in the intensely ironic scene when Martelle (now enthusiastically championing a romance between his daughter and the supposed soldier) insists that the Abbé should kiss Maria. "I must do it, but in all purity, as a parent would kiss a child" the Abbé tells the audience in an aside (Planché 1838: 15). As he kisses her lips, however, the Abbé becomes aware of new (unpriestly) emotions toward Maria; in her turn, Maria begins to fall in love with the Abbé's disguise. Later, of course, the Abbé reveals his true identity, Martelle repents of his hasty conclusions, and the relationship between Carl and Maria is reinstated. Nevertheless, *A Hasty Conclusion* cleverly deploys an offstage marriage as a means by which to license a *risqué* dramatization of ambivalent sexual feelings.

Plate 4. Madame Vestris as Don Giovanni. A toy theatre portrait
published by J. Dyer.

What did Céline Céleste and Eliza Vestris have in common? Both
were foreigners: Vestris of Italian extraction, born in London into an
artistic, professional family; Céleste, born in Paris of Spanish
parents, arrived in England for the first time in 1830. Striking
physical features, and the status of an exotic outsider undoubtedly

smoothed their paths to dramatic success. Vestris's career began as a mezzo soprano at the King's Theatre, and her rich, pellucid singing voice helped to bring her wide acclaim; Céleste, initially unable to play speaking parts in England (such was her halting command of the English language) first came to public attention through her talent in the mute expression of pain and suffering. Transvestite roles – for Vestris, as Giovanni in Moncrieff's adaptation (see J. Dyer's suggestive and scandalous image of Vestris in this role) and as Macheath, and for Céleste as the dumb boy Maurice and in her various roles in *The French Spy* – brought both women fame, and, at least as importantly for their managerial ventures, fortune. For the rise of women managers in London was made financially possible by the capital of theatrical transvestism. Céleste's highly successful tour of America between 1834 and 1837, for example, was reputed to have made her thousands of pounds. Whereas, at the Olympic, extravaganza incorporated and refined Vestris's transvestite stage history, Céleste's most famous Adelphi roles as Miami (1845) and Cynthia (1847) submerged that stage memory of masculinity in the creation of women on the very edges of femininity. The violence and wildness of these characters, strongly reminiscent of mute wild men like Orson on the late Georgian stage, evokes a self-destructive femininity which has turned against itself.

Female management transformed the institutional relationships between Vestris and Céleste, now directors and producers of performance as well the dramatic star of their establishment, and a predominantly male community of dramatic authors. In other ways, however, Vestris and Céleste fared no better than many male actor-managers of this period. Vestris's personal extravagance, together with the corrupt practices of certain Olympic employees, had rendered her insolvent by 1837: the stock of the Olympic – its whimsical clouds, carpets, and elegant chairs – were sold in fulfillment of her debts. Céleste, too, quickly lost the profits of her stage performances in her joint managerial ventures with her lover, the eminent actor-manager and playwright Benjamin Webster.

With the exception of the Olympic, where Vestris was the sole lessee, theatrical management for these two women represented a complex and unstable confusion of public and private life. Vestris and her second husband, Charles Mathews, jointly managed Covent Garden (1839–42) and, at least in name, the Lyceum (1847–55). Céleste's periods of theatrical management, first at the Theatre

Royal, Liverpool (1843–44), then at the Adelphi between 1844 and 1858, were both conducted as partnerships with Ben Webster. Having quarreled with Webster in 1858, Céleste briefly managed the Lyceum theatre alone. Though they were later reconciled, and she continued her acting career, Céleste did not embark on theatre management again.

CÉLESTE'S MUTENESS

SCENE: *A woman stands on the edge of a forest, dressed in short red petticoat, black hunting shirt, and hunting cap made of panther's skin. Unobserved, she watches in horror and amazement as her lover embraces another, unknown woman. She puts her rifle to her shoulder, only to lower it again, raising the weapon repeatedly, only to let it fall again. Suddenly, jealous passion overwhelms hesitation. The woman fires, and her lover is shot through the heart.*[5]

The sound of Miami's rifle breaks the silence during which the audience have witnessed through gesture and expression, but not through language, her terrible anguish. At some level, the rifle sound is the most articulate "speech" which Miami makes in the entire play. In the second half of the drama, which takes place in Ireland, Miami (now in the person of Madame St. Aubert) again retreats into silence – the silence of atonement. Having reunited Geraldine (the unknown woman of Act 1) with Geraldine's daughter, and given them all her property, Miami dies in silence with the secret of her crime. "Seek not to know," she tells Geraldine, "I wish my story to die with me" (3.5: 62).

In January 1845, audiences gathered at the Adelphi to watch the first performance of Buckstone's play, *The Green Bushes; or, A Hundred Years Ago*. Set at the time of the Irish rebellion, the play dramatizes the escape of Connor to the Mississippi where he falls in love with a French–Indian huntress (Miami). Connor successfully conceals his past until one day when his wife Geraldine, whom he had left behind in Ireland, appears from out of the forest. *The Green Bushes* and *The Flowers of the Forest* came to exemplify what became known as the "Adelphi drama." Unlike the Olympic pieces discussed earlier, these plays, originally designed as "vehicles" for Céleste, rapidly became stock pieces which were performed widely both in Britain and in America. But what interests me here is the suddenness with which Miami or Cynthia appear in theatrical history. Where does the primitive violence of Miami come from? How can we interpret the self-division and self-torment of Cynthia, the Italian Gipsy Queen?

According to the model of authorship implicit in the Dramatic Copyright Act, the dramatic author of these two plays was John Baldwin Buckstone, famous low comedian, a prolific and versatile playwright, and later the successor to Webster as the Haymarket's manager. Turning back the pages of the Adelphi repertoire, we might be struck by the very different female roles being created in the early 1830s through Buckstone's authorship for the Adelphi company, and especially for Elizabeth Yates, in plays such as *Henriette the Forsaken* (1832) and *Isabelle; or, Woman's Life* (1834). Here, Adelphi drama began to explore, with powerful psychological realism, the emotional pain of women within marriage: the discovery and acceptance of a husband's infidelity, the patience and fortitude of a wife in the face of betrayal. These plays dramatize a femininity which is graceful, hopeful, gentle, forgiving, and slow to despair.

In 1844, however, the Adelphi theatre opened, "Under the Direction of Madame Céleste." In a much more discreet typeface, readers were informed that the theatre was being leased by Ben Webster. Unlike Vestris, who possessed sole authority for the selection of both performers and playwrights, Céleste inherited at the Adelphi a well-known and highly popular company including Fanny Fitzwilliam (who as Geraldine, the forsaken lover in *The Green Bushes* subtly offsets the character played by Céleste), "O." Smith, J. B. Buckstone, and Elizabeth Yates. Whereas, at the Olympic, Vestris evolved a new kind of illegitimate drama featuring elegant burletta and luscious extravaganza, Céleste and Webster remained loyal in their choice of repertoire to the idiosyncratic blend of melodrama known as Adelphi drama. What is remarkable about the institutional relationship between Céleste as directress and star, and Buckstone, as the Adelphi's stock writer, is the originality with which Céleste's instinctive, sometimes violent stage history passes into Adelphi dramaturgy.

Céleste's management of the Adelphi has all but disappeared from theatrical history. The unusual title of *directress* suggests either a genuine theatrical partnership with Webster, or, more plausibly given that Webster continued to act as manager of the Haymarket (by then open for ten months of the year), overall control. Céleste, we can surmise, was commissioning plays from dramatic authors such as Buckstone, as well as being responsible for casting, rehearsal, and production. Playbills certainly drew attention to her authority as directress, announcing for example, "The Action, the Dances, & the entire Mise en Scene Invented, arranged & directed by Madame Céleste."[6] To what extent did Céleste's new position of theatrical power enable her – either through a process of active collaboration or in more unconscious ways – to author her own theatrical representations in roles such as Cynthia and Miami?

Céleste's own stage history in mute characters powerfully shaped the speaking parts later written for her. Her early roles included Julio, the deaf and dumb boy in Thomas Holcroft's *Deaf and Dumb; or, The Orphan Protected*, Julietta in John Farrell's play, *The Dumb Girl of Genoa*, and Fenella, in the opera of *Masaniello*, adapted from Scribe and Auber's *La Muette de Portici*. Playwrights then began to create mute "vehicles" especially for Céleste, such as her multiple roles in the military drama, *The French Spy*, by John Haines (Queen's, 1831), Narammattah in Bayle Bernard's *The Wept of Wish-ton-Wish* (Adelphi, 1831), dramatized from James Fenimore Cooper's novel, and Maurice in *The Child of the Wreck* (Drury Lane, 1837) adapted from the French by J. R. Planché.

Audiences, reviewers, and, no doubt, playwrights too marveled at the expressive power of Céleste's pantomime action – the capacity of this performing body to speak the emotions of her characters without the intervention of language. As *The Times* (9 October 1837) reported of Céleste's performance as the hesitant, falsely accused Maurice, "her 'dumb show' . . . is anything but inexplicable. She expressed by her varied and appropriate action, and by her swiftly changing features, the various passions of love, despair, indignation, and joy, with touching fidelity." Whereas my exploration of Vestris's playwrighting highlights a self-conscious, ironic form of theatrical production exemplified by the renunciation of Perseus, my claim for Céleste as an Adelphi playwright rests on a still more intangible form of authorship which comes about when a performing body, especially a body associated with the representation of mute action, begins "wrighting" theatrical production.

Genteel transgression, whether sexual or criminal, had been at the heart of Vestris's cross-dressing roles. By contrast, Céleste's theatrical apprenticeship took place in roles of wordless passion at the center of which lay that characteristic melodramatic tension between knowledge and powerlessness. But Céleste's fame as a mute performer also raises important questions about the authorial integrity of these dramatic "vehicles." To what extent, for example, did

Céleste improvize her mute action rather than perform according to directions from a preexisting text? For acting editions are of course a production text "as performed" at a particular theatre, "correctly printed from the prompter's copy," complete with cast lists, descriptions of costumes, and images from drawings "taken during the representation." But how much of Céleste's pantomime was actually written or even notated by Planché or Bernard? In the absence of play manuscripts, the authorship of mute action (like the authorship of other nontextual performances, such as Cynthia's dance in *The Flowers of the Forest*), remains a mystery.

Céleste's most striking and successful early role was as the General's daughter, Mathilde de Meric, disguised first as Henri St. Alma (the French Spy) and then as Hamet (an Arab boy) in *The French Spy; or, The Siege of Constantina*. J. P. Hall's lithograph (plate 5) depicts Céleste in the last of these roles, her solemn, almost haunted gaze and dignified pose evoking both the experience of strangeness and also a calm resolution. As a flirtatious French lancer, as a deranged Arab boy who performs a wild Arab dance and whose expressive dumb show mimes the action of desperate warriors in battle, and finally as a woman confronting a terrible conflict between the desire to save her lover and the dishonor of submitting herself to the despot Achmet, the emotional variety of these roles is remarkable. Crossing boundaries of sex and of ethnicity, Céleste's transvestite roles reveal a new depth of inner conflict and human pain within the conventions of melodrama.

The origins of characters such as Miami and Cynthia can be traced in Buckstone's earlier forsaken women, and in the dramatization of clashing nations and unspoken, wordless emotion in Haines's play. Further back in theatrical history, too, the gentle, simple Yarico whom the mercurial Inkle was all too ready to betray in George Colman's play about slavery offers a plangent dramatic precedent. Several important features, however, distinguish Miami and Cynthia from these earlier characters. First, both are ethnic outsiders, driven from their original homes by persecution (Cynthia's gypsy tribe) or, as in Miami's journey to Ireland, by the desire to expiate the crime of having killed her husband. Secondly, the romantic passions of Miami for Connor and Cynthia for Alfred, although leading to psychological self-destruction, and eventually to death, are endowed with a compelling, almost redemptive emotional authenticity. Full of fervent, poignant emotion, their pain, wild grief, and jealousy verge

Plate 5. Madame Céleste as the Wild Arab Boy.
Lithograph by J. P. Hall, 1834.

on the edge of madness, and also on the edge of language. Though both are speaking parts, their expressive dramaturgy of wild gazes and stupefied glances, shudders and silences, powerfully evokes Céleste's earlier mute stage history.

The pivotal discovery scene in both plays takes the form of a sudden transition from the mute action of the silent eavesdropper to a memorable outpouring of passion and rage. In *The Flowers of the*

Forest, Cynthia, then concealed within the foliage, hears Lemuel confessing to Bess that he is the murderer of Hugh (3.1). Cynthia's face appears and disappears behind the foliage, her eyes fixed "with wild intensity" upon Lemuel. Suddenly, this scene of powerless, expressive mute action is transformed. Cynthia's passivity explodes and, her movements punctuated by music, she rushes through the foliage to seize and accuse Lemuel. Similarly, the shocking climax of the play takes place without dialogue in a long attenuated silence broken only by thunder, and Cynthia's own bitter sobs. Grasping her knife, she looks intently at Alfred; the eyes of the tribe watch her closely. Then "with a sudden effort" Cynthia raises the knife, "and plunges it into her own heart" (3.7: 62–63). The play's denouement explores the tragic intersection of powerless silence and violent action. Whereas the falsely accused mute characters of melodrama end the play morally triumphant, both Miami and Cynthia die in a final gesture of atonement. For having reconciled the child and the wife of the man whom she killed, Miami dies and takes her secret to the grave with her, whilst Cynthia's death is presented as the ultimate act of expiation, both for loving Alfred, and, in doing so, for betraying her tribe.

How do we attribute authorship here? What these plays represent, I think, is a turning point in Adelphi dramaturgy through which new and unsettling images of femininity are being produced. From a particular collision of individuals and cirumstances – Buckstone's role as stock author, Céleste's stage history, the conventions of Adelphi melodrama, and Céleste's new authority as the Adelphi's directress – arise the haunting, original roles of Miami and Cynthia.

PLAYWRIGHTING AND HISTORIOGRAPHY

"Madame Celeste had the indelicacy to tell me, that 'I had been paid for the piece. *I took my money* and ought to *do my duty.*' I informed her that an author is under no positive obligation to attend rehearsals."[7] So wrote the disgruntled Dion Boucicault in a letter to Ben Webster concerning a rehearsal for his play, *The Willow Copse* (Adelphi, 1849). Boucicault's correspondence, together with a later, nostalgic account of his debut as a dramatist, offer some tantalizing clues about the playwrighting careers of Céleste and Vestris. Céleste, explains Boucicault indignantly in this letter, "so far forgot herself as a lady, as to address me before the company in a tone to which as a gentleman I could not reply" (quoted in Jackson 1989: 313).

The dispute between dramatist and acting manager concerned Boucicault's absence from rehearsals of *The Willow Copse*, and in particular his refusal to write a concluding "tag" for Céleste to speak at the end of the play. According to Céleste, it would seem, this combination of dilatoriness and downright uncooperativeness amounted to a breach of Boucicault's authorial responsibilities. To Céleste, Boucicault insisted that, in his view at least, an author's participation in rehearsal was strictly voluntary; to Webster, however, Boucicault admitted a more pressing reason for his absence, namely his desire to hide from his creditors (one of whom was Webster himself). Indeed, having decided to stay out of the public gaze, Boucicault seems to have abandoned his dramatic authorship to Céleste and Webster. "I have not interfered with *the arranged business*," he commented resignedly in his letter to Webster, "although diametrically opposite to my written instructions in the piece – I have only suggested inflexions of voice & manners of utterance" (quoted in Jackson 1989: 313).

When might "arranged business" begin to constitute a form of shared authorship? Boucicault's annoyance over *The Willow Copse* (a play which, ironically, was written in collaboration with Charles Lamb Kenney and, perhaps significantly, never published) can usefully be juxtaposed against his rather different interpretation of *London Assurance*'s production in 1841. For, as an inexperienced playwright, Boucicault had heaped gratitude on the Covent Garden company for making his first play a success. Although Vestris and Mathews jointly managed the theatre, Mathews seems to have been solely concerned with his own stage part. "[P]assages which I never intended as hits, were loaded, primed, and pointed, with an effect as unexpected to me as it was pleasing," Boucicault declared of Mathews. By contrast, Vestris's contribution to *London Assurance* seems both more inchoate and also much more extensive: "I am well aware that to her judgment, taste, and valuable suggestions, with regard to alterations of character, situation, dialogue, expunging passages, and dilating others – to her indefatigable zeal, I owe my position" (Bourcicault [*sic*] 1841: viii). Vestris, we may surmise, struck out parts of Boucicault's text, and extended others (whether by rewriting them herself, or by providing dialogue to be written by Boucicault we do not know). Boucicault's self-congratulatory memoir of his debut, published decades later in 1889, reveals that *London Assurance* was indeed radically rewritten in the green room, the performers being handed scenes before the ink was dry on the manuscript. Within a collaborative form of production, the dominant part in the making of *London Assurance* seems to have been played by Eliza Vestris.

In "The Death of the Author," Roland Barthes famously declared that *writing* is the place "where all identity is lost, starting with the very identity of the body writing" (Barthes 1977: 142). My argument has suggested that the identity of the authorial body in dramatic texts may itself be uncertain. The disappearance of authorial identity here, however, produces not anonymous textuality but rather its opposite: a dramatic author whose bold claim to the text's legal ownership brings about the death of other authorial voices.

The Olympic and Adelphi plays explored in this chapter reveal and simultaneously conceal a form of feminine authorship. That authorship is predicated not on writing, but rather on the agency and authority exerted by Céleste and Vestris as actress-managers. Signs of authorship include the expressive forms of mute action incorporated into the roles of Miami and Cynthia, or Vestris's equivocal renunciation of Perseus. My concept of playwrighting highlights the institutional and also the physical character of play-making – the incorporation or translation of foreign materials, consecutive or simultaneous work by several hands, the disappearance of these individual artisans in the finished physical object.

By questioning distinctions between male and female authorship, this chapter disrupts one of the fundamental assumptions of feminist criticism. Playwrighting, I have argued, throws into doubt the certainty of such discrimination; legal ownership of a dramatic text (and its performance copyright) may not be synonymous with authorship. On the contrary, plays such as *The Green Bushes* and the Olympic extravaganzas seem to represent the appropriation, or silent assimilation of feminine authority into what is subsequently presented, particularly in acting editions, as a male-authored text. In seeking to define the contribution of women as playwrights in the nineteenth century, we need to examine our own assumptions about the nature of theatrical authorship. The elusive playwrighting of Eliza Vestris and Céline Céleste, I would argue, reveals the invention of dramatic authorship to be a theatrical fiction.

NOTES

For collaborative advice, I am grateful to other contributors in this book, and especially to Tom Crochunis who responded so generously to my ideas at an earlier stage.

1 For contemporary disputes over copyright, see Foote 1829: 105 ff.
2 "Bill to amend Laws relating to Dramatic Literary Property," in Cockton 1988: vol. III, 977. See further, Barrett 1988; Stephens 1992.
3 Ben Jonson's introduction of the word *playwright* into several of his epigrams (Jonson: 1988, 49, 56, 69) however interestingly predates the *OED*'s first recorded usage. Jonson's coinage ("Playwright me reads, and still my verses damns, / He says, I want the tongue of epigrams" [49]) is wryly self-conscious and slyly ironic. For Jonson, the notion of the dramatic author as playwright offers a conspicuous neologism through which to explore questions of authorial self-definition, especially in relation to Jonson's own stage rivals. It is notable, too, that Jonson is experimenting with the concept of the playwright within poems whose relationship to translation (here from the Latin poet, Martial) also provokes questions about the nature of writerly authorship.
4 On these addresses, see reviews in *Dramatic Magazine*, 3 (April 1831): 90–91; *Examiner*, 1314 (7 April 1833): 215; *New Monthly Magazine*, 40 (1834): 531–32.
5 My description of Act 2 Scene 3 of *The Green Bushes* (Buckstone [1845]) draws on evidence from within the published text and from a review in the *Morning Chronicle*, 29 January 1845.
6 Playbill for 10 January 1848 advertising a piece by Charles Selby entitled *The Pearl of the Ocean; or, the Prince and the Mermaiden*.
7 MS letter, 24 November 1849, University of Pennsylvania Library, cited in Jackson 1989: 313.

REFERENCES

Adelphi playbill, 10 January 1848, Playbills 368, British Library, London.
Baillie, Joanna 1812, *A Series of Plays*, vol. III, London: Longman, Hurst, Rees, Orme and Browne.
Barrett, Daniel 1988, "The Dramatic Authors' Society (1833–1883) and the Payment of English Dramatists," *Essays in Theatre*, 7.1: 19–33.
[Bernard, W. Bayle] [1884], *The Wept of Wish-ton-Wish*, London: Dicks' Standard Plays, 546.
Barthes, Roland 1977, "The Death of the Author," *Image-Music-Text*, ed. and trans. Stephen Heath, London: Fontana.
Boucicault, Dion 1889, "The Debut of a Dramatist," *North American Review*, 148: 458–63.
Bourcicault [*sic*], Dion 1841, *London Assurance*, London: printed for the author.

Buckstone, John Baldwin [1840a], *Isabelle; or, Woman's Life*, London: Acting National Drama, vol. VIII.

Buckstone, John Baldwin [1840b], *Henriette the Forsaken*, London: Acting National Drama, vol. VIII.

Buckstone, John Baldwin [1845], *The Green Bushes; or, A Hundred Years Ago*, London: Acting National Drama, vol. XI.

Buckstone, John Baldwin [1847], *The Flowers of the Forest*, London: Acting National Drama, vol. XIII.

Cockton, Peter (ed.) 1988, *Subject Catalogue of the House of Commons Parliamentary Papers 1801–1900*, 5 vols., London: Chadwyck-Healey.

Cole, John William 1859, *The Life and Theatrical Times of Charles Kean F.S.A.*, 2 vols., London: Richard Bentley.

Colman, George (the Younger) [1829], *Inkle and Yarico*, London: Cumberland's British Theatre, vol. XVI.

Dance, Charles, and J. R. Planché 1879, *The Extravaganzas of J. R. Planché Esq.*, ed. T. F. Dillon Croker and Stephen Tucker, 5 vols., London: Samuel French. See vol. 1 for *Olympic Revels; or Prometheus and Pandora, Telemachus; or, The Island of Calypso*, and *The Deep, Deep Sea; or, Perseus and Andromeda*.

Dramatic Magazine 3 (April 1831): 90–91.

Examiner; A Sunday Paper on Politics, Domestic Economy, and Theatricals, 1314 (7 April 1833): 215.

Fitzball, Edward 1859, *Thirty-Five Years of a Dramatic Author's Life*, 2 vols., London: T. C. Newby.

Foote, Horace 1829, *A Companion to the Theatres; and Manual of the British Drama*, 2nd edn, London: W. Marsh and A. Miller.

Haines, John [1884], *The French Spy; or, The Siege of Constantina*, London: Dicks' Standard Plays, 680.

Howard, Jean 1993, "Cross-Dressing, the Theater, and Gender Struggle in Early Modern England," *Crossing the Stage: Controversies on Cross-Dressing*, ed. Lesley Ferris, London: Routledge, 20–46.

Jackson, Russell (ed.) 1989, *Victorian Theatre*, London: A. & C. Black.

Jonson, Ben 1988, *The Complete Poems*, Harmondsworth: Penguin.

Morning Chronicle, 29 January 1845.

New Monthly Magazine and Literary Journal, 40 (1834): 531–32.

Olympic playbill, 3 January 1831, Playbills 329, British Library, London.

Orgel, Stephen 1981, "What is a Text?," *Research Opportunities in Renaissance Drama*, 24: 3–6.

Planché, Eliza 1834, *The Welsh Girl*, London: John Miller.

Planché, Eliza 1838, *A Hasty Conclusion*, London: Chapman and Hall.

Planché, J. R. [1850], *The Child of the Wreck*, London: Lacy's Acting Editions, 39.

Planché, J. R. 1872, *The Recollections and Reflections of J. R. Planché*, 2 vols., London: Tinsley Brothers.

"The Play-Houses and their Prospects," 1836, *New Monthly Magazine*, 48.3: 165–77.

Rede, Leman T. 1836, *The Road to the Stage*, new edn, London: J. Onwhyn.

Stephens, John Russell 1992, *The Profession of the Playwright: British Theatre 1800–1900*, Cambridge: Cambridge University Press.

Thackeray, T[homas] J[ames] 1832, *On Theatrical Emancipation, and the Rights of Dramatic Authors*, London: C. Chapple.

The Times, 14 February 1831, 9 October 1837.

Tomlins, F. G. 1840, *A Brief View of the English Drama*, London: C. Mitchell.

Watson, Ernest Bradlee 1926, *Sheridan to Robertson: A Study of the Early Nineteenth-Century Stage*, Cambridge, MA: Harvard University Press.

CHAPTER 6

Sarah Lane: questions of authorship

Jim Davis

Authorship and translation, when defined in theatrical terms, are complex, collaborative processes. The romantic notion of the solitary (male) writer, quill in hand, is misleading when applied to the complicated, multifaceted processes involved in bringing a dramatic text to performance. A form of translation is occurring – a rendering of new significances, new interpretations, new possibilities – a rewriting or recreation of text. In effect the authorship of a performed text is an act of translation, of adaptation and of dramaturgical skill, a further act of playmaking collectively achieved by actors, stage managers, scene-painters, costumiers and, in the nineteenth century, managers. Inevitably, similar processes are also implicit in the audience's reception of what they see performed, mediated in turn through the varied cultural assumptions which they bring with them to the theatre.[1]

Many nineteenth-century plays were translations and/or adaptations in the narrowest sense. The French and German theatre, penny dreadfuls, novels, and newspaper accounts all furnished the British stage with the raw material out of which new plays were concocted. Yet what appeared on stage often reflected more than the mere process of literary transformation and was made possible by a range of agencies. Just as Holcroft's *A Tale of Mystery* (Covent Garden, 1802) or Sheridan's *Pizarro* (Drury Lane, 1799) appropriate and rewrite Pixérécourt and Kotzebue to make certain political points relevant to a British audience, so the plays in performance took on moral and iconographic significances beyond those intended by both the original authors or their nominal translators. In effect the ultimate acts of translation and authorship transcend those attributable to any one individual and are better defined as processural phenomena within the theatrical context.

The complexity with which we need to imbue such terms as

Plate 6. Caricature of Mrs. Sarah Lane of the Britannia Theatre,
subtitled "Rule, Britannia!" Source and date unknown.

authorship, *translation*, *adaptation*, and *dramaturgy* is strikingly embodied
in the career of the nineteenth-century actress, manager, and
dramatist, Sarah Lane, a significant figure in east London theatre for
over fifty years. A popular and talented actress, she had married
Samuel Lane, manager of the Britannia Theatre, Hoxton, in the
1840s. Her nephew A. L. Crauford states that she had been of great
assistance in advising on the development of the Britannia in its
early days (Crauford 1933: 253); Britannia prompt copies reveal that
she also had considerable influence on the way that plays were
staged. Her comic roles in pantomime, melodrama, farce, and
burlesque, not to mention her focal appearance in the Britannia
Festival every December, further enhanced her reputation and that
of the theatre. Yet, from 1873 to 1881 her name began to appear on

the playbills as the author of a series of plays translated and adapted from the French. The implications of this new development in what was already an enormously successful career raise a number of issues, not the least of which are questions of authorship and translation in both the specific and broader terms outlined above.

Sarah Lane is one of the more privileged of nineteenth-century women playwrights, in that her works are actually recorded and attributed to her in Allardyce Nicoll's handlist of plays (Nicoll 1959: vol. v, 448). In his study of nineteenth-century British playwriting, John Russell Stephens also gives her a special mention:

After 1850 there was no shortage of female dramatic authors, but they were amateurs and few achieved any dramatic distinction ... Among the exceptions to the majority was Sarah Lane ... who energetically ran the Britannia and wrote a cluster of melodramas for the theatre in the 1870s and early 1880s. (Stephens 1992: 4)

Yet it is quite possible that Sarah Lane never actually translated or adapted (in the literal sense) any of the plays attributed to her. On 16 February 1873, the Britannia's stage manager, Frederick Wilton, sceptically commented in his diary: "By Mrs. Lane's desire, read 1st Act of a piece which, she informed me, she had *herself* translated from the French!" (Wilton 1863–86). His diary entry for 10 November of that year, when the play in question, *Taken from Memory*, was first performed, is equally incredulous: "Taken from the French by Mrs. S. Lane!" (Wilton 1863–86). On 12 February 1874, he recorded: "Received last night of Mr Robinson the 1st Act of a drama called *Patrie* translated from the French by Mrs S. Lane (credat judens)!! to prepare for Easter"[2] (Davis 1992: 216). A. L. Crauford, who managed the Britannia Theatre from 1882, not only makes no reference to her dramas in his account of the Lanes, *Sam and Sallie*, but claims that *Patrie*, staged as *Dolores* at the Britannia, was written by the son of Sarah Lane's friend, the bookmaker Johnny Gideon (Crauford 1933: 316). (The younger Gideon also provided a version of *Les Deux Orphelines* for the Britannia's Whitsun presentation in 1874, although this fell through after Henry Neville of the Olympic Theatre informed Sarah Lane that he held the sole rights to the piece (Davis 1992: 217).)

All of the plays attributed to Sarah Lane were written in the period immediately following the deaths of her husband (Samuel)

and her father (William Borrow), both of whom had played a strong
role in the theatre's policies. Crauford asserts that

The reputation and prosperity of the theatre for a few years was well
maintained, but gradually a decline began to show itself, the cause of which
was as follows. There was no longer a manager with the flair for the
selection of attractions. An outside sinister influence took a hand in
selecting the plays and this soon made itself felt ... Now that Sallie was a
widow he (Gideon) thought he would help her by selecting plays from
Paris, and which he imagined would bring in the shekels to the Britannia
coffers. He was an ardent theatregoer and fancied he knew all that was to
be known on the subject, so that it became a hobby with him. (Crauford
1933: 316)

The first play Gideon sent to the Britannia was Sardou's *Patrie*,
which no other theatre had then presented:

This was magnificently produced on a scale hitherto unknown at the
Britannia and, being a great romantic play, was a considerable success. On
the strength of this Gideon bombarded Sallie [Sarah Lane] with French
plays. But they were not *Patries*; they were utterly over the heads of the
Hoxtonians and consequently quite unsuitable.
    Yet Sallie considered Gideon was infallible and unwisely tried to force
indigestible food upon her patrons. (Crauford 1933: 316–17)

Crauford states that this influence began to be felt in pantomime
subjects, again with disastrous results. Crauford's predecessor,
William Robinson, alarmed at the way business was falling off,
"ventured to protest strongly against these French importations.
Sallie resented his interference. Quarrels arose. Business became
worse and worse" (Crauford 1933: 318–19). Since Crauford replaced
Robinson as manager, his account may be rather partisan. However,
the diaries of Frederick Wilton also attest to Gideon's interference in
the Britannia repertory and staging of plays and to the quarrels this
provoked.[3]
    Yet, as Clive Barker points out, the home-grown repertory also
remained in place and it was only in the 1880s, when the theatre
began to present West End successes, that its policy changed
fundamentally (Barker 1979: 30). Moreover, both *Taken from Memory*
and *Dolores* had very successful runs, which suggests there was a local
market for French as well as English plays. Sarah Lane herself was
well aware of changing tastes, but equally insistent that the drama
should retain a moral tone. Considering the moral ambivalence
associated with the French drama in England, it may seem surprising

that she should want to associate herself with such plays. However the issue here was not just morality: when *Frou-Frou* was performed at the Britannia Theatre in March 1873, with Marian Lacey as Gilberte, it was a complete failure: "unfit for a Britannia audience – '*all talkee-talkee*'", according to Frederick Wilton (Davis 1992: 211). The real problem may well have been the greater emphasis on language than on physical action, an emphasis for which the Britannia audience was unprepared. Yet, from 1873 onwards, Sarah Lane's name became associated with a series of adaptations of plays in many of which language was predominant over action.

It is quite possible that Gideon and his son, who may have contributed a further ten plays and farces to the Britannia (not counting pantomimes) under the pseudonym of E. Manuel between 1875 and 1879 (Newton 1927: 271), were the authors of the plays attributed to Sarah Lane. Some, but not all, of E. Manuel's plays are similar in style and content to those of Sarah Lane. *Expiation* (Manuel 1876), with its emphasis on adultery, repentance, forgiveness, and on language rather than action, has affinities with Lane's work, whereas *Two Sons* (Manuel 1877) has little in common with her plays other than its historical setting. Moreover, all the E. Manuel manuscripts in the Frank Pettingell Collection are in a notably different hand from those manuscripts attributed to Sarah Lane. The handwriting of Sarah Lane's own plays is certainly very similar (although not always identical) from manuscript to manuscript, but not consistent with her handwritten and signed interventions in a number of scripts by other dramatists. Of course, it is possible that the final draft of each of Sarah Lane's plays is her own (regardless of the handwriting), even though she may have been working from someone else's version or translation. However, since the handwriting of the manuscripts submitted to the Lord Chamberlain is similar to the Pettingell manuscripts, a copyist may have been responsible for both written versions, with the result that the question of Sarah Lane's authorship still remains ambiguous.

There are several questions that need to be asked. Did Sarah Lane translate and/or adapt the plays attributed to her? Certainly, the announcement that a major attraction had been written by so popular an actress-manager would have had publicity value in its own right. Yet the Britannia hardly prided itself on nurturing the drama. It presented formulaic plays, written speedily and for little financial return, to supply the needs of a stock company and the public demand for continual novelty. Was Sarah Lane in fact attempting to raise the tone of the Britannia's repertory by the importation of French plays? Was she attempting to "remake" both herself and her theatre in the aftermath of her husband's death? Was she hopelessly under the spell of Johnny Gideon? Is her contribution to the stage as a dramatist, even if she wrote the plays, as significant as her contribution as an actress and manager? And why did none of the plays she allegedly translated or adapted contain roles of the sort she was so famous for playing?

On a number of levels Sarah Lane did translate and adapt not only the plays attributed to her, but many more besides. The incredulity of Wilton and the comments of Crauford may raise doubts about the "authenticity" of the plays attributed to her, but this in turn raises the issue of what we mean when we talk about the "authenticity" of the theatrical text. The fact remains that, during the period in which these plays were performed, Sarah Lane was the controlling force at the Britannia Theatre. She ultimately decided not only *what* was performed but also *how* it was performed. As manager or actress or (putative) dramatist she uniquely raises the conundrum of what translation or adaptation actually mean within a theatrical context. Even if Gideon or his son translated and adapted the plays attributed to her, she made the decision to stage them and possessed the expertise to make them work on stage. Equally, regardless of who translated and adapted the plays from the French, the absence of roles specifically tailored for her talents need not be regarded as an oversight, since this would have freed her to retain tighter control over all aspects of production.

Sarah Lane's supposed dramatic output is not particularly prolific by the standards of her contemporaries. All the plays were performed at the Britannia Theatre, commencing with *Taken from Memory* (1873), followed by *Dolores* (1874), *Albert de Rosen* (1875), *The Faithless Wife* (1876), *St. Bartholomew; or, A Queen's Love* (1877); *The Cobbler's Daughter* (1878); *Red Josephine; or, A Woman's Vengeance* (1880); and *Devotion; or The Priceless Wife* (1881). All but *Albert de Rosen* were mounted at key moments in the Britannia's calendar: Easter, Whitsun, or early November. None of her plays were published and they survive only as licensing copies in the Lord Chamberlain's Collection and (with the exception of *Dolores*) as prompt copies in the Frank Pettingell Collection.

The first drama, *Taken from Memory*, was not a particularly original choice of play to translate. It had already been performed on the London stage in other versions, including *The Four Stages of Life* (1862–63) at the Surrey Theatre, where it was revived in a reduced form as *The Hunchback Doctor* in 1866. The Britannia version won Sarah Lane praise in the *Era* (16 November 1873) for the skill with which she had adapted Vollaire's original, but also criticism for the superabundance of talk, the lack of heightened action, and the use of four acts when three would have done. However, the *Hackney and Kingsland Gazette and Shoreditch Telegraph* (15 November 1873) praised the play, because

without a single sensation scene, or even a comic man, [it] relies for its success upon its merits and its construction and diction alone, and considering that a Hoxton audience, [who] ordinarily delight in strong situations, with the action moving swiftly forward, is opposed to the verbosity of ordinary comedy, that success is worthy to be noted, as the authoress is to be complimented.

The plot centers on two sons – the legitimate, who is profligate, and the illegitimate, the more noble Albert, who is disowned by his father, suspected of a crime that he witnessed but did not commit. Beloved by two women – Genevieve, who enters a convent, and Louise, whom he marries – Albert suffers much hardship, exacerbated by temporary blindness, but is eventually reconciled with his father, whilst his half-brother is revealed as the cause of all his woes. Overall, *Taken from Memory* suffers from too much dialogue and too little dramatic action, although packed full with obstacles and complications, moments of great pathos and sentimentality, a strong moral concern and some good character parts.

Taken from Memory was not a typical Britannia piece; nor was *Dolores*, the next French play to be attributed to Sarah Lane. Presented as a new piece for the Easter holidays in 1874 and set during the Spanish occupation of Brussels in the 1560s, *Dolores* was highly praised by the *Era* (12 April 1874) as "a careful, appreciative and scholarly adaptation." Sardou's play centers on Dolores, who betrays her husband to protect her lover, not realizing that the lover is actually in league with her husband against the Spaniards. Brander Matthews described Dolores as "the wretchedly vicious heroine" of the play, whilst Sardou himself claimed apologetically that "imposed on me by the action of the play, she long haunted my sleep to reproach me for having made her so vicious" (quoted in

Matthews 1901: 192–93). *Patrie*, first performed at the Porte Saint-Martine in 1869, was successfully revived at the Chatelet in 1872 and in 1886 was turned into an opera. Yet, at the time of the Britannia production, none of the larger West End theatres had taken up the play, to the surprise of the *Era* (12 April 1874):

Well placed on the stage, with the advantages of the battles, processions, and exciting scenes with which it is filled, *Patrie* must have obtained success purely as a spectacular play. But still there were dissentient voices ... Many protested against the essentially disagreeable character of the heroine – a strong character part, but one utterly unsympathetic to an English audience. Mrs S. Lane deserves some credit for testing the question of conventionality before a most conventional audience. The theory is that an East-End audience will tolerate no play which does not "come all right in the end," but here is a melodrama played at the Britannia where the leading characters drop off one by one, and the termination is as tragic as the opera of *The Huguenots*, which it very much resembles in tone and situation.

According to the *Hackney and Kingsland Gazette and Shoreditch Telegraph* (11 April 1874):

The enterprising Manageress of the "Great" Theatre, Hoxton, has long realised the fact that her special patrons are able to appreciate the highest delineations of the drama. The new piece, with which Mrs S. Lane delighted her Easter audiences on Monday, is in accordance with that idea, and, consequently, owes its claims for success to its effect upon the mind rather than upon the eye.

If Sarah Lane had flattered her audiences and wooed her critics by choosing to stage *Dolores* at the Britannia, the achievement was due in part to the excellence of the acting and the scenery. The snow-covered exterior of the battlements of Brussels and the huge interior of the Brussels town hall were excellently depicted, whilst the acting of the three principal characters, Count Rysoor (Joseph Reynolds), Karloo (Edgar Newbound), and Dolores (Marie Henderson) was thought equal to the best West End acting. Marie Henderson won acclaim for "her power to portray the deep and stormy passions of love and hate" (*Hackney and Kingsland Gazette and Shoreditch Telegraph*, 9 May 1874). The *Standard* (7 April 1874) drew attention to her effective handling of a difficult and morally ambiguous role:

The scenes in which the expressions of her love for her husband's supplanter were most marked, and which, of course, from their very nature, were difficult to portray in a manner satisfactory to an English audience, were entirely successful. The audience, however, we are bound to say, appeared rather to sympathise with the difficulties of the actress, and the genius she displayed in surmounting them, than in the moral obliquities which they involved.

The *Era* (12 April 1874) was particularly impressed by the way in which she had worked up her death scene, "with all the horrible details of tragic realism, terminating in a magnificent 'backfall.'" If the play itself was an unusual choice for the theatre, its meticulous staging and casting ensured its success. It was obviously a tremendous coup for the Britannia to be the first to stage one of Sardou's most notable dramas; if their attempt to stage *Les Deux Orphelines* six weeks later had not been forestalled by Henry Neville, perhaps the theatre would have consolidated a reputation for the staging of major new French dramas. As it is, *Dolores* remains the exception rather than the rule.

The Britannia version of *Patrie* stays faithful to Sardou's original, both in dialogue and action. The prompt copy does not survive, so that the Lord Chamberlain's manuscript is the only version still available. Since stage directions and details of setting were often omitted from the Lord Chamberlain's copy and dialogue was not always complete, any deductions made from this version are necessarily speculative. If the cuts in dialogue are indicative of what was actually spoken in the Britannia Theatre, then the play was shortened slightly and dialogue that emphasized the psychological states of the main characters or was self-reflective was removed. Even Rysoor's key speech, "*Patrie*, you can have no doubt of my devotion. I have set your affairs in order before my own," disappears. Any slow build up to moments of intense passion is sacrificed for the sake of pace. The acts of the play are also reorganized: Sardou's five acts are reduced to four and the eight scenes of the original are reduced to five. This means that less time is lost to scene changes and that each act in the new version now ends at a key moment in the development of the action, providing strong and effective climaxes, usually emphasizing Dolores's situation rather than the theme of "patrie." The retitling of the play as *Dolores* also indicates the Britannia emphasis, doubtless exploiting Marie Henderson's popular following in the East End. The Britannia playbills were soon billing *Dolores* as "The most successful Drama produced for years. Powerful Diction, Passion & Pathos – Admirably drawn Characters and Superb *Mise*

en Scène. A Rich Emotional and Intellectual Treat!," and were
referring to its being eulogized as "the most powerful drama on
the London stage (Vide *Standard, Telegraph, Morning Advertiser, Sunday
Times, Era, Graphic, Figaro, Hornet* &c, &c.)" (Britannia cuttings). It
had an exceptionally long run (six to seven weeks) by Britannia
standards and was revived in subsequent seasons. In its tale of
passion, jealousy, and revenge, unfolded through a series of highly
dramatized set speeches, it verged on the tragic rather than the
melodramatic. It is very different from the standard Britannia
melodramas, many of which were based on models from an earlier
era and had more in common with the world of Pixérécourt than
with that of Sardou.

Of Sarah Lane's six remaining dramas, five can be dealt with
fairly concisely. *The Faithless Wife*, a version of the well-known French
play, *Le Centenarie*,[4] was like *Dolores* produced as the Britannia's Easter
Monday melodrama. According to the *Hackney and Kingsland Gazette
and Shoreditch Telegraph* (24 April 1876):

There have been several versions, but this produced at the "Brit" obtains a
merit for following somewhat more closely the French original, and
consequently is more effective, at the same time the style and language are
thoroughly English.

Set in France, the play centers around two sisters, Juliette and
Camilla, and their 100-year-old grandfather. Juliette is very much
the passive, suffering victim, whilst Camilla withstands the mis-
placed wrath of her father and the machinations of the play's
villain. The play is conventionally moral: adultery and illegitimacy
are punished by death, whilst honor is rewarded with life and
reconciliation. A principal focus is once again a strong female
character, Camilla, played by Bertha Adams, who had previously
played the title role in a revival of *Dolores*. *Albert de Rosen*, adapted
from the French play *Les Couteaux d'or* and set in Paris and the
Mexican gold-fields, is rather a disappointment. This long and
convoluted drama about betrayal, abduction, and revenge features
a group of prospectors called the "golden dagger"; an Indian
woman, Cora, training her panther to avenge her father's death;
and a heroine, Ellen Talbot, whose degradations empower her and
turn her into a figure of strength. In many ways an ineffective play,
its major interest perhaps resides in its strong female characters. *St.
Bartholomew* is centered on the St. Bartholomew's Day Massacre and

therefore on the conflict between Huguenot and Catholic and on the intrigues of the French royal family. Combining friendship, loyalty, revenge, treachery, selfless love, self-sacrifice, torture, and poisoning, this historical drama is highly formulaic, relying heavily on elaborate and varied settings, a large cast and a sensation scene in a torture chamber for its effect. *The Cobbler's Daughter* was described by the *Hackney and Kingsland Gazette and Shoreditch Telegraph* (29 March 1878) as another success attributable to Sarah Lane's "good taste and management":

The incidents are laid in France at the early period of the last century, but, actually, they are more of an English nature, and more abounding in traits to enlist English sympathies than it is possible would ever have been associated with our friends across the Channel. Some of the situations perhaps are by no means novel, but they are treated by the fair authoress in a way that makes them quite fresh and original as though they were new.

The play concerns a cobbler, Papillon, and his relationship with his adopted daughter, Genevieve. Although enhanced by the performances of J. B. Howe and Bertha Adams in the principal roles, it is rather a contrived piece, overreliant on coincidence and effusively sentimental. *Devotion; or, The Priceless Wife*, the last adaptation from the French, concerns a soldier, Bernard (J. B. Howe), who is separated from his wife Marianne (Bertha Adams) in battle and, presuming her dead, later remarries. Bernard, who has been blinded in battle, is unaware that his second wife, Helen, is unfaithful. The arrival of his first wife, who has in fact been wrongfully imprisoned, and the exposure of the second wife's duplicity, lead to the play's resolution. The play's focus is on the "devotion" of the first wife, as both wife and mother, and on the restoration of the true family after the "wicked woman's" infidelities and false accusations resolve in her suicide.

Despite its description as "a new and powerful drama," *Red Josephine*, taken from the French of M. Ponson du Terrail, had already been performed in England as *Baccarat; or, the Knave of Hearts* (Suter 1865) at Sadler's Wells in 1865, with Alice Marriott in the role of Red Josephine, and a year later at the Grecian as *Rocambole; or, The Companions of Crime*. Red Josephine is a strong female character – a gambler, hopelessly in love with the play's hero, whose life she saves, even though her love is unrequited, after an attempted murder instigated by the play's villain, Rocambole. Until its final act, *Red*

Josephine follows Suter's version very closely, sometimes almost word for word: it is difficult to tell whether the Britannia play is a translation or a carefully disguised adaptation of Suter's play. However, whereas Josephine expires at the end of the Britannia version, in Suter's play the last act leaves the villain and his mother trapped in a cavern amidst rising waters, followed by a scene in which the plot is resolved through Josephine, who remains alive, even though she cannot have the man she loves. Bertha Adams, who played Josephine at the Britannia, was highly praised by the *Era* (14 November 1880) for her rendering of the title role and for the quality of the stage pictures she created at the end of the second and fourth acts, when she respectively witnesses a murder and dies in the arms of the man she loves. In pursuit of the villain, Rocambole (or Dubois in this version), she finally confronts him in an underground cave, which is in imminent danger of being flooded (hence providing a spectacular conclusion to the play):

ROCAMBOLE: Josephine!
JOSEPHINE: Yes, Josephine.
ROCAMBOLE: My saviour!
JOSEPHINE: No, your executioner. [*Darts on him, seizes him by the shirt collar with the left hand, draws a concealed dagger with the right*] I have you now, escape if you can, the evil one has assisted you often, what aid will he bring you now, assassin? [*Stabs him twice in the breast*] (Act 4 Scene 3)

At this point, officers and Armion, the man she loves, appear:

JOSEPHINE: The cards have this time been fairly dealt. The Knave of Hearts has been taken by Red Josephine [*Faints into the arms of* ARMION *– slightly recovers, sees him, expresses her happiness at dying with him and dies in his arms*].

Red Josephine, the last but one of the dramas attributed to Sarah Lane, demonstrates a movement back to older sources and to an emphasis on the sensational rather than the psychological.

Nevertheless, Sarah Lane's notes in the prompt copy of *Red Josephine* usefully reveal her authorial role in translating the written text into performance, indicating a strong theatrical sense, specifically in relation to makeup, continuity, and setting. At the end of Act 3, Josephine, alone with Rocambole, attempts to get possession of his dagger. She is dragged around as she attempts to bite his hand, but is saved as the door is broken from outside and Rocambole retreats. The prompt copy notes:

In struggle JOSEPHINE pulls ROCAMBOLE across the stage by his neckerchief – he strikes her on the forehead and blood should be seen on her brow – JOS[,] frequently in the struggle and fight calls ROC, villain, assassin, murderer – this left to the discretion of the actress. When JOSEPHINE comes on in next act she has the scar from blow on her forehead.

Equally specific instructions are given for the final act of the play:

When JOSEPHINE comes on in the last scene she must be made up hollow under the eyes &c., shewing she is near her death from sorrow. This will account for her dying as soon as she has been revenged. The lady who plays MADAME ANDREW (ROCAMBOLE's mother) must be made up to look the age ROCAMBOLE's mother would be.

The beam … must be iron, and when ROCAMBOLE strikes the wall he must strike on an iron plate painted same as it so that its sound is heard by the audience, and when he throws the bar down (being iron) it will sound as it should.

Sarah Lane's theatrical sense and attention to detail are also apparent in her notes for other plays attributed to her. At the end of *Taken from Memory* she added a memorandum on the disposition of characters in the final tableau:

Disposition of characters at end. ALBERT lifts JULIETTE on to his one knee. DUPERRIER with upraised hands stands over them [R.C.] D'ARCY [LG], with his face to audience. LOUISE and GENEVIEVE kneeling to him in thankfulness, their backs to the audience, each holding his hand.
N.B. ALBERT should, I think, keep his eyes firmly fixed on JULIETTE till the curtain is down.

In the prompt copy of *Devotion*, there is a note to the prompter concerning a crucial letter, to be "careful that this note be properly sealed each night," and a memorandum concerning Helen's suicide in the last act, that there is "very short time for making up her face." *Devotion* also contains a note at the end of the last act that all the scenes should be "enclosed" and instructions on the speed with which the dialogue should be spoken as Act 1 approaches its climax. Similar instructions, again revealing a concern with the pace of the performance, occur in Act 3 of *The Cobbler's Daughter*, when Genevieve is reunited with her mother: "The latter part of this act played quickly." Such evidence continually demonstrates Sarah Lane's practical sense, her knowledge of stagecraft, her awareness of what will be effective, and her careful attention to detail, authenticating the broader claims of theatrical authorship made on her behalf.

Whilst the plays attributed to Sarah Lane are consistent in their

French sources, their romantic tone, their sentiments, and their formulaic construction, it is difficult to discern amongst them collectively an individual voice. They are solid French romantic melodramas, often set historically and requiring a degree of spectacle in their staging, whilst also relying more heavily than the average Britannia melodrama on dialogue and character development. Like many of the popular domestic pieces performed at the Britannia, most of these plays feature strong female roles, whether they stress constancy, courage, jealousy, or passion. Thus Louise, Camilla, Ellen, and Marianne reveal hidden reserves of strength in adversity, whilst Dolores, Red Josephine, Cora, and Helen are driven beyond the boundaries of social convention by their passions. Only Genevieve in *Taken from Memory* (who becomes a nun when she realizes the play's hero does not love her) and Juliette in *The Faithless Wife* (whose adultery is expiated by her own death and that of her child) receive more traditional treatment. In many ways these plays (with the exception perhaps of *St. Bartholomew*) reflect the paradox of the melodramatic heroine, "helpless and unfriended," yet rebellious and yearning for independence, that Martha Vicinus has so eloquently investigated (Vicinus 1989: 174–86). The newspaper reviews, which praise Sarah Lane without condescension, further indicate an ability to adapt the plays successfully to English taste (whilst remaining close to the French originals) and to extend the paramaters of dramatic fare offered to the Britannia audiences.

Sarah Lane acted in none of the plays that appeared under her name at the Britannia. The sort of comic roles in which she specialized did not feature in any of the above adaptations from the French, which were all singularly lacking in comic relief or in characters that embodied the piquant, sprightly, vivacious, brisk, hearty, happy, sparkling, arch, and graceful qualities for which critics so often praised her.[5] Whereas other dramatists created roles especially for her, the plays discussed above quite clearly separate Sarah Lane the actress from Sarah Lane the nominal dramatist. There are no roles requiring singing, dancing, or male impersonation, all of which were significant in many of the characters she embodied in melodrama, pantomime, and burlesque.[6] In fact, insofar as Sarah Lane's performances bore any immediate relationship to the plays attributed to her, they did so through her appearances in other pieces on the same bill. Thus *The Faithless Wife* was followed on its opening night by an "opera bouffe" entitled

Women's Rights (Marchant 1876) about a land in which the position of the sexes is reversed – "Men are the gentle and women the stronger sex" (*Hackney and Kingsland Gazette and Shoreditch Telegraph*, 24 April 1876). Female impersonator Fred Foster, "the Girl of the Period," played the Queen, Rose d'Eté (burlesquing *The Grand Duchess of Gerolstein*) and Sarah Lane was a dashing young French gentleman, Frivolin, who has to fend off the Queen's advances. After lots of jokes about men being tender, poor, and helpless, risking seduction because of their "sparkling eyes," being fit only to stay at home and do the washing and turn the mangle whilst the women get on with politics; the men revolt and assert their authority and the play concludes with the tag "that woman shall bless the day / She learned to love, to honour and obey." Despite the gender reversals, the burlesque points toward as conventional a conclusion as the melodrama that preceded it. *St. Bartholomew* was followed by a "vaudeville," *The Spanish Page* (1859), in which Sarah Lane played Queen Isabella, who disguises as a handsome page boy, Flirtillo, in order to satisfy her curiosity about the man to whom she is betrothed. It was as if, after witnessing the high seriousness of her role as author, the audience was brought down to earth again by her skills as a burlesque performer. The role of author may also have been an insurance policy against the day when she could no longer attract audiences as a performer, but since she was still donning Flirtillo's black tights when she gave her last performance at the age of seventy-six (Crauford 1933: 335–36), her appeal on stage does not appear to have waned. Normally she was no longer playing juveniles by the early 1880s, but Crauford states that "she was as vivacious as ever in pantomimes and in suitable parts in all plays" (Crauford 1933: 323).

The *Theatrical Journal* (9 January 1851) claimed Sarah Lane as "a second Madame Vestris." Yet, whilst Vestris and Marie Wilton have received far more acclaim, on account of their so-called "reforms," Sarah Lane certainly vied with them in stature both as a performer and as a manager. In 1863, a biographical account claimed that

Mrs. Lane's talent is remarkable alike for its excellence and its versatility. She plays in so many parts of such an opposite character, that one scarcely knows in which she most excells ... although the performance of Peter Spyke has been frequently pronounced her most perfect part, yet her personations of Irish characters never fail to be greeted with enthusiastic approbation; whilst probably no other actress since the days of Mrs.

Jordan, and her successor, the late Miss Davison, has made such a hit in Nell, in *The Devil to Pay* ... In smart singing chambermaids she has been popularly styled the "Vestris of the East"; and has won for herself a deservedly high reputation in the dashing cavaliers of musical burlesque ... There is a *naivete* and grace in her appearance, an ease and elegance in her movements, and a finish in her acting, which stamps her as a true artist. (*Players*, 17 March 1860)

Her ability to combine comedy and pathos (Crauford 1933: 253) and her versatility as a performer were particularly admired. Yet this versatility did not extend to the heroines or adventuresses of melodrama; ironically, the very plays with which she drew audiences, because she had allegedly written them, were those in which no part existed for herself. Despite this anomaly, the moral concerns of her own plays are equivalent to those which her characters in other plays embodied. There is no ambivalence: whilst her plays deal with adultery, infidelity, treachery, and revenge, they never endorse them. This much vaunted concern with morality and instruction was an important factor in the public reputation that Sarah Lane fostered for herself.

In fact, Sarah Lane's authorial presence at the Britannia is consonant with the authorial presence that Jane Moody argues for Vestris and Céleste (see above, chapter 5). The plays of other Britannia authors could certainly be defined as collaborative ventures insofar as they created characters and moral perspectives dependent on Sarah Lane's involvement. In 1876, Sarah Lane's policies as actress, manager, and playwright were discussed in the *Saturday Programme* (29 April 1876):

Directing one of the largest theatres in the metropolis, having to cater for those who prefer strong meat to milk-and-water, Mrs. S. Lane has wisely enough directed her attention chiefly to melodrama. Visitors to the Britannia will seek in vain for the thinly disguised suggestiveness which, until lately, was the staple food of many West-End playhouses ... In many cases Mrs. S. Lane is her own authoress, and her works have the advantage of being exactly suited to the tastes of her patrons. In still many more cases the popular directress is the chief actress in the plays she produces, and it is this hearty and complete identification of herself with the work of her own theatre that has done a good deal to place it in its present popular position. No one ever heard of a failure at "the Brit," because the good judgment of the directress is unfailing.

Perhaps the most successful embodiment of Sarah Lane's prestige in both the theatre and the community – by the end of her life she was known as the "Queen of Hoxton" – was the annual Britannia Festival, which was a central part of Sarah Lane's benefit every December. The last of these occasions is recalled in an unidentified clipping by a member of the audience writing on 16 December 1952:

At last the big moment arrived – the Festival Scene. The stock company assembled on the stage in a big semi-circle with Sarah Lane in the centre ... Every one on the stage would step forward in turn to greet Mrs. Lane with a kiss on her outstretched hand. She would then thank them for their performances during the year, and they would each address the audience with a specially written verse. There were thunders of applause when the verse finished. After that, Mrs. Lane would make a present to each artist, and there was a second greeting to the audience. The response to this was staggering. (Britannia cuttings)

The regal nature of this occasion is further described in another unidentified clipping, dated 31 March 1890, entitled "Women of the World no.v. – Mrs. Sarah Lane":

No work-girl in north-east London is so poor but that she will bring her tribute to lay at the feet of this noble-hearted lady, who has lightened many sorrows – not only with laughter, but with an open purse. No deserving cause appeals to Mrs. Lane without receiving ready response. She plays not only the good fairy of the pantomime, but the far more practical part of good fairy of real life. (Britannia cuttings)

This aspect of Sarah Lane's work and reputation, together with the roles she performed at the theatre, the type of programme she encouraged, and the plays she possibly wrote, effectively reveal her as the author of both her onstage and offstage persona. A caricature (plate 6) depicts her as Britannia: immediately in front of the theatre itself, but with the dome of St. Paul's and the London skyline in the background, she seems to epitomize national as well as local endeavor.

Sarah Lane also strongly influenced the way plays were staged at the Britannia. Thus, whether or not she translated or adapted the plays attributed to her, she would certainly have had a hand in their final representation, if surviving evidence of her intervention in other plays is anything to go by. The manuscript plays in the Frank Pettingell Collection (many of which are Britannia prompt copies) often contain requests by Sarah Lane to her stage manager for cuts or for changes in staging to facilitate backstage maneuvers or even concerning the content of the playbill for the play in question. The prompt copy of *The Left-Handed Marriage* (Hazlewood 1864), which commences with a paragraph describing morganatic marriage, includes a note from Sarah Lane stating "Mr. Wilton, please put this in the bill," whilst a note in *Red Josephine* requests that red ink be used in the title on the playbill. On the script of *The Volcano of Italy* (Hazlewood 1865) Wilton notes of Act 2 Scene 2, set in a ballroom:

For the first month the supers and the Ladies of the Ballet all came on here to begin this scene and continued promenading about the Ball-Room & sometimes in the garden & until the Countess entered ... But at the end of the 4th week Mrs. S. L., considering that the promenade distracted the attention of the audience, cut them.

The Old, Old Story (Marchant 1868) contains a request from Sarah Lane to include all the business in the script and also a request to Wilton to set one of the scenes so that "I can get across at the back of it instead of having to go under the stage." There are also instructions from Sarah Lane not to set the second act with a Terrace, if this will save time, and that she will herself provide a piece of blue silk ribbon that is needed in the first act.

The dramaturgical skills with which Sarah Lane oversaw the translation of plays from page to stage are equally apparent in the cuts that she ordered, many of which are recorded in the Pettingell manuscripts. Thus *Faith, Hope and Charity* (Hazlewood 1863), the first play to use Pepper's Ghost in a dramatic representation, contains many cuts made by Sarah Lane on the second night of its run, in order to take forty-three minutes off the running time. The problems of getting sheet glass into place for Pepper's effect and the time taken to dismantle it had entailed a running time of 3 hours and 58 minutes on the play's first performance. Lane's cuts are also evidenced in *The Old Maid and the Winding Sheet* (Hazlewood 1862), *The Dark King of the Black Mountains* (1866) and *The Old Cherry Tree* (Hazlewood 1866), *Turned Out to Starve* (Webb 1870), *Truth* (Pitt 1871), *Cast Aside* (Hazlewood 1871) and *To the Green Isles Direct* (Akhurst 1874). If Sarah Lane was responsible for the final scripts of *Dolores* and *Red Josephine*, then her skills at editing and cutting are again very evident, especially in the latter.

The ability to cut plays quite ruthlessly to reduce running time, to avoid repetition and to enhance narrative clarity reveals once again how skilled Sarah Lane was dramaturgically. Whilst all the plays attributed to her are adaptations or translations from the French and there are indications that some or all of them may have been partly or totally the work of other hands, the Pettingell manuscripts of these and other plays reveal a significant dramaturgical ability. The theatrical fare offered at the Britannia would have been much less successful if deprived of the flare and attention to detail that Sarah Lane brought to it. Yet, although Crauford acknowledges her contribution to the success of her husband's management (Crauford 1933: 253), he later claims that she "was wanting in judgment as a manageress," that "no woman has ever won reputation" in the profession of theatrical management and that "the flair of the showman – would appear to be a masculine prerogative" (318). In Crauford's view he was the power behind the throne in the later stages of Sarah Lane's management and it was due to his intervention that the presentation of French plays ceased. Nevertheless the performance of all eight plays that appeared under Sarah Lane's name embodied three qualities that were at the center of the Britannia's reputation: a concern with effective and meticulous staging, a consistent moral perspective, and the presentation of strong, independent female characters. These concerns were also at the heart of the Britannia's managerial policies (presumably influenced by Sarah Lane despite Crauford's assertions) and embedded in the roles Sarah Lane played as an actress. In order to appreciate Sarah Lane's authorial impact we need, in fact, to look beyond any logocentric obsession with the written word to her influence on how Britannia plays were prepared for performance and staged, and on the values which they represented. Whether or not she was responsible for the final draft of each play attributed to her, it was her understanding of the transitional process of translating the plays from page to stage which was at the center of her achievement.

Ironically, through the agency of Nicoll (1959: vol. v, 448), Sarah Lane is one of the most visible of nineteenth-century women playwrights. She is also amongst the more visible of nineteenth-century actresses and managers. In considering not only the eight plays attributed to her, but also those in which she intervened dramaturgically and/or as a performer, the question of what actually constitutes authorship within the collaborative process of theatrical performance is inevitably raised. In the case of Sarah Lane, the implication that she did not translate the plays is not a denial of her voice, which is manifest much more emphatically as a "translator" through her functions as manager and actress. In part, any neglect of Sarah Lane as dramatist must also be attributed to the social and critical prejudices against which neigborhood theatres battled both in their own times and subsequently. Moreover, the revival of old French pieces, such as *Taken from Memory* or *Red Josephine*, is arguably not very significant, regardless of who translated them, other than for raising the question as to why the Britannia attempted them so much later than theatres like the Surrey and Sadler's Wells. The presentation of *Dolores*, in a relatively literal but substantially cut version, is significant not as a contribution to dramatic literature but for the extraordinary policy decision that its first English performance should be at the Britannia. This act of daring and the outstanding success of the production, both of which are presumably attributable to Sarah Lane, are the achievements we should be honoring. Rather than argue an erroneous or spurious case for the authenticity or quality of a group of generally nondescript plays (*Dolores* apart), we would better serve the memory of Sarah Lane by fuller investigation of the role she played in bringing these plays and others to the stage and interpreting them in performance. In so doing, we do not diminish the notions of authorship and translation, but expand them in a more representative and inclusive way.

NOTES

1 According to Fortier (1997: 89), "Recent translation theory expands the idea of translation from its traditional limited sense to include rewriting in all its forms (the production of a dramatic text on a stage, for instance) and what may be called the recontextualization of the work of art."

2 "Credat judens": "A Jew might believe!"

3 Gideon's provision of French plays is also verified by Chance Newton (1927: 270) and Soldene (1897: 52–53), whilst Wilson (1954: 58) implies Sarah Lane was not much of a French scholar and did not translate the plays herself.

4 A version of this play had also been given at a Saturday matinee performance in the West End in July 1875 at the Olympic Theatre.

5 For a brief discussion of Sarah Lane's acting, see Davis 1991: 385.

6 Male impersonation was often a significant element in Sarah Lane's roles. As Florence Langton in *The Mother's Dying Child*, she managed to thwart and ultimately expose the villain by adopting a series of disguises, which included a Somerset servant girl, an old nurse, an inebriated fast young man and an Irish boy, Barney O'Brian. In *The Flirt*, which played for her 1871 benefit, she impersonated a country boy, Jack Fleam; in *Woman, Her Rise and Fall in Life*, she disguised as a young

and good-looking military officer "sporting a handsome pair of whiskers," to thwart villainy and aid the distressed. As Clotilda Phipps in *The Marriage Certificate*, she pretended to be a drunken sailor in order to resolve the plot, whilst in *The Old Cherry Tree*, as Selina Hawthorne, she disguised as Terence O'Grady, a cab driver, and as Tommy Tod, a sporting man. In *The Old, Old Story*, as Dorothy Dibbles, she disguised in male attire and went in pursuit of her friend's seducer, whom she discovers and shoots. In pantomime and burlesque she regularly assumed male attire, as in *Old Daddy Longlegs*, when she played Sir Regent Circus, a languid swell.

REFERENCES

Akhurst, W. M. 1874, *To the Green Isles Direct*, Tm29, reel 72, Frank Pettingell Collection of Plays, University of Kent, Canterbury: Harvester Press Microform Publications.

Barker, Clive 1979, "The Audiences of the Britannia Theatre, Hoxton," *Theatre Quarterly*, 9.34: 27–41.

Britannia cuttings, Hackney Archives, Rose Lipman Library, London.

Britannia playbills, Hackney Archives, Rose Lipman Library, London.

Crauford, A. L. 1933, *Sam and Sallie*, London: Cranley and Day.

Davis, Jim (ed.) 1992, *The Britannia Diaries 1863–1875: Selections from the Diaries of Frederick C. Wilton*, London: Society for Theatre Research.

Davis, Jim 1991, "The Gospel of Rags: Melodrama at the Britannia 1863–1874," *New Theatre Quarterly*, 7.28: 369–89.

Entr'acte, 12 January 1894.

Era, 16 November 1873, 12 April 1874, 14 November 1880.

Fortier, Mark 1997, *Theory / Theatre: an Introduction*, London: Routledge.

Hackney and Kingsland Gazette and Shoreditch Telegraph, 15 November 1873, 11 April and 9 May 1874, 24 April 1876, 29 March 1878.

Hazlewood, Colin H. 1862, *The Old Maid and the Winding Sheet*, Om22, reel 62, Frank Pettingell Collection of Plays, University of Kent, Canterbury: Harvester Press Microform Publications.

Hazlewood, Colin H. 1863, *Faith, Hope and Charity*, Fm7, reel 23, Frank Pettingell Collection of Plays, University of Kent, Canterbury: Harvester Press Microform Publications.

Hazlewood, Colin H. 1864, *The Left-Handed Marriage*, Lm22, reel 39, Frank Pettingell Collection of Plays, University of Kent, Canterbury: Harvester Press Microform Publications.

Hazlewood, Colin H. 1865, *The Volcano of Italy*, Vm2, reel 83, Frank Pettingell Collection of Plays, University of Kent, Canterbury: Harvester Press Microform Publications.

Hazlewood, Colin H. 1866a, *The Dark King of the Black Mountains*, Dm7, reel 15, Frank Pettingell Collection of Plays, University of Kent, Canterbury: Harvester Press Microform Publications.

Hazlewood, Colin H. 1866b, *The Old Cherry Tree*, Om10, reel 51, Frank Pettingell Collection of Plays, University of Kent, Canterbury: Harvester Press Microform Publications.

Hazlewood, Colin H. 1871, *Cast Aside*, Cm11, reel 11, Frank Pettingell Collection of Plays, University of Kent, Canterbury: Harvester Press Microform Publications.

Lane, Sarah 1873, *Taken from Memory*, Tm3, reel 74, Frank Pettingell Collection of Plays, University of Kent, Canterbury: Harvester Press Microform Publications.

Lane, Sarah 1874, *Dolores*, Lord Chamberlain's Plays, British Library, London.

Lane, Sarah 1875, *Albert de Rosen*, Ao2, reel 103, Frank Pettingell Collection of Plays, University of Kent, Canterbury: Harvester Press Microform Publications.

Lane, Sarah 1876, *The Faithless Wife*, Fm8, reel 23, Frank Pettingell Collection of Plays, University of Kent, Canterbury: Harvester Press Microform Publications.

Lane, Sarah 1877, *St. Bartholomew; or, A Queen's Love*, Sm4, reel 66, Frank Pettingell Collection of Plays, University of Kent, Canterbury: Harvester Press Microform Publications.

Lane, Sarah 1878, *The Cobbler's Daughter*, Cm29, reel 13, Frank Pettingell Collection of Plays, University of Kent, Canterbury: Harvester Press Microform Publications.

Lane, Sarah 1880, *Red Josephine; or, Woman's Vengeance*, Rm10, reel 63, Frank Pettingell Collection of Plays, University of Kent, Canterbury: Harvester Press Microform Publications.

Lane, Sarah 1881, *Devotion; or, The Priceless Wife*, Dm33, reel 17, Frank Pettingell Collection of Plays, University of Kent, Canterbury: Harvester Press Microform Publications.

Manuel, E. 1876, *Expiation*, Lord Chamberlain's Plays, British Library, London.

Manuel, E. 1877, *Two Sons; or, A Tale of the Monmouth Rebellion*, To9, reel 112, Frank Pettingell Collection of Plays, University of Kent, Canterbury: Harvester Press Microform Publications.

Marchant, Frederick 1868, *The Old, Old Story*, Om24, reel 52, Frank Pettingell Collection of Plays, University of Kent, Canterbury: Harvester Press Microform Publications.

Marchant, Frederick 1876, *Women's Rights*, Wm66, reel 91, Frank Pettingell Collection of Plays, University of Kent, Canterbury: Harvester Press Microform Publications.

Matthews, Brander 1901, *French Dramatists of the Nineteenth Century*, New York: Scribner & Sons.

Newton, H. Chance 1927, *Cues and Curtain Calls*, London: John Lane.

Nicoll, Allardyce 1959, *A History of English Drama 1660–1900*, 3rd edn, vol. v, Cambridge: Cambridge University Press.

Pitt, W. H. 1871 *Truth; or, The Spells of Love*, Tm38, Reel 77, Frank Pettingell Collection of Plays, University of Kent, Canterbury: Harvester Press Mircroform Publications.

The Players 17 March 1860.

Saturday Programme 29 April 1876.

Soldene, Emily 1897, *My Theatrical and Musical Recollections*, London: Downey.

The Spanish Page 1859, Sm70, reel 72, Frank Pettingell Collection of Plays, University of Kent, Canterbury: Harvester Press Microform Publications.

Standard, 7 April 1874

Stephens, John Russell 1992, *The Profession of the Playwright: British Theatre 1800–1900*, Cambridge: Cambridge University Press.

Suter, William 1865, *Baccarat; or, The Knave of Hearts*, Lord Chamberlain's Plays, British Library, London.

Theatrical Journal, 9 January 1851.

Vicinus, Martha 1989, " 'Helpless and Unfriended': Nineteenth-Century Domestic Melodrama," *When They Weren't Doing Shakespeare: Essays in Nineteenth-Century British and American Theatre*, ed. Judith L. Fisher and Stephen Wyatt, Athens, GA: University of Georgia Press, 174–86.

Webb, T. H. 1870, *Turned Out to Starve*, Tm40, reel 78, Frank Pettingell Collection of Plays, University of Kent, Canterbury: Harvester Press Microform Publications.

Wilson, A. E. 1954, *East End Entertainment*, London: Arthur Baker.

Wilton, Frederick C. 1863–86, *Diaries*, MS1181, Mitchell Library, State Library of New South Wales, Sydney.

PART 3

Geographies of production

CHAPTER 7

Staging the state: Joanna Baillie's "Constantine Paleologus"

Beth H. Friedman-Romell

> Our desire to know what men are in the closet as well as in the field; by the blazing hearth and at the social board, as well as in the council and the throne, is very imperfectly gratified by real history.
>
> Joanna Baillie, "Introductory Discourse," 5

The plays of Joanna Baillie (1762–1851) reveal the hidden, domestic, and personal elements motivating public human action. In her most explicitly historical tragedy, *Constantine Paleologus; or, The Last of the Caesars* (1804), Baillie departs from Edward Gibbon's "real" historical account of the fall of the fifteenth-century Greek emperor by staging the conflicted relationship between domesticity and the state (Gibbon 1789). Baillie transforms the traditional tragic formula of the male protagonist's struggle to choose between love and honor, and in so doing raises questions of pressing concern to British audiences living through the Napoleonic wars and their aftermath. What is the individual's responsibility to the state, and vice versa? What kinds of leaders do we need? What sort of government best serves the public? Are we citizens, subjects, or slaves?

During the quarter-century following its publication, adapted versions of *Constantine* appeared on four stages in the British Isles: a benefit for actor Daniel Terry, at the Theatre Royal, Liverpool (November 1808); a successful melodramatic adaptation called *Constantine and Valeria*, performed at London's Surrey Theatre (July 1817); John William Calcraft's benefit performance at the Theatre Royal, Edinburgh (June 1820); and Calcraft's restaging of his Edinburgh adaptation at the Theatre Royal, Dublin (June to July 1825).[1] By examining these different productions and their receptions across time and space, we discover that managers' stagings undermined Baillie's challenging dramaturgy, while reinforcing culturally dominant ideologies of gender and politics.

Baillie's works have enjoyed a critical renaissance in the past decade, as scholars of British Romanticism have begun to redefine the generic, aesthetic, thematic, political, and historical contours of the field. Much exciting recent scholarship challenges traditional assumptions about the tenets, forms, and creators of Romantic cultural production, questions the validity of the notion of Romantic antitheatricality, and suggests that there are many "romanticisms" to be explored. Scotland's Joanna Baillie, one of the most popular and widely respected writers of the age, is a central figure in this revisionist project. By contrasting Baillie's rational female characters with her irrational, emotional male ones, Anne K. Mellor asserts that Baillie both challenges traditional gender definitions and supports Mary Wollstonecraft's thesis that men and women are equally capable of reasoned thought and action (1995: 409). Useful materialist approaches by Burroughs (1997) and Watkins (1992) focus on Baillie's exploration of the socially constructed, performative nature of gender roles. However, while Baillie's texts invite feminist interpretations, their staging and reception often did not.

Critics are also struggling to redefine what Baillie and other Romantic writers meant by "the closet," arguing variously that

(1) Romantic playwrights, especially Baillie, desperately wanted their work staged, but could not find appropriate venues, competent companies, educated audiences, or a receptive press. Therefore, they were consigned against their will to the status of "closet" dramatists (Burroughs 1997: 86–94; Donkin 1995: 159–83; Donohue Jr. 1970: 81, 88–89).

(2) "Closet" may refer to a wide range of theatricalized performances which happened to lie outside the realm of the "public," for-profit theatre (Burroughs 1997: 8–20).

(3) "Closet" encompasses one state through which all dramatic texts pass and repass – first in the writing, then in the reading/imagining. So-called "closet" drama foregrounds the "split allegiance to its existence as both textuality and theatrical bodily performance."[2]

(4) "Closet" may mean the revelation of what is conventionally private – the personal, the domestic, the emotional (Mellor 1994); the subtextual expression of repressed homoerotic desire (Bur-

roughs 1997: 126–29: Crochunis [1996]), or even the writer's own social or sexual "closeting" (Crochunis 1996). We must always imagine *Constantine* as a "performed closet drama" existing simultaneously on page and stage, and concerning itself with gender, sexuality, and power. Ironically, despite the recent attention to the Romantic closet and the homo*sociality* found in Baillie's plays, critics on the whole remain oddly reluctant to consider the potential homo*sexuality* of either Baillie or her characters.[3]

Previous discussions of Baillie's work are also limited both by a narrow focus on the dramaturgy of a handful of the *Plays on the Passions*, and by the lack of sustained analysis of actual performances. Such selectivity underestimates the importance managerial control and state censorship played in late eighteenth- and early nineteenth-century productions, and masks the potentially hegemonic power theatrical performance wields over audiences (Backscheider 1993; Cox 1990; Russell 1995). The result is a useful, but only partial understanding of both *what* and *how* the plays "meant" during the playwright's own time. The discussion of *Constantine* that follows demonstrates that performances repressed Baillie's questioning of the politics of gender, religion, and the state, and substituted an aggressively heterosexual, patriotic reading.[4]

Constantine transforms elements of Edward Gibbon's 1789 description of the defeat of the Greek Empire by the Turks, in order to explore questions of individual identity and group responsibility. In Baillie's version, the brave but peace- and home-loving Constantine, supported by a tiny band of foreign Christian followers, stages a valiant but futile resistance to the Muslim siege. Constantine and his men serve as foils to several other groups in the play: the Emperor's traitorous advisors, Petronius and Marthon; the craven, luxury-loving citizens of Constantinople; the tyrannical Mahomet himself; and the Sultan's slavish subjects. Baillie departs from Gibbon by creating the strong and passionate Empress Valeria, who commits suicide in order to avoid becoming Mahomet's bride after Constantine's death. Baillie also invents a romance between Petronius' daughter, Ella, and Rodrigo, the Genoan sailor who aids the Greek cause. Finally, and most significantly, Baillie develops at length the "manly" love between Constantine and his followers.

THEATRE ROYAL, LIVERPOOL, 1808

As spectators attended the Theatre Royal on a chilly November
evening, they were preoccupied by Britain's 1808 abolition of the
slave trade, upon which Liverpool's economy largely relied. They
also were contending with the British government's wartime
blockade of neutral countries' merchant ships, which resulted in a
rapid decrease in trade and an increase in inflation, unemployment,
and horrendous poverty for the lower classes. The population
explosion (and its attendant overcrowding, squalor, and sectarian
violence), and the continued activities of the naval press-gangs were
also problems. Finally, the specter of Napoleon and his invading
armies dominated the public imagination (Drescher 1988; Muir
1907; Power, 1992). All of these concerns resonate with the stage
action in *Constantine*.

In 1803, new proprietors Lewis and Knight elegantly refurbished
the Theatre Royal on Williamson Square. Unlike its cramped and
indecorous predecessor, this building aspired to the commodious
gentility of a London patent house. Although a fairly large theatre,
its acoustics and sight lines met Baillie's demands for proper reception of serious drama (Broadbent 1969: 111–12). The new theatre
continued to attract a broad cross-section of the town's population,
and audiences on occasion continued to demonstrate rowdy, even
riotous behavior. The pit was well attended by clerks and appren-
tices; however, the more genteel boxes often went empty (Broadbent,
1969; Midwinter, 1971). The town generally supported four nights a
week, except for race week, when the company offered six performances. The newly established resident company was adequate, but
uneven. Reviews suggest that the company did better overall in
comedy than in tragedy; there were some talented but unseasoned
performers; these actors' shortcomings and inexperience were foregrounded when they appeared alongside visiting London "stars";
and a young actor named Daniel Terry (who played Constantine)
showed much promise (*Monthly Mirror*, August and September 1808).

SURREY THEATRE, 1817

The first euphoria of Waterloo long over, Londoners in 1817 faced
high prices, low wages, and intense overcrowding caused both by
postwar demobilization and an influx of rural workers displaced by

enclosure and industrialization. With the threat of Napoleonic tyranny no longer a source of patriotic cohesion, the sense of class awareness which had been growing since the 1780s intensified, leading to dissatisfaction, conflict, and repressive government measures. Although Britain's elite and professional classes emerged from the wars more wealthy and powerful than ever, they could no longer ignore questions of Catholic emancipation, electoral reform, the problem of slaveholding in British colonies, and the elite's apparent desertion of customary patriarchal responsibilities.

The Surrey Theatre of 1817, like the Theatre Royal, Liverpool, had recently undergone a transformation. Under Thomas Dibdin's management, the Surrey enjoyed a reputation for respectability and quality unequaled in either its previous or subsequent history. When Dibdin took over management from Elliston in 1816, he renovated the theatre, improved the acting company, and revamped the repertoire (*British Stage and Literary Cabinet*, January 1817). At this time, the Surrey drew fashionable as well as local "middling" and lower-class patrons. The company, particularly male and female leads Huntley and Taylor, were regarded as equal to those of the patent houses, and the quality of material presented was considered "generally far superior" (*British Stage*, September 1817). Although Dibdin was still compelled by the patent laws to adapt "straight" drama by adding music and dance, the skilled performers, the splendid scenery, and the variety of entertainments – a combination of melodrama, pantomime, comic sketches, spectacular pageantry, and interludes of music and dance – attracted large audiences to what was "by far the most profitable theatrical concern in the metropolis" (*British Stage*, July 1817). Dibdin's 5 July 1817 presentation of *Constantine and Valeria* was a melodramatic adaptation of Baillie's text.[5] The production's scenery, especially that of the burning of Constantinople, was outstanding (*British Stage*, July 1817). The famous French actor Talma attended the performance, and praised "the splendour and elegance of what is termed a *minor* theatre" (*British Stage*, August 1817).[6] Dibdin's version of the play appears to have fulfilled its audience's expectations in terms of acting, plot, staging, and moral import.

THEATRE ROYAL, EDINBURGH, 1820

We find the Theatre Royal, Edinburgh of 1820 in the hands of Harriot Siddons and her brother, William Murray. Harriot Siddons was a beloved actress and capable company manager; Murray distinguished himself as an excellent producer who paid particular attention to scenic detail. Located since 1811 in Shakespeare Square, the Theatre Royal continued to offer patrons an intimate auditorium and gaslit stage in which actors were seen and heard clearly (Macleod 1976: 135–36). Alongside the more traditional repertoire of comedy, tragedy, pantomime, and "novelties" such as rope-dancing and exotic displays of "savages," Murray's programming emphasized Scottish patriotism (Macleod 1976: 266–70).

Why might Calcraft have selected *Constantine* for his benefit? *Constantine*'s patriotism is not explicitly pro-Scottish in the manner of *The Family Legend* (adored by Edinburgh spectators in 1810),[7] although the fame of its native author, its opportunities for pageantry, and the elegance and high tragic tone of the text may have attracted Calcraft. The recent innovations in lighting promised greater control of mood in this atmospheric play, and the small space and good acoustics ensured that Baillie's verse would be heard and appreciated. Finally, Calcraft opted to play Rodrigo, not Constantine – a choice reflected in the editing and staging of the text, and which encouraged the audience to interpret the more conventional and patriotic character as the hero of the play.

THEATRE ROYAL, DUBLIN, 1825

Whereas Edinburgh citizens were able to affirm patriotic and imperialist impulses vicariously through witnessing theatrical performances, Dublin spectators' relationship to Britain and Empire was more vexed. Union with Great Britain in 1800 brought no economic or political benefits to the vast majority of Irish citizens. Parliamentary, legal, and administrative power resided in the hands of the ten percent Protestant minority, who themselves were in a colonized position with respect to England. The 1820s was a time of widespread sectarian and agrarian unrest and violence. Daniel O'Connell began organizing for Catholic emancipation in 1823. Bad harvests, enclosure, absentee landlords, depressed trade, and lack of industrial development created extreme poverty and hunger. A particularly bad year was 1824, when the establishment of free trade within the British Isles damaged the Irish economy further, thus triggering periodic violent "disturbances" among the starving populace (Foster 1988: 292–95; 320; Kee 1976: 27, 170–85).

The Theatre Royal was anything but insulated from this strife. Its Protestant and aristocratic Anglophile supporters hoped the theatre would civilize the masses and uplift "national taste," although in reality the theatre had a long history of factional strife, disorder, and riot (Stockwell 1938: 167–224; *The Dramatic Argus* 1825). The anonymous author of *The Dramatic Argus* claims to be an impartial servant of the public's interest, who believes that his[8] just criticisms could improve the caliber of theatrical performance and lead to an elevation of Irish national culture. *The Dramatic Argus* complains that the noisy and indecorous upper gallery would often disrupt performances in order to harass performers, argue with the new manager, or express political sentiment. The author is outraged by this factional impropriety, and fears "the gods" will drive away the "superior ranks, who are, bona fide, the true supporters of the Theatre and true taste" (*The Dramatic Argus*: vol. II, 10–11).

By 1825, most of the remaining fashionable set who had not moved to London preferred operas and concerts to dramatic performances, but they still turned out for guest artists like Madame Vestris, or extravagant, patriotic afterpieces like *The Battle of Waterloo*. As for the company, critics generally agreed that the actors ranged in ability from adequate to poor, and that the company did better in comedy than tragedy. In any case, tragedy was never well attended, and almost nothing drew for more than a few nights (which may attest to the fact that most people could not afford to go to the theatre at all). From time to time, other entrepreneurs would open up small rival houses, but these ventures were generally short-lived. These factors ensured that upper- and middle-class patrons could not segregate themselves into separate theatres (*The Dramatic Argus*: vol. I, 66–67). Moreover, because the audience was politically, economically, and religiously diverse, the ideologically charged *Constantine* had unpredictable ramifications in Dublin.

In his letter to Baillie transcribed into the promptbook (24 May 1820), Calcraft explains that his cuts and character conflations are motivated by the conventional demands of contemporary theatres and audiences – the text is far longer than most "acting tragedies"; some "beautiful" poetry fails to further the plot; the company does not have enough competent actors to fill all the principal roles; and modern spectators' tastes demand rapid action, striking spectacle, and immediate, vehement delineation of passion. According to Calcraft, both the 1820 and 1825 performances were successful, pleasing audiences, the press, and the author herself (Calcraft, April 1851: 532–36). Calcraft explains that in Dublin he had

more extensive means than in Edinburgh. New scenery was painted, and much pageantry introduced. A splendid banquet in the imperial palace, in the first act; a singularly well organised mob, in the second; a grand military procession, in the third; the Bosphorus, with the imperial fleet and galley, in the fourth; and in the fifth, the storming of the city, and bearing off of the body of the slain Emperor by his devoted band of brothers. (Calcraft 1851: 534)

From this description, and from examining the promptbook, we discern that Calcraft structures the adaptation in terms of spectacle and climax, rather than interior character development. Both the *Freeman's Journal* (1 July 1825) and the *Dublin Morning Register* (28 and 30 June 1825) praised the production and the good taste of the management in offering a play of such merit to the audience. The play ran for three nights, not bad for a serious drama in Dublin in the middle of the summer. Like Terry and Dibdin before him, Calcraft seems to have found ways to please specific audiences by adapting Baillie's "closet" text for representation. What were these strategies, why did they work, and how did they affect reception?

VALERIA: FEMININITY AND ROMANCE

Baillie's Valeria is a curious blend of "masculine" and "feminine" traits; however, this potential androgyny was undermined in performance by her portrayal as a hyperfeminine woman. Valeria possesses a noble courage that awes friend and enemy alike. She models the courage necessary for British women to send their loved ones off to war (or after 1815, on imperial conquest), although she fears for her husband's safety.   Towards the end of the play, Mahomet's vizier, Osmir, remarks that Valeria "does indeed a wondrous mixture seem / Of woman's loveliness with manly state" (429). Following her death, Mahomet himself exclaims, "Great God of heav'n! Was this a woman's spirit / That took its flight?" Rodrigo replies, "Let ev'ry proudest worship be upon her, / For she is number'd with the gallant dead!" (434). Yet Valeria often succumbs to her passionate, emotional nature. She first puts her love before the needs of the community in wanting to prevent her husband from facing the rebellious mob (1.2), then irrationally places faith in pagan sorcery (2.3). Unlike, for example, the Countess Albini of *Count Basil*,

Valeria has no identity independent of her wifely status. She ignores the titles Mahomet applies to her ("Thou sorrow-clouded beauty," "empress," "sov'reign dame") until he calls her "Widow of Constantine" (427). The gaping self-inflicted dagger wound in her breast is the quintessential emblem of female suffering, a trope familiar from Restoration tragedy. Losing Constantine has wounded her heart irreparably, and she has very properly taken her life to avoid Mahomet's bed. Now she is fulfilled:

> I now am what my soul desires to be,
> And what one happy moment of strength wound
> Beyond the pitch of shrinking nature makes me;
> Widow of Constantine, without reproach,
> And worthy to partake the honour'd rest
> Of the brave lord whose living love I shared.   (431)

Thus Valeria's behavior throughout displays "womanly" foibles alongside "womanly" valor – she is strong, but not "manly" in any traditional sense.

In the hands of Sarah Siddons, for whom Baillie wrote the role, Valeria's strength and passion would have counterbalanced her femininity in interesting and complex ways. However, the actresses who were actually cast in the part possessed quite different physical attributes and acting skills. For example, in the Edinburgh production, Harriot Siddons would have been a movingly feminine Valeria (see plate 7). Her physical style and presence was the antithesis of her famous mother-in-law. Petite, demure, and possessing a mellifluous voice, Harriot Siddons excelled in witty comedy and pathetic roles. According to William Murray, his sister "could impart deep interest to scenes of quiet pathos ... still she did not aspire to the more impassioned and lofty sphere of the drama. Her style was the beautiful, not the grand, which she willingly resigned to her great relative" (Murray 1851: 31).

Similarly, Miss Jarman of the Theatre Royal, Dublin, was admired for her work in genteel comedy and moments of pathos in serious drama (*The Dramatic Argus*: vol. 1, 33, 49). She had "graceful and gentle deportment," but not the "abstract contemplativeness of the tragic heroine ... Her gestures are uncharacterised by that excitative violence of manner, which is indispensable to the adequate personification of the agonized spirit" (*The Dramatic Argus*: vol. 1, 18–19). Therefore she must have been more affecting in her tender scenes with Constantine than her final moments of distracted grief

Plate 7. Engraving of Harriot Murray (Siddons), *c.* 1800.

and vindication. Miss Taylor of the Surrey likewise excelled in innocent comic and pathetic roles such as Lady Touchwood in *The Belle's Stratagem*, Rebecca, "the fair afflicted Jewess," and Jeanie Deans in *The Heart of Midlothian* (*Theatrical Inquisitor*, March 1820). She could, however, move audiences in grand tragic roles, as "a mistress of the deeper passions [who] continually sways them with a commanding earnestness, which is ever the characteristic of true genius" (*British Stage*, August 1820). Thus Miss Taylor's performance may have come closest to Baillie's conception of the part.

Such "femme" casting of Valeria supported managers' increased emphasis on romance. The altered title of the Surrey melodrama, *Constantine and Valeria*, suggests a heightened focus on heterosexual love relationships. Unlike the complex lead couple, Rodrigo and Ella are cardboard ciphers of conventionally gendered virtues: he the courageous, valiant, and rough seaman; she the soft, pliant, and obedient maiden in distress. Calcraft and Terry rendered Ella even

more absent and silent than she is in Baillie. In choosing the role of
Rodrigo over Constantine, then "beefing" up Rodrigo's part by
reassigning lines from other characters, Calcraft made the sailor the
hero of the play. (It is telling that one of the only scenes Calcraft left
virtually untouched was the long declaration of love between Ella
and Rodrigo in Act 4 Scene 5.) In both Terry's and Calcraft's
versions, Constantine died with Valeria's name on his lips (not in
Baillie); Terry concluded the entire play with a new line for Valeria:
"Now Constantine I am thine again!" Spectators received the image
of the conventional young and virtuous lovers, Rodrigo and Ella,
united over the dead body of Valeria. The elimination of Baillie's
final discussion of the nature of power left the audience with an
image of "properly" gendered romantic love as central to the
restoration of moral order.

CONSTANTINE: MASCULINITY AND QUEERNESS

Baillie insists that if she had followed her natural inclination, her
entire drama would have centered on the love between Constantine
and his men, "those 'cords of a man' binding together the noble
Paleologus and his brave imperial band" (Baillie 1805: xviii–xix). It
is clear that critics and managers were uncomfortable both with
Constantine's domestic bent, and the homoerotic undertones
beneath the surface of the many homosocial scenes in the play. This
discomfort led to staging decisions which rendered the potential
queerness of Baillie's text less readable to spectators.

In three long interior scenes (1.2, 2.4, and 4.4) set in Constantine's
apartments and the church of St. Sophia, Baillie shows the Emperor
and his men demonstrating fellowship, loyalty, compassion, and
mutual respect. Far more than the pomp and privileges of empire,
Constantine loves hearth, home, and the companionship of his wife
and friends, priorities which nonetheless endanger the welfare of the
state, as Heugho observes (1.2: 293–94). Constantine immediately
removes his armor upon his first entrance and invites his men to do
the same, commenting ruefully, "Mine armourer, methinks, has
better skill / To mar men's heads than save them" (297–98). More
than a quip on the discomfort of his garb, this remark indicates the
Emperor's regret at exposing his men to certain death, while his
gesture enacts his openness and vulnerability before them. When the
men follow his lead, we find a group of human comrades beneath

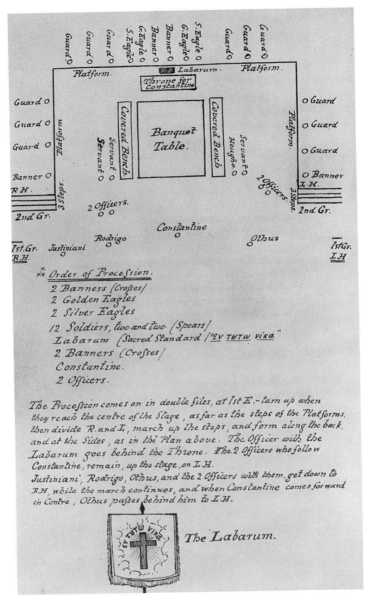

Plate 8. A page from the Calcraft promptbook for *Constantine Paleologus*
by Joanna Baillie.

the brutal and impersonal trappings of war. Both Terry and Calcraft cut not only this important disarmoring moment, but most of the references in Act 1 Scene 2 to the domesticity which masks Constantine's "manly faculties" (294). Calcraft replaced the moment with a formal procession including about thirty extras, who arranged themselves around Constantine's imperial throne and banquet table (see plate 8). Thus Calcraft failed to create the sense of privacy, intimacy, and equality between Constantine and his followers that Baillie's text demanded, and substituted a distancing and impersonal scene of state.

Managers made a similar alteration to Act 4 Scene 2, set in the church of St. Sophia, when Constantine most explicitly shows his sense of Christian brotherhood. There immediately follows a contrasting outdoor scene which critiques the Turkish barbarians and the Greek traitors, Petronius and Marthon. As the mournful bell tolls, Constantine's men join their leader "in gen'rous love and brotherhood united" (375). Unlike the self-interested citizens, the men's love is "generous," given without thought of glory or reward. In return, Constantine divests himself of the last traces of hierarchical earthly status. In a long and eloquent speech, Constantine reminds the men that earthly rulers are, like everyone else, "As children of one grand and wondrous house" ruled by God (377). He humbly begs forgiveness for any pride, impatience, or harshness he may have shown his followers while he was in power (377–80). He embraces each man, then asks pardon and blessing from his old servant Heugho, who "bursts into tears and falls upon his master's neck" (380). After another round of general embracing, Constantine prevents his men from kneeling in fealty to him, redirecting their worship toward its proper, heavenly object. The scene concludes as they go off to worship together as brothers before God. Again, Constantine exposes a vulnerability and humility unexpected in a ruler. Again, his men demonstrate tender, "feminine" sensibilities in lush, passionate language. And again, managers cut the scene, thereby eviscerating Baillie's demonstration that earthly devotion to individuals or even nations must give way to faith in and service to God. Also suppressed is Baillie's important but subtle move toward Unitarian philosophy, which is embedded in the scene's dialogue and its representation of virtuous Orthodox (i.e., non-Protestant, but non-Catholic) Christians.[9]

Focus on political, religious, or even psychosexual concerns was likewise deflected by drastic cuts and conflations of the supporting characters, supposedly prompted by lack of company depth. For example, Terry, producing for a wartime audience, severely curtailed the stage time given to Petronius and Marthon, who commit the most heinous form of treason – instigating domestic rebellion. The Liverpool audience did not hear about the "fickle, wavering herd" whom the traitors manipulate (1.1: 291); instead, they saw a unified, patriotic front resisting Muslim tyranny. Terry also all but eliminated the hypermasculine warrior, Justiniani. The audience experienced neither Justiniani's overzealous, aggressive devotion to Constantine and the cause (1.2), nor his weak and cowardly (but all too human) retreat from the front lines once he is wounded, although he knows his desertion will have a ripple effect on the troops (5.1).

Baillie carefully delineates different types of masculinity within the band of followers. Their responses to Mahomet in Act 3 Scene 2 (364–65) are indicative:

OTHUS: And with our chief in that tremendous ruin
        If it must be, we will sink lovingly.
JUSTINIANI: We will sink honorably.
RODRIGO: We will sink gloriously.

These three warriors each represent a different aspect of manhood, which Baillie demands must be blended in a successful ruler. Rodrigo, the naval pillar, seeks glory; Justiniani, the old soldier, seeks honor. And as for Othus? On an abstract level, he stands for tender devotion to one's country. But this court-poet-turned-soldier also invites a "queer" reading. Something of a fifteenth-century man of feeling, Othus, for love of his emperor, has cast aside his "Grecian lute, and pen, and books of grace" in favor of the "rude lance" which he now grasps (1.1: 289). It is to Othus that Constantine bares his innermost secret turmoil (2.3); it is Othus with whom Valeria makes her peace in her dying moments (5.2). If we imagine Othus in love with Constantine, we might plausibly read the subtext of Act 2 Scene 3 as a scene of frustration and of unrequited love. Constantine first weeps freely in front of his friend. Then, oblivious to Othus' feelings, Constantine raises his hopes:

              O this doth press my heart!
        A heart surcharg'd with many cares, and press'd
        With that besides, which more than all – with that
        Which I have wrestled with – which I have strove –
        With that which comes between me and myself –

> The self that as a christian and a man
> I strongly stove to be –　　　　　　　　　　　　　　　(337–38)

Eagerly Othus presses him:

> You have before some secret cause of trouble
> Hinted to in broken words: will not your highness
> Unto a faithful friend –　　　　　　　　　　　　　　(338)

Constantine then reveals his tormented dreams and fantasies about Mahomet and Valeria to his loyal retainer. Dismayed, Othus responds, "Alas, I know it all!" (338), which may signal his disappointment that Constantine does not or will not reciprocate his feelings, or even allude to Othus' own tortured imaginings about Constantine and Valeria.

The scene raises expectations for a great revelation, then disappoints them. Constantine's fear that Mahomet will rape his wife seems commonplace and even logical, given the Sultan's personal reputation, combined with the predominant image of the lascivious Muslim male circulating in British society at the time (Allison 1995: 61–85). Does the shock lie in the implied eroticism of the fantasy, or the hint that Constantine is afraid Valeria will "like it?" Or rather, are we disappointed along with Othus that something *else*, that which cannot be named, "that which comes between me and myself," is not revealed? What is there about Constantine's *expressed* fear that would make him less of a Christian? Edinburgh and Dublin audiences did not even ponder these questions because Calcraft cut these "odd" moments. Both he and Terry also cut the poignant final scene between Valeria and Othus, her potential, undeclared rival for Constantine's affection. Calcraft, as Rodrigo, added insult to injury by appropriating much of Othus' dialogue for himself, which further blurred Baillie's distinctive characterizations. Thus the homoerotic potential of the play remained locked in the closet.

CHRISTIANITY AND ISLAM

Also closed off in performance was Baillie's refinement of Christian Stoic philosophy, a Scottish Enlightenment version of pagan Stoicism. Christian Stoicism emphasizes the values of benevolence and civic virtue, and transforms the pagan acceptance of one's fate into Christian faith in a providential plan behind worldly injustice (Sher 1985: 175–86). According to Adam Smith, uncomplaining self-sacrifice for one's country, whether in battle (like the men), or through suicide (like Valeria) is the noblest action one may take ([1790] 1976: 238–39). Unlike the pagan Stoics, who were expected to suppress emotional response, Christian Stoicism requires a sympathetic understanding of other people in order to foster compassionate action (Smith [1790] 1976: 11–13). However, for Smith, men of "self-command" must feel, but not demonstrate, emotion. Both Constantine's demonstrative affections and Valeria's reliance on sorcery and its power to alter fated outcomes represent their departure from Christian Stoic principles; ultimately, their sacrifices present a triumphant outcome to their struggle. Unlike Smith, Baillie believes it is important to witness this most human struggle – she predicates her dramas on the idea that by arousing their natural "sympathetic curiosity," audiences derive instructive morals (Baillie 1853: 3–7). Yet managerial cuts and one-dimensional acting both flattened the characters (whose self-command in performance was never really in doubt), and prevented the play from doing all of its emotional work on spectators.

Another relevant component of Christian Stoic doctrine is the belief in Christianity's historical role as a civilizing force (Sher 1985). The struggle between Christian "civility" and Muslim "barbarism," central to the play, taps into long-standing Western fears about the corrupting influence of "Mahometism." The relationship between Mahomet and his people is one of mutual distrust, fear, and loathing. His troops are so much "garbage ... good enough for filling ditches up" (346). He stations "grizzly hangmen" armed with cords and hatchets in the rear guard, should any Turkish soldier lose his nerve and attempt desertion in the face of certain slaughter (346). Torture is *de rigueur* for disobedience; suspected traitors are blotted from life with an arbitrary swipe of the pen. There is no trial by jury for Mahomet's slaves/subjects (347).

In consequence, the Turks admit they fight for fear or spoil, not for love of country, religion, or ruler. Mahomet is therefore openly envious of his "weaker" rival, Constantine, and infuriated that he cannot command the love and loyalty of slaves:

> They arm them for to-morrow's fight, 'tis true,
> With much alacrity, and talk of conquest,
> Carnage, and spoils; but for their Sultan's name,
> The name of Mahomet, through all the camp
> I've scarcely heard its sound. Nay once I heard it

In accents harsh pronounced, but as to listen
I nearer drew, my steps the speaker scared,
And all was into fearful silence hush'd.
Their Sultan's name! – Pest seize the stupid slaves!
O Constantine! it is not thus thy soldiers
Do arm themselves for thee.   (369)

When Mahomet meets Constantine's small but loyal envoy, and witnesses Othoric's brave and stoic self-sacrifice (3.2), his disturbance grows. "And Constantine is served by men like these!" becomes Mahomet's distracted refrain (364–66). It is clearly better to die in the defense of liberty, surrounded by loyal subjects, than to reap the fruits of aggressive conquest earned by slaves one cannot trust.

Baillie's text reifies dominant British stereotypes about Muslim government, and reminds audiences of the contemporary international political struggle for control of the Mediterranean, a vital strategic and commercial region. Britain partially justified its own imperialism by asserting its moral superiority and capability to rule. In the case of the Mediterranean and the Ottoman Empire, the British sought to push back Napoleon and "liberate" Christian Greeks from Muslim rule. The wartime Liverpool audience easily may have seen Napoleon in Mahomet's lust for power and assault on Christianity, and therefore enthusiastically cheered the Greek struggle for survival against oppression. Postwar spectators in London or Edinburgh were perhaps more likely to respond to the call to preserve and extend the empire. One wonders how differently that call would have resonated in Dublin for Protestant versus Catholic spectators, or Unionists versus those desiring Irish independence.

LIBERTY AND LICENSE

The parallels between Greek and British citizenry could be uncomfortable. With the exception of Constantine's small band of true patriots, the indolent and degenerate Greek populace fail to rise and defend their liberties, but rather, are lured by Mahomet's promised luxuries into a life of thralldom. Ironically, the patriots in the play are largely comprised of sympathetic foreigners – native citizens fail to stand up for their property and their children's birthright. Worse yet, in a counterrevolutionary British worldview, the Greeks often act as a mob. The first crowd scene (2.1) paints an ugly portrait of the Greek citizens:

[An open street before the imperial palace. A crowd of men, women, and children discovered, bearing in their hands torches, with clubs, sticks, &c., and the stage entirely lighted by the red glare of their torches cast up against the walls of the building. The confused noise and clamour of a great crowd is heard as the curtain draws up.]

> 1st CROWD: Holla! let them come forth who trouble us
> And love they blood and beating, they shall have it.
> 2ND CROWD: Surrender! bread and wine, and peaceful days!
> Surrender, devils, or ye shall pay the cost!

[All the crowd call out clamorously, and brandish their torches, &c., in a threatening manner against the palace.]   (310)

Baillie's irrational mob is as threatening to the Greek state as the Muslim menace. Constantine confronts the crowd first by appealing to the loyalty they owe their ruler, relying on the traditional patriarchal comparison between king and father, subject and child (312–13). This argument works only on some of the citizens, who threaten to combat the opposing faction. Constantine next makes an appeal to their sense of civic responsibility and patriotism:

> O there still be amongst you men sufficient
> To save your city, your domestic roofs,
> Your wives, your children, all that good men love
> Were each one willing for a little term
> To face but half the dangers which perforce
> Not doing this, he stands exposed to;
> To bear but half the toils which I bear daily,
> And shall bear lovingly!   (313)

All must sacrifice something for the common good – follow your leader's example, urges Constantine. *Still* the crowd is undecided. Mahomet's luxury beckons. Constantine takes the ultimate risk – he descends unarmed from the palace steps, to inspire his people's trust and sense of solidarity with their ruler. Even this gesture is inconclusive – the divided crowd begins to fight, and Constantine's men must spring into the conflict, rally those who have decided to fight for the Emperor, and disperse the rest.

How did managers treat the mob? In 1808, Terry retitled the work *Constantine Paleologus; or the Band of Patriots*, clearly appealing to loyalist shipping interests who were profiting from the war, along with any sailors who might be in the audience. Terry eliminated many of the slavery references, whether they refer to Mahomet's troops or the "slavish" cowardice of the Greek citizens. Perhaps the mere mention of the word was too controversial for a town wondering how Britain's recent abolition of the slave trade might effect their economy. Significantly, Terry also cut the crowd's calls for "bread and wine and peaceful days" (310), which may have reminded spectators not only of the starving French peasants of the Revolution, but also of Britain's own periodic bread-rioters (1795, 1800–1), mutinying Spithead sailors (1797), or Irish insurrectionists (1798). Finally, Terry invented the following speech for Rodrigo, who probably delivered it directly to the audience:

> And 'ere the Tyrant places his standard here
> O'er our fallen bodies, his steps shall find
> A dangerous and bloody path – come friends
> We will all join, – ye all love valiant worth
> Give me your voices, in a brave man's cause
> – For Constantine and Glory!

The Liverpool stage directions read, "Othoric and the whole crowd shout 'Constantine and Glory' long live brave Constantine," whereas in the original, the crowd remains menacingly divided.

In 1808, management self-censored menacing images of civil discord. Surprisingly, despite the postwar economic downturn and periodic civil unrest, Calcraft's adaptation was less squeamish than Terry's about potentially inflammatory references to slavery or insurrection. In the 1820 and/or 1825 context of unpopular monarchs and aristocrats who were seen as abandoning customary responsibilities, Constantine's exemplary behavior toward the mob functioned as a collective fantasy of what a patriarchal ruler should do: love and defend the "children" in his care. But the patriarchal contract is mutually binding: whereas rulers must remain vigilantly aware of their subjects' needs, subjects should eschew desire for luxury and rise up to serve their country at home and abroad, lest liberty, in the absence of discipline become license.

On the surface, heaven lets Constantine down: the Turks win, the Emperor is slain, the Empress commits suicide. However, Mahomet's victory is hollow. The Sultan ultimately learns that "The willing service of a brave man's heart, / That precious pearl, upon the earth exists, / But I have found it not" (436). Of the loyal band, only Othus and Rodrigo remain alive (and the former, Kent-like, will soon join his commander in death). In a noble gesture, Mahomet rewards Rodrigo with his freedom, while Othus' final speech predicts dire, "gothic" consequences for a Muslim empire built on tyranny:

> ... heaven ofttimes
> Success bestows where blessing is denied.
> A secret spirit whispers to my heart,
> That in these walls your weaken'd wretched race,
> Slaves of their slaves, in gloomy prison'd pomp,
> Shall shed each other's blood, and make these towers
> A place of groans and anguish, not of bliss:
> And think not when the good and valiant perish
> By worldly power o'erwhelm'd, that heav'n's high favor
> Shines not on them.   (437)

Othus' speech predicts a providential history that ultimately will reward the good and valiant Christians and punish the "weaken'd wretched race" of fratricidal slaves. Baillie's text presents a paradox: the model Christian is not the winning king, nor can the successful Sultan maintain the loyalty of his people. If the failure of both of these systems indirectly praises the virtue of the Protestant British constitution, it also emphasizes that this form of government requires morality, sacrifice, and personal commitment from leaders and subjects alike, if it is to thrive.

Regrettably, Othus' expression of Christian Stoic philosophy was excised from the Liverpool, Edinburgh, and Dublin texts (and probably at Surrey as well). In performance, the play ended with the image of Mahomet and everyone else marveling at the courage of Constantine, Valeria, and the patriots to sacrifice their lives for their country. In Terry's version, Valeria got the last word; the Sultan was no longer a complex character capable of moral insight but a dehumanized enemy. Calcraft cut all but one speech in praise of the honored dead, which he reassigned from Rodrigo to Mahomet. Both Othus' prediction and his final explanation of the moral lesson to be gained from watching the tragedy were cut, in favor of a more dramatically flashy and pathetic ending. Perhaps managers could not risk any factionally inclined spectators making the connection between the tyranny represented in the play and Britain's own "tyrannical" measures and policies: the suspension of *habeas corpus* (1794); imposition of the income tax (1799); anticombination laws (1799–1800); the Corn Law (1815); the periodic violent quashing of popular protests, culminating in the Peterloo Massacre and subsequent "Six Acts" repressing public meeting and printed protest (1819); or especially in Dublin, the continued oppression of Catholics.

This case study of *Constantine Paleologus* encourages consideration of the effects of specific time, place, and production choices on the making of meaning. The productions examined here downplayed gender and sexual ambiguity, foregrounded romance, eliminated potentially subversive readings about British state repression of reform agitation, and simplified Baillie's political discussion of the domestic and Christian roots of good government. How individual spectators responded to these changes would have depended on gender, class, nationality, religion, degree of familiarity with Baillie's original text, and sensitivity to the text's encoded subversions. However, it is clear that heterosexual, male, middle-class managers produced a sanitized, patriotic version of *Constantine* for imagined spectators who were very much like themselves. Substantial interventions in the script, casting, and staging marginalized nondominant spectators and prohibited alternative readings. These adaptations no doubt contributed to the persistent critical framing of Joanna Baillie as a "closet" dramatist whose works, though beautifully and powerfully poetic, were "unstageable" in their natural state. By uncloseting Baillie and her work, we promote her own agenda to stage the unstageable.

NOTES

1 Actor-playwright Henry Siddons submitted the Liverpool manuscript for licensing (Huntington Library, MS LA 1557) and probably contributed to the adaptation. However, Terry is billed as the adaptor in the playbill for the production (Carhart 1932: 154). Calcraft's promptbook is held by the University of Pennsylvania's Furness Library (MS C59 B15c). My archival research was supported by the North Atlantic Conference on British Studies, Huntington Library, Northwestern University, and the Society for Theatre Research.

2 I am grateful to Tom Crochunis for permitting me to quote from his 1996 manuscript, "Byron, Baillie, and Closet Drama's Ambivalent Dramaturgy."

3 Burroughs and Crochunis are exceptions.

4 Subsequent references to *Constantine* cited within the main text are from the 1805 edition, unless otherwise stated. All references cite page number(s).

5 I have not uncovered a manuscript or prompt copy of this version.

6 See also Dibdin's account of Talma's visit (1828: 62–63).

7 For Baillie's deployment of competing Scottish and British identities, see Friedman-Romell 1998.

8   I do not have any direct evidence of the author's gender, but infer that
    he is male based on the tone of the work and also on the virtual
    nonexistence of professional female drama critics at this time.

9   For more on Dissent in Baillie's dramaturgy, see Friedman-Romell
    (1998).

REFERENCES

Allison, Robert J. 1995, *The Crescent Obscured: The United States and the Muslim World 1776–1815*, Oxford and New York: Oxford University Press.

Backscheider, Paula R. 1993, *Spectacular Politics: Theatrical Power and Mass Culture in Early Modern England*, Baltimore: Johns Hopkins University Press.

Baillie, Joanna [1804] 1805, *Constantine Paleologus; or, The Last of the Caesars: A Tragedy in Five Acts*, in *Miscellaneous Plays*, 2nd edn, London: Longman, Hurst, Rees, and Orme.

Baillie, Joanna [1851] 1976, "Introductory Discourse," *The Dramatic and Poetical Works of Joanna Baillie*, Hildesheim: Georg Olms.

British Stage and Literary Cabinet, January and July–September 1817; August, 1820.

Broadbent, R. J. 1969, *Annals of the Liverpool Stage from the Earliest Period to the Present Time*, New York: Benjamin Blom.

Burroughs, Catherine B. 1997, *Closet Stages: Joanna Baillie and the Theatre Theory of British Romantic Women Writers*, Philadelphia: University of Pennsylvania Press.

Calcraft, John William (adaptor) 1820, *Constantine Paleologus; or The Last of the Caesars: A Historical Tragedy in Five Acts*, C59 B15c, Furness Library, University of Pennsylvania.

Calcraft, John William 1851, "Leaves from the Portfolio of a Manager No. IV. Joanna Baillie," *Dublin University Magazine*, 220: 529–36.

Carhart, Margaret Sprague 1923, *The Life and Work of Joanna Baillie*, Yale Studies in English, 64, New Haven: Yale University Press.

Cox, Jeffrey N. 1990, "The French Revolution in the English Theatre," *History and Myth: Essays on English Romantic Literature*, ed. Stephen C. Berendt, Detroit: Wayne State University Press, 33–52.

Crochunis, Tom [1996], "Byron, Baillie, and Closet Drama's Ambivalent Dramaturgy," unpublished manuscript: the author.

Dibdin, Thomas 1828, *The Reminiscences of Thomas Dibdin*, 2 vols., New York: J. and J. Harper.

Donkin, Ellen 1995, *Getting Into the Act: Women Playwrights in London 1776–1829*, London and New York: Routledge.

Donohue Jr., Joseph 1970, *Dramatic Character in the English Romantic Age*, Princeton: Princeton University Press.

Dramatic Argus 1825, 2 vols., Dublin: J. Scott.

Drescher, Seymour 1988, "The Slaving Capital of the World: Liverpool and National Opinion in the Age of Abolition," *Slavery and Abolition*, 9.2: 128–43.

Dublin Morning Register, 28 and 30 June; 1 July 1825.

Foster, R. F. 1988, *Modern Ireland 1600–1972*, London: Penguin.

Freeman's Journal, 28 June; 1 July 1825.

Friedman-Romell, Beth H. (1998), "Dueling Citizenships: Scottish Patriotism v. British Nationalism in Joanna Baillie's *The Family Legend*," *Nineteenth Century Theatre*, 26.1.

Gibbon, Edward 1789, *The History of the Decline and Fall of the Roman Empire*, vol. XII, Basil: J. J. Tourneisen.

Kee, Robert 1976, *The Green Flag*, vol. I, *The Most Distressful Country*, Harmondsworth: Penguin.

Macleod, Joseph 1976, *Mrs. Henry Siddons and the Edinburgh Theatre Royal*, unpublished typescript, London: Theatre Museum.

Mellor, Anne K. 1994, "Joanna Baillie and the Counter-Public Sphere," *Studies in Romanticism*, 33.4: 559–67.

Mellor, Anne K. 1995, "A Revolution in Female Manners," *Romanticism: A Critical Reader*, ed. Duncan Wu, Oxford: Basil Blackwell, 408–33.

Midwinter, Eric 1971, *Old Liverpool*, Newton Abbot: David and Charles.

Monthly Mirror, August and September 1808.

Muir, Ramsay 1907, *A History of Liverpool*, Liverpool: Liverpool University Press.

Murray, William 1851, *The Farewell and Occasional Addresses Delivered by W. H. Murray, Esq.*, Edinburgh: James G. Bertram and Co.

Power, M. J. 1992, "The Growth of Liverpool," *Popular Politics, Riot and Labour: Essays in Liverpool History 1790–1940*, ed. John Belchem, Liverpool: Liverpool University Press, 21–37.

Russell, Gillian 1995, *The Theatres of War: Performance, Politics, and Society 1793–1815*, Oxford: Clarendon Press.

Sher, Richard B. 1985, *Church and University in the Scottish Enlightenment*, Princeton: Princeton University Press.

Smith, Adam [1790] 1976, *The Theory of Moral Sentiments*, ed. D. D. Raphael and A. L. Macfie, Oxford: Clarendon Press.

Stockwell, La Tourette 1938, *Dublin Theatres and Theatre Customs 1637–1820*, Kingsport, TN: Kingsport Press.

Terry, Daniel (adaptor) 1808, *Constantine Paleologus; or, The Band of Patriots*, Larpent MS LA 1557, Huntington Library, San Marino, CA.

Theatrical Inquisitor, March 1820.

Watkins, Daniel P. 1992, "Class, Gender, and Social Motion in Joanna Baillie's *De Monfort*," *Wordsworth Circle*, 23.2: 109–17.

CHAPTER 8

The "lady playwrights" and the "wild tribes of the East"

Female dramatists in the East End theatres, 1860–1880

Heidi J. Holder

In the field of nineteenth-century British theatre, the contributions of both female playwrights and East End dramatists have long been underanalyzed. In fact, research into these two subjects reveals an unexpected and compelling conjunction: despite the reputation of the Victorian theatre as a realm hostile to female dramatists, the East End theatres produced at least two – Sarah Lane and Mrs. Henry Young – who established considerable reputations as playwrights, and staged plays by at least a dozen others (see appendix 2). The theatrical terrain of the East End proved to be distinct, in crucial ways, from its counterpart in the more fashionable West End. Furthermore, many East End dramas mimicked the patterns of West End plays, while making some shifts in detail, shifts that rearranged London's moral map; gender and class stereotypes would prove to be a key factor in the drawing of that map, and would, I think, provide an opportunity for women – even as dramatists – in East End venues. The ideology of "separate spheres" that proved so limiting for women playwrights in the West End theatres was virtually absent in the East End, where the ideal of the "lady" was not dominant and women's public role was more flexible.

London's East End theatres struggled toward respectability and financial security in the 1840s and 1850s, first attaining legitimate status after the Theatres Regulation Act of 1843, then gaining the right to be called "theatres" in the 1850s and 1860s (previously they were labeled "saloons"). Managers such as Thomas Rouse, of the Grecian Saloon, fought a hard battle for the right to call their places "theatres" (Rouse 1842–49). The importance of the title as a marker of legitimacy and status was known full well by managers and by the public; *Knight's Cyclopaedia of London*, one of the many guides published primarily for visitors to the Great Exhibition of 1851, surveys

London's theatres – including the Pavilion and the Standard, both in the East End – and quickly dismisses other places of entertainment: "there are in addition a number of taverns at which dramatic performances of a humbler kind are exhibited, such as the Eagle Tavern, City Road, the Britannia, Hoxton, and many other places. They are not theatres, however, and so we leave them" (*Knight's Cyclopaedia* 1851: 827).

The view of the East End theatres inherited from nineteenth-century critics and journalists is riven by contradiction. There was an enduring fear, on the part of reviewers and government authorities, that members of the working-class audiences would be easily corrupted by representations of vice. Journalists coming to the East End theatres to provide their middle-class readers with a glimpse into the abyss would often emphasize the squalor of the setting and the vulgarity of the audience; Thomas Erle, for instance, is notable for his sneering images of East End audiences (Erle 1880). A reporter for the *Thespian*, for example, made a journey "to the more oriental part of the metropolis" to visit the Garrick Theatre in "Vitechapel," where he complained of the presence of Jews and the variety of smells in the theatre (10 June 1857). G. A. Sala made a point of noting that the audience at the Effingham was "even dirtier" than the theatre itself (Sala 1859: 268). At the same time, however, the citizens of the East End, and their choice of entertainment, were sometimes held up as an example to the more jaded and sophisticated audiences to the west. In reviews of dramas at the Effingham, the Standard, the Britannia, and the City of London, the reviewers for the *Era* often stressed the audience's taste for "simple" plays extolling the virtues. Later in the century, Shaw would use his review of the Britannia's famous annual pantomime to castigate the cynicism and lewdness of the "expensively dreary" shows of the West End (Shaw 1898: 487).

At the Effingham Theatre on Whitechapel Road in Stepney, managed by Morris Abrahams, a woman named Mrs. Henry Young had at least *twenty-five* plays staged between 1861 and 1868; several of these also appeared at the Pavilion, the City of London, and the Britannia in the East End, and two also appeared at the Victoria on the South Bank.[1] In his handlist of plays from 1850 to 1900, Allardyce Nicoll records only two plays by Mrs. Young; research in the *Era*, the Lord Chamberlain's Plays, and in playbills at the Theatre Museum, the British Library, the Guildhall, Lambeth

Public Libraries, and Hackney Public Archives has uncovered twenty-three more.[2] Young's husband was a minor actor in the Effingham company and an occasional playwright himself;[3] there is no evidence that Mrs. Young was an actress. All of her plays found thus far are melodramas, often domestic melodramas, of a violent and intricate kind. This fact in itself is of interest, since rather few women of the time had any success in writing melodramas for the stage (among plays produced by women during this period, comedy was the dominant genre).

Young wrote with an eye to popular themes and stories. She wrote a Sweeney Todd play, a Jonathan Wild play, and a George Barrington ("the gentleman pickpocket") play. Very often she chose her subject matter from tales that were currently popular in the penny press; her first "hit," a play entitled *Jessie Ashton; or, The Adventures of a Barmaid* (Effingham 21 April 1862), was drawn from a story in *The Welcome Guest* (see plate 9). It appears that this was her third play at the Effingham, and it ran for seven weeks; its popularity inspired D. W. Sawyer to pen a version for the Surrey Theatre the following December. The reviewer for the *Era* called the play "an excellent drama of its class, and one entirely suited to the taste of the frequenters of the place ... The incidents are too numerous to particularise – they comprise assault, robbery, murder, lunacy, and a fire" (27 April 1862). The play was much touted in the *Era*'s theatre listings during the weeks that followed: "The prolonged and rapturous applause bestowed on the Drama of 'Jessie Ashton' from the rise to the fall of the curtain fully justifies the management in announcing it 'the great hit of the season'" (4 May 1862); "'Jessie Ashton' universally acknowledged to be the best and most effective drama ever produced in the East End" (11 May 1862).

In the late summer of 1861, Abrahams closed the Effingham for renovation. A playbill of 19 October touts the theatre as "extensively enlarged! Newly decorated and improved!" (British Library, hereafter abbreviated as BL). After staging two of Mrs. Young's plays in 1861, Abrahams was apparently willing to give her play *Jessie Ashton* an Easter Monday opening that spring. *Jessie Ashton* ran for at least forty performances (through Whitsun) at the Effingham – the last performance was 7 June. Following this success, Abrahams relied heavily on Mrs. Young for melodramas: six more plays appeared under her name that year. She was clearly a draw following her success with *Jessie Ashton*, enough so that her early drama *Pride,*

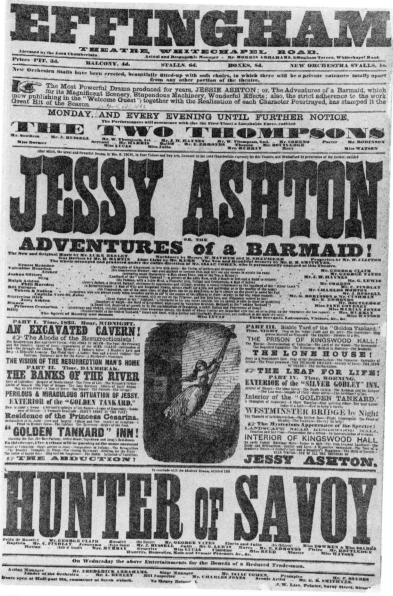

Plate 9. Playbill for Mrs. Henry Young's *Jessy* [*sic*] *Ashton, or the Adventures of a Barmaid*. Effingham Theatre, 28 April 1862.

Poverty, and Splendour, staged at the Victoria in 1856, was revived at the Effingham. The bills refer to Mrs. Young as "the authoress of the Great Drama Jessie Ashton" (playbill, BL). An early play by Henry Young, *Bertha Gray, the Pauper Child; or, The Death Fetch* (originally staged at the Bower Saloon in July 1851), was quite possibly revived at this time at the Effingham under his wife's name, in order to capitalize on her popularity: *The Death Fetch; or, The Pauper's Child*, "by Mrs. H. Young," appears on an Effingham bill for 23 June 1862 (BL). I have found no licensing copy for this play. By 12 July Mrs. Young's version of the Sweeney Todd story, entitled *The String of Pearls*, is billed as "an entirely new drama"; hereafter her plays are often described on the Effingham bills as being "written expressly for this theatre."

Young's female characters are remarkably active and often violent. In *Jessie Ashton*, the heroine brandishes pistols, leaps from windows, and beats the villain with a boat hook. In *The Mescican [sic] Bandit; or, The Silver Digger of Perate* (staged at the Pavilion in October 1863), the heroine "Viva Torre" repeatedly rescues her lover, usually by threatening her enemies with pistols. In *The Bravoes of London* (Effingham, October 1863), the villainess Phoebe Coomb, working as a lady's maid, notes her own uncanny resemblance to her mistress, the Duchess of Calverton. Phoebe schemes to imprison the Duchess, take her place, and marry her fiancé. When the family agent, Campbell, notes that Phoebe lacks a tell-tale birthmark on her hand, she beats him about the head with a mallet, then gives her lackeys instructions to dump him in the sewer. She imprisons the Duchess in a garret, and very nearly tricks her fiancé into marriage. And in *The Pick-Lock of Paris* (Effingham, October 1866), the heroine, a picklock and housebreaker, spends much time waving pistols, and, at one point, a spear. However, she should not be judged too harshly by the audience, since she also qualifies as a persecuted woman. Her husband – exploiting her amazing abilities as a picklock – is forcing her to engage in crime, at one point by threatening their child (she is made to hammer at the forge while her daughter cries piteously in the background), in a scene that the reviewer for the *Era* called "a tableau of immense interest to Whitechapel playgoers" (4 November 1866).

Young's plays – compared with those of other East End dramatists such as Colin Hazlewood, Edward Towers, William Suter, and William Travers – show a marked tendency toward plots featuring elaborate and horrific persecution of women, female villainy, and violent action by women, whether for good or ill. All these are, of course, recognized features of melodrama; the 1860s, in which Young did most of her work, was the decade of *East Lynne* and *Lady Audley's Secret*, two female-authored texts that led to innumerable representations of female vice, violence, and suffering on the Victorian stage. What is noteworthy about some of Young's characters is their blending of the qualities of the melodramatic "heroine" and "heavy," a merging of character types that would remain highly popular in the East End theatres (Aston and Clarke 1996: *passim*). Adele in *The Pick-Lock of Paris* is a case in point: while her actions are those of a villainess, running about in a mask, robbing houses, and threatening her enemies with assorted weapons, she is motivated throughout by her desire to protect her child. She suffers and fights back to the end, at one point threatening her villainous husband with a pistol: "lay but a finger on me and I'll shoot you like a dog" (Young 1866: 21). Ultimately, the ambiguity of her role is dispelled. Adele will not be happily reunited with her first love – the closest thing the play has to a hero – who has reappeared on the scene; instead, she dies, for no particular reason, and her one-time lover marries her daughter.

These dramas make frequent use of the urban, London milieu; precise locations – Westminster Bridge, Newgate, St. Paul's – are commonly used. Mrs. Young's female characters also display the contradictory characteristics of the "public female" in the mid-Victorian period. As Deborah Nord has pointed out, the "woman of the streets" and the "fallen woman" were typically conflated categories, a fact which suggests the circumscribed nature of urban female types (Nord 1995: 15). The negotiation of urban space was quite a different matter for East End women, however, a fact reflected in Young's dramas. In the chaos of the city, women could either be seen as liberated, or as threatened; the city could represent danger or opportunity. The eponymous Jessie Ashton, for instance, is seen at the opening of the play imprisoned by "resurrectionists" (body snatchers) in a Lambeth cellar, and she is pursued doggedly by them when she makes her escape (in a sensational scene in which she must climb down the side of a building); however, it emerges that Jessie is in London because she is fleeing a villain who disrupted her happy life in the countryside. "I became the victim," she laments, "of plots and machinations" (Young 1862: 21). In this case, London is not a place where country wives and maids meet their doom (as in Watts Phillips's *Lost in London*), but a redemptive space, where all is eventually put right.

This counterimage of London provides a context for female characters who seem almost protean in their ability to shift identities. In *The Dark Woman* (Effingham, May 1861), one of Mrs. Young's first plays for the Effingham Theatre, the title character has multiple identities: she is "Linda" a seduced Italian peasant girl, who has escaped death and made her fortune as "the Dark Lady," leader of a gang of thieves known as Paul's Chickens (their hideout is in a vault under St. Paul's); in daylight hours she poses as a countess. Such female characters as the Dark Woman, or Phoebe Coombs in *The Bravoes of London*, whose identities have become unmoored, provide models of female agency that are very much tied to their context. These women literally emerge from the ground: Young was extremely fond of elaborate underground sets, and her characters often have a kind of "underground existence" in vaults, cellars, and sewers.

In the 1870s another woman, Sarah Lane, wrote eight melodramas for the Britannia Theatre, in Hoxton, where she was herself the manager (1872–98) after the death of her husband Samuel Lane.[4] In addition to her own compositions, Lane also staged plays by Charlotte Crauford, Jessie Wilton, Kate Wilton, Mrs. Henry Young, Valentina Roberts, and Edith Sandford. Lane's plays provide a useful contrast to Young's. They are, superficially, more "decorous," as befits a theatre that carefully cultivated its status as a respected institution in the East (most were in fact adaptations of French plays); yet they also show a similar preoccupation with the elasticity of female melodramatic roles. Take, for example, Lane's *The Faithless Wife* (1876). From the title one might expect a "fallen woman" play, and Lane does indeed furnish us with a wayward wife. When the play begins, at the 100th birthday party of the head of the Fauvel family, Juliette's fall has already taken place, and she soon makes an impassioned confession: "Alas, I, who have always lived among you, under your protection – I who exhausted my strength in your love, in your looks, found myself so much alone in my married life. I felt abandoned, and weak" (Lane 1876: 15). Significantly, she is speaking to her sister, and it is that sororal relationship that provides the focus of the play. It is worth noting that this is as close as Lane or Young came to writing a "fallen woman" play, an extremely popular subgenre and one that provided many of the major female roles of the time. Lane, however, used the genre to create an image of woman's constancy to woman, an unusual application of this standard plot.

Melodrama encourages its audience to indulge in fantasies of persecution, and both Lane and Young exploit this feature in their creation of female-centered plotlines. Lane's *Devotion; or, The Priceless Wife* (1881) features a woman who, separated from her husband by war, returns years later to find him married; he convinces her to pose as a servant in his household (a situation reminiscent of *East Lynne*) to avoid a scandal, leading to moments of extreme pathos when she must conceal her identity from her son. But Lane, like Young, also created violent and transgressive female characters. In *Red Josephine* (1880), one of Lane's later plays, the title character is a gambler – she got her name by always betting on red in Baccarat – who will do anything to protect and possess her lover (we see more drawn pistols here); ultimately, exhausted by her efforts, she dies at the play's conclusion. In the play's "sensation" scene, the villain is trapped in an underground cavern with his mother; as the cavern begins to fill with water, the villain attempts to escape, only to be stabbed to death by Josephine. Lane was ready to seek out unusual heroines, as in her adaptation of Sardou's *Patrie*, *Dolores* (1874). *Dolores*, with its decidedly unpleasant female lead, and final scene of murder and martyrdom, was one of Lane's successes.

Lane was a beloved actress and manager who became, over the years, a virtual institution in the East End, so it is not surprising that she would successfully stage her own works and that her plays would be promoted using her name; indeed, she is prominently identified as author on the Britannia's playbills. Jim Davis, in this volume, raises the possibility that Lane was not in fact the author – or the sole author – of the dramas presented under her name. This question of authorship prompts us to ask why Lane's name would be connected with these plays. In addition to asking what the role of author might do for Lane's career and public persona, we might wonder how the Britannia as an institution might benefit by staging plays under a woman's name. Was a woman's name, Lane's in particular, deemed a "selling point" in the East? Mrs. Young is a much more obscure figure, but her name also appeared in reviews and notices as early as 1856, and her work received very favorable attention in the *Era*. There seems to have been no question of hiding her identity; indeed, she evidently became something of a draw for the Effingham. She was considered an adept but "tasteful" sensation dramatist, and a skilled adapter of stories from the popular press.

Given the emergence of women playwrights in the East End, it is necessary, I think, to consider the gender politics always deeply embedded in the discussions and debates over the working classes and the East End. There are two crucial threads to follow: one from the rhetoric of Chartism – mainly from the 1830s and 1840s, but with long-term influences; the other from the literature and journalism of "outcast London." The writings related to the former movement are not primarily focused on the East End, but provide a wealth of disturbing images of the intersection of class and gender. The latter movement reveals the emergence of the East End as the nightmarish realization of the disintegration of normative gender and family roles feared by the anti-Chartists. The canon of writings on London's urban poor includes such works as Dickens's *Sketches by Boz* (1837), Henry Mayhew's *London Labour and the London Poor* (1861–62), and James Greenwood's *A Night in the Workhouse* (1866) and *The Seven Curses of London* (1868).

The Reform era saw gender used as a potent rhetorical weapon. Those opposed to even the more moderate reformist goals such as universal male suffrage eagerly seized on images of unruly *women* to make their points about the dangers of working-class unrest. Responding to the so-called "Plug Plot" revolts of August 1842, in which workers were encouraged to disable steam boilers by removing their plugs, the appearance of marching, protesting women was quickly seized on by the opposition. Samuel Smiles wrote that woman's work outside the home inevitably led to a working-class population that was "uneducated, turbulent, and discontented" (Smiles 1843: 426, cited in Clark 1995: 242). Anna Jameson would use the occasion to raise the possibility of a complete breakdown in gender categories:

the girls of some of our manufacturing districts are ... wearing the garb of women, but actuated by the worst passions of men, in every riot and outbreak the women are the leaders and exciters of the young men to violence. (Jameson n.d.: 201–2, cited in Clark 1995: 242)

The activity of women workers during the Chartist period was clearly alarming to middle- and upper-class citizens. The counterbalancing working-class movement was one of domesticity, in which working-class male suffrage was posited as necessary for the maintenance of a patriarchal male-dominated household. Rather than allowing fear of female activism and violence to work against them, many working-class male activists created a strategy by which that fear could be harnessed in an effort to bolster support for a universal male franchise (Clark 1995: 247).

This same combination of gender-based attack on the part of the middle and upper classes and reactive strategy on the part of the lower classes can be seen in the 1860s through 1880s, when the poor of London became an object of intense interest to the reading public. Commencing with Mayhew's series of pieces in the *Morning Chronicle* and followed by innumerable articles, series, and books, even on through the Edwardian period, the obsession with London's poor had from the very beginning a strong focus on gender and family. As with the anti-Chartist writers, the chief spectacle was the danger of the disintegration of gender and family roles. James Greenwood, in *The Seven Curses of London*, is typical in his view of the plight of the "gutter population," asking, "who are the mothers?" (13). Of young working girls, such as flower sellers, he observes, "Here they come, unabashed by the throng, as though the highway were their home, and all mankind their brothers" (18). He goes so far as to insist that the spurning of matrimony is not so much by choice as by nature:

The state of matrimony is not good for such folk. It was never intended for them. It may be as necessary for healthful life as eating is, but no one would think of taking a man starved, and in the last extremity for lack of wholesome aliment, and setting him before a great dish of solid food. It may be good for him bye-and-bye, but he must be brought along by degrees, and fitted for it. (25)

Here again, the accusation is that the working and lower classes have abandoned, or are incapable of adhering to, the norms of proper sexual and domestic behavior – a situation that, it was often argued, made them ineligible to vote.

Inevitably, the debate over the nature of the lower classes was framed in geographical terms: the problem lay in the *East*. That the theatres were seen as a possible civilizing influence is evident in Mayhew's own writings, when he praises the Effingham Theatre and its salutary effects on its audience. Mayhew expresses the hope that "by innocently amusing them, [the theatre might] soften their manner and keep them out of mischief and harm's way" (Mayhew 1968: vol. IV, 477–78). Clement Scott would later offer a similar defense of the Britannia: "The Brit, by its entertainments, examples of heroism, pluck, bravery, and unselfishness, has helped in a remarkable way to humanize the sad-hearted people down East" (Scott 1899: vol. I, 89).

It was in this climate of intense concern with the "civilizing" of audiences on the part of writers and readers from outside of the poorer districts, and of defensive reaction from citizens of those districts, that Young and Lane saw their plays staged, advertised, and reviewed. I find it striking that these women playwrights made their mark at a time when anxiety about the poor and the working classes was at its height, sustained by ever more shocking exposés in the press. And, of course, rhetoric of "civilization" and "domesticity" intersected with the interests of the theatre managers and theatregoers in that district. The managers, and Lane in particular, put themselves forward as an elevating presence in their communities; Lane, as "Queen of the Britannia," was presented, in later years, as a benevolent mother figure both within the company (which was very tight-knit), and in the community, where she was known for doing good works.

So in the context of contemporary anxiety over how best to "humanize" the East End, the appearance and success of "lady dramatists" (as they were called) makes a certain amount of sense. After all, Mayhew and his fellow reformist journalists always stressed the vital role of women in the "taming" of the East.

In the dramas of London life that emerged in both the East and West, paralleling the growth of reports on "outcast" London, the character most representative of the London poor was the "street Arab." This archetypical urban figure, without home, family, or settled occupation, represented all that was most dangerous in the lower orders. Christopher Herbert, in his analysis of Mayhew's anthropological exercises among the poor, sees this characteristic rootlessness as an "almost debilitating disorder, a compulsive malaise and a state of persistent disorientation" (Herbert 1992: 213). Herbert argues that this lack of purpose and direction exhibited by the poor very nearly derailed Mayhew's mammoth project. It is ironic, then, that the type of the street Arab became central to East End drama, very often as a source of knowledge and restorer of order. As with the often dizzying identity shifts enacted by Mrs.

Young's female characters, a quality typically denigrated or reviled is shown to have laudable effects: rootless, changeable women and boys of the streets can become, surprisingly, champions of justice and order.

The street Arab character was even more common in the East (and South) than in the West; sometimes he in fact claimed a central role, instead of remaining a mere plot facilitator. He generally spoke with the voice of common sense and popular morality. He also tended, in the East and South, to be played by women; cross-gendered casting of his role does not seem to have been as common in the West End. Actresses can be found playing street Arabs in John Wilkin's *St. James's and St. Giles's* (City of London, 1853), William Travers's *A Poor Girl's Temptations; or, A Life on the Streets* (City of London, 1858), J. B. Johnstone's *How We Live in the World of London* (Surrey, 1856), Valentina Roberts's *Jack Mingo, The London Street Boy* (Britannia, 1866), and William Travers's *The Boy Detective; or, The Crimes of London* (Effingham and Britannia Theatres, July 1876).

The increased emphasis on the street Arab character – his elevation, in the East End, into a central figure more clearly representative of a kind of London ideal – is balanced by that character's portrayal by a woman. I find it striking that so many of these champions of the poor who appeared on East End or South Bank stages were played by women, and I would suggest that this pattern in casting may well have been adopted by managers in order to make the class critique of the plays more innocuous on the surface by creating a disjunction between words and bodies. In *Jack Mingo*, for instance, the theatre manager's wariness of representations of crime can clearly be seen in the excisions made in the prompt copy of the text: a scene in Act 2, in which Jack Mingo ponders knifing and robbing one of the women who has come to his aid, is trimmed so that Jack does not actually stand over the sleeping woman with a knife. Instead, he admits later in the scene that he was tempted to commit murder. Even as it stands, the scene shows the kind of criminal behavior that made the Examiner of Plays so nervous. However, in this scene the stereotypical viciousness of the street Arab is embodied in female form, placing it squarely in the less threatening and more jocular tradition of the breeches role.

Even such a thundering critic of lower-class entertainments as James Greenwood clearly considered depictions of crime less dangerous – perhaps less serious – when cross-gendered casting was employed. In *The Seven Curses of London*, Greenwood, who had earlier attacked the penny gaffs in a series in the *Morning Star*, sternly characterized them as "dangerous dens of amusement"; "the broadest and deepest pitfall," he warned, "is the theatrical entertainment known as the 'gaff'" (Greenwood 1868: 67–68). However, his account in *The Wilds of London* of a gaff production of *Gentleman Jack; or, The Game of High Toby* is quite lighthearted; this change in tone may be due to the casting of the leading role:

It was Mrs. Douglas Fitzbruce fully equipped for the "High Toby Game." She wore buckskin shorts, and boots of brilliant polish knee-high and higher, and with spurs to them; her coat was of green velvet slashed with crimson, with a neat little breast pocket, from which peeped a cambric handkerchief; her raven curls hung about her shoulders, and on her head was a three-cornered hat, crimson-edged with gold; under her arm she carried a riding whip, and in each hand a pistol of large size. By way of thanking her friends in the boxes and pit for the generous greeting (it is against the law for actors to mutter so much as a single word during the performance of a "gaff" piece), she uttered a saucy laugh (she could not have been more than forty-five), and, cocking her firearms, let fly at them "point blank" as it seemed; however, the whistling and stamping of feet that immediately ensued showed that nobody was wounded – indeed that the audience rather enjoyed being shot at than otherwise. (Greenwood 1876: 15)

Mrs. Fitzbruce's character goes on to blow out the brains of a miller, gun down a coach driver, marry a damsel, and snatch her father's wealth. Greenwood's amusement at these actions is striking, given his earlier condemnation of the violent entertainments at the gaffs, and one wonders whether he would have found the piece to be more objectionable, more *dangerous*, were the highwayman in question played by a male actor.

The cross-gender casting of suspect or criminal male characters is not the only juggling with gender found in East End theatres. East End dramas suggest a remarkable awareness on the part of audiences, playwrights, and managers of the significance of gender roles in public debate over the theatre and the poor. Side by side with the intricate sexual politics of Chartist rhetoric and the gendered view of the poor in contemporary journalism, there existed a theatrical response to such ideas and images. If the explorers of "outcast London" reported the utter degradation of women in the East, especially at the hands of their male counterparts, the theatre could tell another story. Theatre historians have duly observed contemporary accounts and reviews that praise the "simplicity" of East End audiences, particularly their delight in the triumph of virtue. They may be missing, however, the larger context for this "simplicity." Take, for instance, Blanchard Jerrold's approving picture of the Garrick, usually considered one of the lowest and roughest of the East End theatres: "Virtue is always rewarded in these humble dramatic temples; manly courage gets three times three; and woman is ever treated with respectful tenderness ... the helper of the 'female in distress' (dismissed from the West End long ago) is sure of his rounds of applause" (Jerrold [1872]1970: 35). Such a view contrasts sharply with the harsh picture of gender relations that emerges in so much of the writing on the East End by the so-called "social explorers" such as Mayhew and Charles Booth. In fact, it seems to be a kind of reverse image.

When one begins to look for such reversals of common gender stereotypes of East End denizens, they are quite easy to find. If the worldly-wise heroes of these plays tended to be cadgers and street Arabs (sometimes played by women), the characters whom they assist are often upper-class females. One particular plot that recurs in the East End theatres has a young woman of privilege fleeing from a forced marriage to a man who is of her class, but clearly criminal. In a "relocating" of vice to the West and the suburbs, the villainy of the rich is often exemplified by their "selling" of their daughters. This reversed rescue plot is featured in *The Courts and Alleys of London* by Frederick Towers (Effingham, 1864), Mrs. Young's *Nobody's Son* (Effingham, 1866), and the anonymous *The Street Arab; or, Adrift on the World* (Garrick, 1871). This was a very popular motif in the East, a region not infrequently accused of selling and degrading its women (the image of the brutal working-class man was a staple of the literature of the poor from Dickens and Mayhew to Kipling and Arthur Morrison).

Audience resentment of this ubiquitous accusation can indeed be seen in plays focusing on the selling of working-class women into prostitution; in William Travers's *A Poor Girl's Temptations*, the impoverished heroine's father is a straightforward representation of the well-known type of the drunken spendthrift cadger who lives off the labor of his female relatives, but, when presented with the possibility of selling his daughter for money, he draws himself up to make a noble speech:

I'm a wretched, fallen, degraded drunkard, but lost as I am I'd sooner starve in the streets and my body rot in a pauper's grave than brand my poor innocent Jessie with the name of Harlot. (Travers 1858: 6)

In this play the villain – an aristocrat – kidnaps the young woman, locking her in a house in Mayfair (in another geographical inversion of the moral norm). The combat between virtue and vice takes place on the bridge over the Serpentine in Hyde Park, where the virtuous – aided by the indispensable street Arab – triumph and happily return to Stepney.

The manipulation of gender roles can also be seen in the treatment of working-class women on the East End stage. To be sure, there is no shortage of helpless maidens, often pursued by low-minded aristocrats and swells (C. H. Hazlewood was particularly drawn to this plotline); however, the East End theatres displayed a fondness for decidedly undowntrodden women. Sarah Lane herself specialized in such roles at the Britannia Theatre, and audiences adored her in such parts as Florence Langton in C. H. Hazelwood's *Mother's Dying Child*, Sally Swinton in George Dibdin Pitt's *The Corporal's Daughter*, Molly Sullivan in Pitt's *Molly Sullivan; or, Poverty and Splendour*, and Celestine in Frederick Marchant's *The Three Perils*. Jim Davis sums up Lane's "high-spirited, comic, eccentric figures":

it is Sarah Lane's characters who stand up to the villains, unmask the seducers, and venture, disguised, into the most degenerate haunts to save the day. "She is never gloomy," commented the *Era* of 15 October 1871, "never one of the despairing ones; never sobbing, sighing, or hysterical; but always bright and intelligent, and gaining favour by the readiness with which she invariably espouses the cause of the weak and oppressed." (Davis 1991: 385)

The image of the East as a land of exploited suffering women and degraded brutish men, as a place where gender roles threaten to dissolve, clearly had an impact and provoked a determined, if oblique, response. Whatever the state of women in the East, female *characters* in the theatre showed a remarkable degree of autonomy and power, and male characters could display a wider range of transgressive and threatening behaviors when they were played by women.

It is in this context, then, that the appearance of women playwrights should be evaluated. The period from the 1850s to the 1880s was one in which the East End theatres struggled to achieve that "rise to respectability" that is the hallmark of the traditional – if vastly oversimplified – history of the West End theatres. Some, such as the Britannia (under Lane) and the Standard, Shoreditch, achieved, with much labor, both a solid reputation and a strong local following. The Effingham, where Mrs. Young's plays were staged, fought an uphill struggle; as Jim Davis has observed, "the Effingham had difficulty in shaking off the unsavoury reputation it seems, somewhat unjustly, to have acquired" (Davis 1990: 239). Young's career at the Effingham thus emerges during a crucial period in the theatre's history, between the time of its transition from "saloon" to "theatre" and its reopening, in 1867, as the New East London Theatre, following rebuilding and renovation. This was a period in which Abrahams struggled both to please his audiences and to build a respectable reputation for his establishment (if only to keep the authorities at bay).

The traditional view of East End theatre is that it was purely escapist. In his valuable survey of East End plays, Michael Booth concludes:

It would appear then that the escape into fantasy, so marked a feature of melodramatic appeal, is strongly evident in plays written for audiences of East London. This would accord with the facts of existence in that the vast East End working class, themselves either experiencing or in daily contact with dirt, discomfort, poverty, and suffering, would probably have no particular desire to see dramatic presentations of the darker social realities in their theatres. (Booth 1976: 65)

This makes perfect sense, as far as it goes. The escapist impulse may, however, have larger implications, if what was being rejected was not only the material facts of the daily lives of the poor, but certain aspects of their cultural context as well. The escapism of much East End melodrama represents a very specific escape, from the confining and damning images purveyed by outsiders from the West. This revision or "backlash" paradoxically permitted a kind of freedom for women, albeit a limited one: actresses got some juicy parts playing the kinds of socially marginal and potentially dangerous males that middle- and upper-class Londoners loathed with a kind of fascination; female roles showed a greater variety, and the saucy, active "second-lead" female achieved greater prominence as a type. Moreover, female playwrights were given an opening, one that they lacked in the West End theatres. If the East End theatres were to be subjected to heightened scrutiny by the Lord Chamberlain's office and by the bastions of West End journalism and publishing, they could respond by putting women, as it were, *on display*, handily refuting common stereotypes of East End masculine brutishness and feminine suffering.

Jacky Bratton has recently remarked on "the ideological forces [in theatre history] that have pushed women so far to the edges that from any distance they are completely out of sight" (Bratton 1994: 12). A closer look at the history of East End theatres indicates that women were, in fact, remarkably visible (see appendix 2). Thus, the conservative "culture of consolation" that Gareth Stedman Jones sees emerging in the post-Chartist period (Jones 1983: 220), in which the working-classes turned away from politics and toward new options in recreation and leisure, clearly had, in fact, a political component. Cultural politics, rather than practical politics, are at issue here, and in the struggle over the imagery and rhetoric of class in the mid-nineteenth century, East End theatres and their audiences seemed happy to give women good roles to play. If their theatres were to be visited by outsiders – be they policemen, journalists, or representatives of the Lord Chamberlain – and if they themselves were to be made part of a cultural spectacle, East Enders could, in a self-conscious appropriation of cultural symbols, arrogate to themselves some degree of control over what was seen and displayed.

NOTES

Research for this essay was funded by a grant from the Society for Theatre Research (London) and a Summer Stipend from the National Endowment for the Humanities.

1 One licensing copy – of *The Mescican* [*sic*] *Bandit* – gives the name "Melinda Young." Given the venue, the handwriting, and the similarity in plot and characterization between this play and others by Young, this work is almost certainly hers; however, I have used the name that appears commonly on licensing texts and playbills: Mrs. Henry Young.

2 Nicoll's listing of only two plays for Young is puzzling. She is clearly identified as an author on numerous playbills, in listings and reviews in the *Era*, and on licensing copies in the Lord Chamberlain's Plays. The erasure of her status as author from the most commonly used list of nineteenth-century plays demonstrates how easily a playwright's career can vanish from the record of theatre history.

3 Henry Young appeared in numerous productions at the Effingham as a supporting actor; he also worked on some Effingham productions as a stage manager, alongside Isaac Cohen. One such production was Mrs. Henry Young's *Left Alone* (see the *Era*, 11 December 1864).

4   For a rather fanciful account of the Lanes' careers, see Crauford's *Sam and Sallie* (Crauford 1933); A. E. Wilson provides some useful information, if not much documentation (Wilson 1954). For further background on the Britannia and its audiences, see Barker 1979 and Barker 1971; Davis 1990, Davis 1991, Davis and Davis 1991; Wilton 1992.

REFERENCES

Aston, Elaine, and Ian Clarke, 1996, "The Dangerous Woman of Melvillean Melodrama," *New Theatre Quarterly*, 12.45: 30–42.

Barker, Clive 1979, "The Audiences of the Britannia Theatre, Hoxton," *New Theatre Quarterly*, 9.34: 27–41.

Barker, Clive 1971, "A Theatre for the People," *Essays on Nineteenth-Century British Theatre*, ed. Kenneth Richards and Peter Thomson, London: Methuen, 3–24.

Booth, Michael 1976, "East End Melodrama," *Theatre Survey*, 17.1: 57– 67.

Bratton, Jacky 1994, "Working on the Margins: Women in Theatre History," *New Theatre Quarterly*, 10: 122–30.

Clark, Anna 1995, *The Struggle for the Breeches: Gender and the Making of the British Working Class*, Berkeley: University of California Press.

Crauford, A. L. 1933, *Sam and Sallie*, London: Cranley and Day.

Davis, Jim 1990, "'Scandals to the Neighborhood': Cleaning up the East London Theatres," *New Theatre Quarterly*, 6: 235–43.

Davis, Jim 1991, "The Gospel of Rags: Melodrama at the Britannia, 1863–1874," *New Theatre Quarterly*, 7.28: 369–89.

Davis, Jim, and Tracy C. Davis 1991, "The People of the 'Peoples' Theatre': The Social Demography of the Britannia Theatre (Hoxton)," *Theatre Survey*, 32: 137–65.

Dickens, Charles [1837] 1967, *Sketches by Boz*, London: Chapman and Hall.

Era, 27 April, 4 and 11 May 1862; 11 December 1864; 4 November 1866.

Erle, Thomas 1880, *Letters from a Theatrical Scene Painter*, London: Marcus Ward.

Greenwood, James 1866, *A Night in the Workhouse*, London.

Greenwood, James 1868, *The Seven Curses of London*, London: Stanley Rivers.

Greenwood, James 1876, *The Wilds of London*, London: Chatto and Windus.

Hazlewood, Colin 1856, *The Wild Tribes of London*, Lord Chamberlain's Plays, 52959AA, British Library, London.

Herbert, Christopher 1992, *Culture and Anomie*, Chicago: University of Chicago Press.

Jameson, Anna n.d., *Memoirs and Essays Illustrative of Art, Literature, and Social Morals*, London.

Jerrold, Blanchard [1872]1970, *London: A Pilgrimage*, illustrated by Gustave Doré, London: Dover.

Johnstone, J. B. 1856, *How We Live in the World of London*, Lord Chamberlain's Plays, 52958cc, British Library, London.

Jones, Gareth Stedman 1983, *Languages of Class: Studies in English Working-Class History 1832–1982*, Cambridge: Cambridge University Press.

Knight's Cyclopaedia of London 1851, London: Charles Knight.

Lane, Sarah 1876, *The Faithless Wife*, FM8, reel 23, Frank Pettingell Collection of Plays, University of Kent, Canterbury: Harvester Press Microform Publications.

Mayhew, Henry [1861–2]1968, *London Labour and the London Poor*, 4 vols., London: Dover.

Nicoll, Allardyce 1959, *A History of English Drama, 1660–1900*, 3rd edn, vol. v, Cambridge: Cambridge University Press.

Nord, Deborah Epstein 1995, *Walking the Victorian Streets: Women, Representation, and the City*, Ithaca, NY: Cornell University Press.

Playbills 1841–63, Playbills/London 3/Playbills, 397 and 398. Effingham/East London Theatre, British Library, London.

Roberts, Valentina 1866, *Jack Mingo, the London Street Boy; or, Try Again*, JO1, reel 107, Frank Pettingell Collection of Plays, University of Kent, Canterbury: Harvester Press Microform Publications.

Rouse, Thomas 1842–49, letters to Lord Chamberlain, L.C. 7/1, Public Record Office, London.

Sala, G. A. 1859, *Gaslight and Daylight*, London.

Scott, Clement 1899, *The Drama of Yesterday and Today*, 2 vols., London: Macmillan.

Shaw, G. B. 1898, "The Drama in Hoxton," *The Saturday Review*, 9 April: 487–88.

Smiles, Samuel 1843, "The Women of the Working Class," *Union*, 1.

Thespian, 10 June 1857.

Travers, William 1858, *A Poor Girl's Temptations; or, A Voice from the Streets*, Lord Chamberlain's Plays, 52972H, British Library, London.

Wilkins, John 1853, *St. James's and St. Giles's*, Lord Chamberlain's Plays, 52942J, British Library, London.

Wilson, A. E. 1954, *East End Entertainment*, London: Arthur Barker.

Wilton, Frederick 1992, *The Britannia Diaries of Frederick Wilton*, ed. Jim Davis, London: Society for Theatre Research.

Young, Mrs. Henry 1862, *Jessie Ashton; or, The Adventures of a Barmaid*, Lord Chamberlain's Plays, 53013S, British Library, London.

Young, Mrs. Henry 1866, *The Pick-lock of Paris*, Lord Chamberlain's Plays, 53054R, British Library, London.

CHAPTER 9

"From a female pen"
The proper lady as playwright in the West End theatre, 1823–1844

Katherine Newey

In this chapter, I discuss a number of women writers in the first half of the nineteenth century whose careers in the theatres of the West End of London exemplify the problematic relationships between the ideology of middle-class femininity, the National Drama, and women's agency and self-identification as playwrights. I begin by looking at the playwriting experiences of Felicia Hemans and Isabel Hill, who came to the theatre as established writers from other genres, and whose dramatic aspirations were deeply involved in the idea of the National Drama as the representative form of English high culture. In contrast, Caroline Boaden and Elizabeth Planché were intimately connected with the business of the theatre through their husbands, brothers, and fathers. However, their professional status and achievements were often obscured by these familial connections and by their preference for writing comedy. Finally, I look at the reaction to plays by Catherine Gore and Emma Robinson, where the struggle to limit the category of playwright by "a newly ascendant hegemonic fraction ... whose project was to recapture the stage" (Bratton 1996: 59) was overt, and in Gore's case, fought explicitly in gender terms. These women's careers were played out principally in the professional formations of the West End theatre, where the "negative symbolic capital" of femaleness (Moi 1991: 1036) was disguised in the idea of the lady. This role seemed to confer both social and professional privilege and protection, but actually worked to restrict women's professional self-identity and agency. All these women were constrained (albeit in different ways) by the necessity of fulfilling the conflicting roles of professional playwright and the "proper lady," whose self-effacement must be produced through the control of her "natural" voracious desires (Poovey 1984: 4, 15–16).

The effects of this ideological construction of femininity were wide-ranging. In public commentary, plays "from a female pen" (*The Times*, 12 October 1829) were consistently linked to the high moral and cultural ground of the legitimate theatre and the National Drama, requiring of women playwrights an approach to theatrical composition which was not expected from male playwrights. In this way, the protection apparently offered to women by the cultural capital of the National Drama brought with it obligations which ultimately served to emphasize the restrictions of the ideology of femininity. There is evidence to suggest that women writers responded to these expectations of the "female pen" by practicing self-censorship before their plays were subjected to state censorship or public critique. And once their plays were in the public domain, adverse criticism tended to cause women playwrights to retreat precipitately from the public sphere. This is not simply a matter of women's lack of strength or stoicism in the face of criticism. Much of the criticism faced by women used their professional status to question their standing as "ladies"; in the cases of Felicia Hemans and Catherine Gore, for example, the "literary fame" of each woman is grounds for stringent attack.

Conversely, the experiences of the women playwrights I discuss make overt the regimes of control and surveillance implicit in the idea of the National Drama, and provide moments in which, in Toril Moi's words, "symbolic violence may be unmasked and recognized for what it is" (1991: 1023). They suggest that the National Drama was less a type of play or a place of performance and more of a site of struggle, its boundaries defined in the light of extratheatrical ideological concerns. The various experiences of these women also suggest that the "imagined community" of the legitimate theatre (Anderson 1991: 6–7), discursively created through debates over the National Drama, must be analysed in terms of gender as well as class.

ADVENTURES IN THE LEGITIMATE THEATRE: FELICIA HEMANS AND ISABEL HILL

Felicia Hemans's theatrical career is exemplary of one mode of engagement with the theatre in the early decades of the nineteenth century in which the ideas of the "proper lady" and the National Drama clash – only finding resolution in the withdrawal of the lady. Hemans's poetry has conventionally been seen as representative of the worst excesses of Victorian sentimentality, although recent scholarship presents another view of her work. Stuart Curran argues that her career exemplifies a new writerly role: "First, Hemans is broadly eclectic in the range of subject matter, more so in fact than any contemporary except Southey. She mined, as she represented, the new cosmopolitanism of the age; which is to say, she read and wrote with equal amplitude on virtually any subject" (Curran 1993: 190). Like Mary Russell Mitford, Sarah Flower Adams, Joanna Baillie, Barbarina Dacre, Maria Edgeworth, Sydney Morgan, and L. E. L. (Laetitia Landon), Hemans attempted historical verse tragedy as part of her repertoire as a woman of letters. She wrote three plays, *The Vespers of Palermo* (1823), *The Siege of Valencia* (1823), and *De Chatillon; or, The Crusaders* (1840), as well as translating other verse tragedies from Italian (*The Alcestis, Il Conte di Carmagnola*, and *Caius Gracchus*), and casting several of her lyric poems in the form of dramatic monologues or dialogues (*The English Martyrs, Flowers and Music in a Room of Sickness, Wood Walk and Hymn, Burial of an Emigrant's Child in the Forests*, and *The Painter's Last Work*). However, Hemans knew little of the practicalities of theatre, had few contacts in the theatre profession, and, living in Wales, could not be (or chose not to be) physically present as advocate and negotiator for the production of her work in London.

Hemans's plays and dramatic pieces were not originally intended for public performance, but she was persuaded by the Reverend Henry Milman and Bishop Heber to put forward *The Vespers of Palermo* for performance at Covent Garden in December 1823. The play was not successful in London, though it achieved much greater success in Edinburgh, with the endorsement of an epilogue by Sir Walter Scott (see Chorley 1836: vol. 1, 77; Wyndham 1906: 31). Reviews ranged from respectful disappointment in the *Drama*, which first commented on the play as "the offspring of female genius, and of a name already known to fame" (December 1823: 244), to the offhand comment in the *The Times* that

As the lady claims in her prologue to be "not unknown to fame," and as she has been honoured with a prize from that very sapient assembly the Royal Society of Literature! and has, moreover, written some poems which really deserve commendation, we must, in courtesy, give her that standing which entitles her to be told of her demerits.

The patronizing tenor of *The Times* review ends with the insulting comment that "such pieces ... ruin us in snuff to keep awake" (12 December 1823); altogether the *Times* reviewer manages to punish Hemans for present failure and past success.

Hemans's reaction to reviews of her play emphasizes the problematic nature of public performance for women writers. On reading the reviews of *Vespers*, Hemans wrote:

> As a female, I cannot help feeling rather depressed by the extreme severity with which I have been treated in the morning papers; I know not why this should be, for I am sure I should not have attached the slightest value to their praise, but I suppose it is only a proper chastisement for my temerity; for a female who shrinks from such things, has certainly no business to write tragedies. (Quoted in Chorley 1836: vol. 1, 76)

This is one of a number of examples of women writers' sense of the public theatre as being no place for them. The nature of Hemans's response to the failure of her play in London is telling, as she characterizes her venture into the theatre as audacious (her "temerity"), and links the staging of her work with the necessity of developing an authorial persona able to cope with adverse criticism. Her comment suggests that such a persona is, for her, not conformable with her identity "as a female." Hemans evinces a quiet desperation in being caught between her artistic ambition and her female nature, but she is unable to discount her investment in contemporary ideologies of femininity. W. M. Rossetti's critical memoir of Hemans neatly summarizes her entrapment: "Perhaps there never yet was a good five-act stage-tragedy written by a woman; and certainly the peculiar tone and tint of Mrs. Hemans's faculty were not such as to supply the deficiency which she, merely as a woman, was almost certain to evince" (Hemans n.d.: xviii). Rossetti's comment reiterates the double standard which Angela Leighton theorizes in her discussion of Victorian women's poetry (1992: 3): the limitations of knowledge and behavior imposed on a gentlewoman are precisely those which precluded women from writing successful drama.

And yet the attraction of the generic possibilities of drama – particularly its polyvocalism, and thus its potential to resist fixed readings – stayed with Hemans, as she produced the series of dramatic poems and verse dramas noted above. She exploited her own sense of authorship "as a woman" to marry the high cultural form of verse tragedy with the inclusion of feeling that marked her poetry as domestic and sentimental. Her participation in the public realm of the theatre, and her commitment to playwriting in the tradition of the "legitimate" drama, can be seen as a strategy by which to assert both her seriousness as a writer and to make a positive impact on the National Drama. Her isolation from the business of the theatre is clear in her letters, as she likens theatre managers to ogres and wolves (Chorley 1836: vol. 1, 69). However, her choice of metaphors is interesting here, suggesting some of the complexities of the woman writer's relationship to the legitimate theatre of the period. While Hemans constructs London theatre managers as fairy-tale monsters, and herself as their helpless victim, such an image is not without possibilities for reversal. Hemans is also the heroine who is persecuted by wicked enemies on her quest to bring the highest art – poetry – to the rescue of the stage. And it is with these "feminine" qualities of refinement, sentiment, and domesticity that Hemans attempts to reform dramatic writing, and which ultimately lead her to abandon her taste for the stage, as in the later years of her life "she thought that the decline of its [the theatre's] popularity must of necessity keep pace with an increase of the refinement and cultivation of thought" (Chorley 1836: vol. 1, 78). As Catherine Burroughs argues in her discussion of Joanna Baillie's theatre theory, we should not see this as a *retreat* to the closet, but as a writerly strategy by which Hemans chose to engage with theatre aesthetics and practices of the period (1994: 283).

Unlike Felicia Hemans's ladylike modesty about having her play performed, Isabel Hill actively sought to write for the theatre of the late 1820s and 1830s as part of her work as a professional writer. Though she derived most of her small income as a writer through poetry and journalism, and particularly as the English translator of Madame de Staël's *Corinne*, Hill was attracted to writing for the theatre, and was assisted by her brother, Earle Benson Hill, a military man and sometime actor. Her brother's account of her career in the theatre highlights the entanglement between Victorian ideas about the National Drama and the concept of women as the moral and spiritual custodians of high culture, as Hill's plays are judged against the ideas of the National Drama. Hill's brief career as a playwright, like that of Hemans, displays a paradoxical combination of persistence against the odds in dealing with theatre managements and a tendency to assume the role of victim. A simple account of a silenced female voice is inadequate, as an interpretation of Hill's career as a playwright must also consider her active determination to participate in a powerful cultural institution.

During the agitation over the threatened closure of Covent Garden in 1829 a subscription was set up to save the theatre for legitimate drama, and writers were encouraged to offer plays for the cause. Isabel Hill offered a comedy, *The First of May; or, A Royal Love Match*, which was performed at Covent Garden for twelve nights in October 1829. At the same time, and considerably less willingly than Hill, Frances Kemble was persuaded to help save her family's business, the management of Covent Garden (Corbett 1992: 109). Her performance of Juliet in *Romeo and Juliet* was probably the most sensational debut of the season. However, Hill's play suffered from Kemble's success as "it was selected for the nights that Miss Fanny Kemble did *not* appear" (Hill 1842: 88–89). *The First of May* received an unfavorable review in *The Times*, which commented on the play's "feeble" dialogue and "few incidents ... none of those ... of a striking or properly dramatic kind." In spite of this opinion, the play is reported to have been very well performed and "frequently applauded" by the audience. As well as emphasizing the play's theatrical shortcomings, *The Times* directed its most stringent comments at the moral defects of the piece.

The dissoluteness of the King is rather too strongly dwelt upon; and from a female pen the development of such a character is peculiarly indecorous and disagreeable. It is not quite enough that because, as a matter of history, Edward IV was unquestionably a libertine, the mere avowal of his opinions on that score is therefore fit material to regale an audience with. (12 October 1829)

Again, the expectation of moral probity "from a female pen" suggests that Hill should write differently from her male colleagues – even though her primary source might dictate otherwise.

Unhelpful managements, bad reviews, and indifferent houses were just some of Hill's difficulties in the working theatre: Benson Hill provides a litany of complaints about the treatment of Hill by theatre managers and critics. He complains of the "Shameless and unwarrantable conduct, on the part of a Manageress ... but I will not pollute pages hallowed by the name of my chaste and virtuous sister in even the bare mention of the person, who so basely wronged her" (Hill 1842: 95), or the critic who, in talking of a play written by Hill with her brother and produced anonymously, "selected her fireside as a fitting place to bray forth his malicious observations, which were as just as his conduct to a gentlewoman was gallant" (92). Such incidents may be typical of the indignities suffered by all playwrights – men or women – but what is significant here is the way in which Hill's gender becomes the focus both of criticism of her as a writer and of her brother's defense. Though Benson Hill does not reveal the identities of the manageress and the critic who have insulted his sister, his contrast of their immoral behavior with that of his sister's chastity and virtue serves to emphasize her possession of those essential characteristics of the "proper lady." Benson Hill's particular fury at the use of his sister's fireside – her private, domestic space – in which to criticize her public work encapsulates the contrary models of sociability between which Hill was caught. She is required to negotiate between the commercial and professional realities of the theatre as an industry, and the expectation that, as a gentlewoman, she will not appear to be publicly active at all.

FROM THE INSIDE: FAMILY NETWORKS

Writers without close connections to the theatre as an entertainment business (rather than as a branch of literature) were exceptions in the early nineteenth century, although their experiences bring into sharp focus the gendered responses to women playwright's work in the theatre. The women playwrights who were most successful in the theatre were usually already involved in the networks and alliances by which the theatre was organized. Gwenn Davis and Beverly A. Joyce find that the "largest identifiable group [of women play-wrights] is the 15 per cent who were actresses or members of theatrical families" (Davis and Joyce 1992: xi). In this model of participation in the profession, women's familial connections provide them with powerful social and cultural capital. However, their family networks, while anchoring them firmly with potentially powerful professional knowledges, also created specifically patriar-chal formations of female identity, which could subsume women into their fathers' or husbands' identities.

Elizabeth Planché, wife of antiquarian and playwright James Robinson Planché, provides a good example of the ways in which potentially diverging female identities are resolved through patriar-chal categories of appropriate feminine behavior. Planché's career as a successful playwright is subsumed into her husband's identity. Her plays – mostly light comedies and farces – were written and performed mainly for Madame Vestris and Charles Mathews at the Olympic Theatre, where they were very popular. Playbills and reviews provide evidence of the success of Planché's writing, and particularly her ability to write scripts which matched performers, theatres, and their audiences. Her plays remained in theatre repertoires until the mid-century. *The Handsome Husband* opened at the Olympic on 15 February 1836, then played in seasons at all the major London theatres until mid-century: Covent Garden in 1839, the Haymarket in 1842 and 1858, Sadler's Wells in 1846, the Lyceum in 1850, and with a successful revival at the Strand as late as 1895 (see Mullin 1987: *passim*; *Era*, 21 September 1895: 8). The *Athenaeum* praised its "busy, bustling little plot, and a succession of good situations, each in its turn, ignited and exploded by a train of dialogue with considerable fire in it" (20 February 1836: 148). *The Ransom* similarly played in seasons over two decades, opening at the Haymarket on 9 June 1836 and revived there at least twice in June 1837 and November 1848 (Mullin 1987: *passim*). Planché's melodrama, *The Sledge Driver*, was "well received" (*Times*, 20 June 1834), and it was felt she "executed her task with considerable force and feeling in the serious parts, and with much ladylike humour in the comic" (*Athenaeum*, 21 June 1834: 476). The play ran for at least twenty-two performances in its first season at the Haymarket in 1834 ("Playbills" 1983). *The Welsh Girl*, another favorite comedy, was first performed at the Olympic in 1833, and was revived in 1842 ("Playbills" 1983).

Planché had the obvious advantage of being married to James Robinson Planché, who was closely connected with the theatre management of Madame Vestris, but while her married name might have secured Planché a first, polite, hearing, it would not have ensured her continued success. Planché's career as a playwright is, however, reduced by her husband to a footnote that she "had amused herself by translating and adapting several French dramas" (Planché [1872] 1901: vol. II, 20). Elizabeth Planché died in 1846, almost thirty years before her husband wrote his autobiography. Like many of the women discussed in this chapter, she did not speak for herself – except through her plays – but is spoken for by her husband. And his account, as he insists on the "Advertisement" to his *Recollections*, is "limited as strictly as possible to ... public and professional matters ... avoiding reference to my own family and private affairs" (vii). His wife, and her career, is a family matter; in spite of her public success, and the suggestions of shared professional interests, she is carefully and decorously placed back into the private realm.

Perhaps because she remained "Miss Boaden," and her plays were produced mainly at the Haymarket, Caroline Boaden's career remained rather more visible than that of Planché, but it was still obscured by the names of her father and brother. Boaden had six plays performed between 1825 and 1838, mostly in the social and professional respectability of the West End at the Haymarket. She was an honorary member of the Dramatic Authors' Society (the only category of membership open to women), and five of her plays were published in popular editions, all signs of a reasonably successful career. Boaden's plays were reviewed favorably in the contemporary press – the *Athenaeum*, the *Literary Spectator*, and *The Times* all published reviews of her plays at one time or another – though her name was consistently misspelt or not mentioned. However, in the *Dictionary of National Biography* she is referred to, but not named, in the entry for her father, James Boaden. Her existence is recorded thus: "[James Boaden] left nine children, of whom John [q.v.] was an artist, and another (a daughter) inherited a facility for play-writing." The entry for John Boaden judges his paintings as "pleasing ... [but they do] not rise above mediocrity" a judgment which could apply just as well to Caroline's plays. However, as an exhibitor at the Royal Academy and the Society of British Artists, John Boaden has both the institutions of high culture and his gender supporting him.

When her playwriting is discussed, Boaden's gender is commented on in ways that serve to diminish her professional status. D.–G.'s (George Daniels) "Remarks" to the Cumberland edition of *Fatality* place Boaden firmly within a feminine tradition, with a typical use of elaborate politeness and a patronising tone which serve to undermine Boaden's achievement.

We never fear to encounter genius – more especially when that genius is centered in a lady. To have compared Miss Boaden to her illustrious predecessors in the dramatic art, the Centlivres and the Cowleys, would have led her to suspect us of *badinage* ... but when we say that she is a spirited and pleasing writer; that her incidents and characters are well imagined and supported; that her language is pointed, and "Quite Correct," *then* she may receive our opinion with complacency, seeing that the public confirm it with their applause. (Boaden n.d.a: 5–6)

Daniels's comments construct the woman playwright as a thing apart, writing to please a male-identified viewer. Such a model of female authorship sets up special criteria for women's success, as is clear in a review of Boaden's 1832 play, *A Duel in Richelieu's Time*, which judged the play to be "as clever and effective as it is offensive to good taste and injurious to good morals ... [a] clever and worthless production ... [which] we are the less inclined to tolerate ... that it is the work of a lady" (*New Monthly Magazine* August 1832: 348). This admonitory response to Boaden's play epitomizes the ways in which women's playwriting faced a combination of prejudices during the period: the persistent antitheatrical suspicion of the theatre as morally corrupting was allied with assumptions about the appropriate form and content of public writing produced by "a lady." Boaden's work here is subject to the conflicting requirements of comic writing and feminine gentility: in the logic of the review, the very cleverness of the play makes it more morally reprehensible. This response demonstrates the way in which the expectations of ladylike behavior could be inimical to theatrical success.

The contradictions implicit in the successful woman playwright as proper lady are particularly noticeable in response to comedy by women. As a genre, comedy was often a focal point for concerns about the propriety of women's playwriting. While writers such as Hemans gained a hearing in the legitimate theatre on the strength of their investment in the high cultural capital of verse tragedy, the work of Boaden and Planché was firmly located in the commercial realities of the stage. Reviews of Planché's comedies note her aptitude for bringing together situation, plot, and character in light comedy, and George Daniels finds this same competence in Boaden's farce, *The First of April*. "Miss Boaden is a decided patroness of the practical joke, and a perfect mistress of its merry machinery. A water-bottle in *her* hands is a powerful engine of mirth; give her *rope*, and she will hang a hundred whimsical jests upon it" (Boaden n.d.b: 5). However, the generic hierarchy which valued comedy much less highly than tragedy or epic converged with anxieties about the "popular" and "low" elements of comedy when written by women. The *New Monthly Magazine*'s comments about Boaden's play being clever but immoral are typical. The pitfalls of comedy writing for women are demonstrated in the experiences of Catherine Gore and Emma Robinson, whose comedies were censured and censored in such ways as to challenge their identities both as authors and as ladies.

THE "PRIZE COMEDY"

In 1844, anxieties about women playwrights and concerns about the National Drama collided explosively in Benjamin Webster's competition for the "best comedy illustrative of British life and manners of the present day" (*Spectator*, 10 June 1843). Webster's attempt at "the encouragement of dramatic literature" (*Athenaeum* 10 June 1843: 552) by the offer of a prize of £500 and a production at the Haymarket was greeted with some satire and cynicism. This became outright hostility when *Quid Pro Quo; or, The Day of Dupes* was announced as the winning play, "by a lady, and one who is by no means unknown to literary fame" (*The Times*, 21 May 1844: 5).[1] This "lady" was quickly identified as the novelist and playwright Catherine Gore. Almost immediately, accusations of favoritism were made (*The Times*, 22 May 1844: 8), which forced one of the judges to reply with a denial of knowledge about the identity of the winner (*The Times*, 24 May 1844: 7). While Gore later claimed the impartiality of the judges as her defense against some criticisms of the play, she could not defend herself completely against the abuse which *Quid Pro Quo* received, for much of the criticism of the play was based on that one part of her reputation that she maintained as a professional identity: her status as a lady. The phrase "a lady . . . by no means unknown to literary fame" was constantly repeated as a description which emphasized Gore's successful public persona, while implying the doubtfulness of her character as a "proper lady" because her success was not the result of accident or untutored genius, but the outcome of professional experience and knowledge.

The mildest of comments about the selection of Catherine Gore came from the *Spectator*: "It is remarkable that out of ninety-eight [or ninety-seven – reports vary] competitors a lady should have carried off the prize" (25 May 1844: 492). The *Illustrated London News* was most scathing in its condescending opinion:

not one writer of any distinguished grade has entered the lists – so that the prize comedy should not be considered as a fair sample of what the dramatic talent of the day could effect . . . Of the comedy chosen we cannot possibly yet give any opinion: it is the production of a lady in a department of literature which has been ornamented by many female pens. Mrs. Sentlivre [*sic*], Mrs. Cowley, Mrs. Inchbald, and several other writers are sufficient to prove that a good comedy *can* emanate from a feminine brain, and we trust there will be another proof of it when Mrs. Gore's is produced.

Still we cannot help regretting that none of the "favourites have been in the field," although we admire the generosity which held them from the contest for the "stakes." (1 June 1844: 356)

As the whole competition was conducted under conditions guaranteeing anonymity, the *News*'s certainty that no writer of any note had entered the competition is interesting. This insinuation of privileged knowledge of the competition and lofty tone of assessment of "many female pens" constructs Gore and other women playwrights as outsiders because of their sex: their work might be an ornament to comedy, but only when it is chivalrously protected from open competition with established (that is, male) writers. The pattern is a familiar one: the social practice of protecting gentlewomen because of their vulnerable femininity is silently converted to a natural deficiency in their capacity to participate on an equal footing with men.

When *Quid Pro Quo* was produced in June 1844, criticism of the play was aimed at Gore's reputation as a "lady" in terms which would have been unthinkable for a male writer – even a gentlemanly one. The *Illustrated London News*'s commentary turns from condescension to outright hostility:

On Tuesday night last the long-talked of "Prize Comedy" was produced ... and unfortunately turned up a "Blank!" ... A thorough knowledge of life – an almost intuitive perception of the *nuances* of character – a perfectly graphic pencil to sketch them – a smack of sentiment – a considerable fund of humour – a deep mine of wit, that does not always exhibit its riches – a vein of corrective, not invective satire – a constructiveness that can invent a probable series of incidents – a felicitous power of making everybody speak after his own fashion ... and above all, Good Taste, are necessary possessions, or equipments, before one may venture on the task of comedy. And were these discernible in the "Prize Comedy"? Not one of them. The piece is incoherent and plotless. (22 June 1844: 395)

The *Athenaeum* was less personally vituperative, but equally dismissive of the play in terms which conflated the moral and the aesthetic, calling the play vulgar, exaggerated and coarse, false and offensive (22 June 1844: 581). Likewise, the *Spectator* railed at the play's vulgarity, but was patronizingly glib about its novelty: "people will flock to see a 'prize comedy' as they do a prize ox, who are as well able to appreciate one as the other" (22 June 1844: 586).

Perhaps the most devastating of all critiques of *Quid Pro Quo* was made by George Henry Lewes in the *Westminster Review*. What is

most significant, underlying Lewes's ostensibly rational and metho-
dical demolition of the whole competition, is his assumption that
Gore intruded on masculine territory:

If we should have the misfortune to pain Mrs. Gore, we would bid her
remember that there are ninety-six authors whose self-love has been
wounded, whose time has been wasted; some, whose hopes ... have been
disappointed by the awarding of the prize: ninety-six angry men who need
consolation, and who, we cannot but think, deserve it. (Lewes 1844: 106)

Lewes admits that he has not seen or read the other entries, nor does
he give any indication of the knowledge on which he bases his
assumption that all the other entrants *were* men, but goes on to argue
that their reputations vouch for them in a way that Gore's cannot.

That a comedy so deplorably destitute of every vestige of comic genius,
destitute even of ordinary literary ability, should have carried off the prize
from ninety-six competitors, some of whose names are guarantees for a
considerable amount of literary excellence at least, is certainly an act
worthy of very serious attention ... We have not seen one of the ninety-six
rival plays; but from all we know of dramatic literature, we find it
impossible to believe that they were worse than "Quid Pro Quo." (111)

For all his tone of disinterested commentary, Lewes's essay demonstrates the way in which gender is figured in the judgment of aesthetic
merit. Of the reviews I have quoted, Lewes's article is the most
blatant in showing how ideas about appropriate female behavior
crowd out considerations of literary or theatrical merit. Perhaps
Lewes's systematic demolition of Gore's work is all the more shocking
because of his professed championship of women's writing. However,
as Nicola Thompson argues, Lewes's support of women's writing is
qualified by rigid notions of what women are best suited to writing: in
his 1852 essay, "The Lady Novelists," he argues that for women to
write as men write "is the aim and besetting sin of women; to write as
women is the real office they have to perform ... women [succeed]
better in finesse of detail, in pathos and sentiment, while men
generally succeed better in the construction of plots and the delineation of character" (quoted in Thompson 1996: 20). If Lewes wanted
to clear away unsuitable competition for his more deserving friends
in the "literary gentleman's club" (Swindells 1985: 91), he certainly
helped to do so: *Quid Pro Quo* was the last play Gore wrote, after a
successful career of some thirteen plays.

In Lewes's analysis of the whole affair, newspaper responses to the
announcement of the winner of the competition, and reviews of *Quid*

Pro Quo in performance, a familiar pattern emerges. Gore's victory over ninety-seven other competitors (all of whom are presumed to be men) is represented as an unfeminine intrusion into a masculine domain; not only to enter, but actually to win, in open competition, is to trespass in the assumed character of equality. It is a moment of crisis for masculine writing, which can no longer define itself in terms of its difference from feminine writing if women can compete and win in open competition against men. The onslaught against Gore is an attempt to protect the boundaries of the field of legitimate dramatic authorship, but is also evidence of their permeability, suggesting that the idea of the National Drama is mobilized as a rearguard action against an already and indeed always present interloper. However, to see Gore as a victim of a patriarchal establishment intent on policing its boundaries is too simple an interpretation. The severity of attempts to deny her the status of playwright can be seen in terms of Pierre Bourdieu's argument that "[T]here is no other criterion of membership of a [literary] field than the objective fact of producing effects within it ... [oppositional] polemics imply a form of recognition" (1993: 42). By the very weight of opposition to her work, Gore can be seen as momentarily central in defining the field of the National Drama, though the price of this focus was a threat to her identity as a "proper woman."

THE "PROHIBITED COMEDY"

I want now to consider the case of a play by a woman which was *not* performed in 1844. Emma Robinson's play, *Richelieu in Love; or, The Youth of Charles I* was refused a license by the Examiner of Plays. While her gender is not the primary reason for the play's suppression, Robinson's response to official censorship is in part framed by her need to negotiate between expectations of her behavior as a "lady" and her self-image as an author. In her protests against the banning of her play, Robinson takes on a series of identities in an attempt to avoid the blurring of public and private character which Gore suffers. She adopts male personae as "the Author," a "Cadet at Woolwich," or the title bestowed on her by the *Athenaeum*: "our young Oxonian." This strategy allows her to protest publicly about her treatment without either misogyny or chivalry obscuring the central issue of censorship. Robinson's dilemma over public knowledge of her identity is the obverse of Gore's, but it is still part of the problem of being a "lady." As she comments to James Robinson Planché: "I am not anxious that any one who hears I am a *lady* in *private* should win a reputation for courage by abusing me as a *gentleman* in *public* ... I am far more afraid of having too hot a champion than of wanting one" (quoted in Planché 1901: 307). While Gore's professional success cast doubt on her private character, Robinson sees the overprotectiveness resulting from her identification as a "lady" as a significant handicap to her professional status. In what must have been a feat of extraordinary management, Robinson kept her anonymity throughout the controversy in 1844, and for eight years until after the play's performance in 1852.

For a brief period, *Richelieu in Love* was the focus of the campaign against the censorship powers of the Lord Chamberlain and the Examiner of Plays. The play was banned by the Examiner on the grounds that "It is calculated to bring 'church and state into contempt'" (Robinson 1844: xi). Robinson protests against this judgment in a long and polemic preface to the 1844 published version of the play, provocatively subtitled *An Historical Comedy in Five Acts, As Accepted at the Theatre Royal, Haymarket and Prohibited by the Authority of the Lord Chamberlain.* Her main objections are to the secrecy of the process, and the prevention of any appeal against the decision. Using the language of liberal democracy, and the freedom of the printed medium, she launches into a broadside against the tyranny and irresponsibility of the Lord Chamberlain's powers, arguing that the Drama is "the only species of literature still marked with the band of slavery," and asking, "is it possible that dramatic literature can flourish, chained and languishing at the feet of a private despotism?" (Robinson 1844: xxvii). It is this call to arms that the *Athenaeum* and the *New Monthly Magazine* take up, linking the censorship of *Richelieu in Love* to the ever-declining state of the Drama: "If ever there was a time, then, in this country when the drama demanded encouragement, and fosterage, and rewards, this is the time; ... this is the very time, O public, when the Examiner of Plays prohibits the representation of a new five-act comedy!" (*New Monthly Magazine,* 1844: 346).

PROFESSIONALISM AND THE "PROPER LADY"

Looked at in isolation, the treatment of the work of Emma Robinson and Catherine Gore by the theatrical establishment of London is

probably no worse than that of their male peers. However, this is to
assume that Gore and Robinson, and other women writers of the
time, worked under the same conditions as their male peers. I hope
to have shown how they did not. Gore's public character as a
woman writer was central to the way her work was received and
evaluated, while Robinson avoided censure by sedulously cloaking
her female identity. That she did so successfully is cause for celebration, as she was enabled to make her case public in a vigorous
manner and enlist others on her side without drawing sex-based
comment. But at what personal cost? This is a question more
difficult to answer.

Moreover, the question of state censorship of women's work cuts
straight into a consideration of the ways in which the maintenance
of the persona of the "proper lady" is brought about by conscious
and unconscious self-censorship. Robinson's public complaint is
that "Every thought, every word must be weighed with an eye at
the 'Examiner.' The taste in office, not the inspirations of genius
must be consulted" (Robinson 1844: xxix–xxx). This hints at the
kind of constraint which Mary Russell Mitford expresses privately
after her play *Charles the First* was similarly banned in 1825. While
Robinson maintains a conscious defiance, Mitford is despairing,
writing to William Harness that "not licensing that play [*Charles the
First*] will do great harm to my next, by making me timid and over
careful" (Chorley 1872: vol. ii, 214). Furthermore, public and
private censorship often took place against a background of strai-
tened circumstances in which professional writing meant financial
survival. John Sutherland's quantitative analysis of a sample of 878
Victorian novelists shows that while only just over 10 percent of
male writers did *not* have a prior or alternative activity, only 10.3
percent of women *did* (Sutherland 1995: 163). The material situations of Hill, Hemans, Mitford, Gore, and many other women
supplied the final irony in the ideology of the "proper lady," in that
these women rarely had alternatives to the professional writing
which provided them and their families with the means to live as
ladies.

Again and again, the identity of "lady" was grounds for public
comment on and castigation of women playwrights. This construction of the middle-class woman playwright through excessively
gender-marked commentary points to the central contradiction of
the "proper lady" which too often proved irresolvable for women

playwrights. Not only did the nature of making theatre generally mean the public identification and discussion of the playwright (in contravention of the requirement for modesty, privacy, and silence on the part of a lady), but also women's attempts to participate in the institutions of national culture were seen as encroachments on a domain which was assumed to be masculine. The investment in the cultural capital of "legitimacy," concentrated in the largely middle-class theatres of the West End of London, by which women playwrights attempted to maintain their class position, was also the means by which their status as ladies could be undermined. For middle-class women playwrights in the early nineteenth century, this meant that they faced great difficulties in inhabiting a professional identity and participating in the cultural community of the legitimate theatre, as they occupied the overdetermined and overlapping roles of "woman playwright" and "proper lady." While these categories are implicitly connected by the category of femaleness, class and gender roles are so entangled as to make successful achievement of this conjunction – in the role of a "lady playwright" – almost impossible in the lives and careers of the women I discuss.

NOTES

1   *The Times* article dated 21 May 1844 was based on an earlier announcement that appeared in the *Morning Chronicle*, suggesting interest in the competition was not just limited to the theatre industry.

REFERENCES

Anderson, Benedict 1991, *Imagined Communities*, rev. edn, London and New York: Verso.
Athenaeum, 20 February 1836, 21 June 1834, 10 June 1843, 22 June 1844.
Boaden, Caroline n.d.a, *Fatality: a Drama, in One Act*, with remarks, biographical and critical, by D.-G. [George Daniels], London: John Cumberland.
Boaden, Caroline n.d.b, *The First of April*, with remarks, biographical and critical, by D.-G. [George Daniels], London: John Cumberland.
Bourdieu, Pierre 1993, *The Field of Cultural Production: Essays on Art and Literature*, ed. Randal Johnson, Cambridge, MA: Polity Press.
Bratton, Jacky 1996, "Miss Scott and Miss Macauley: 'Genius comes in all disguises,'" *Theatre Survey*, 37.1: 59–74.
Burroughs, Catherine B. 1994, "English Romantic Women Writers and Theatre Theory: Joanna Baillie's Prefaces to the *Plays on the Passions*,"

Re-Visioning Romanticism: British Women Writers, 1776–1837, ed. Carol Shiner Wilson and Joel Haefner, Philadelphia: University of Pennsylvania Press, 274–96.

Chorley, Henry 1836, *Memorials of Mrs Hemans*, 2 vols., London: Saunders and Otley.

Chorley, Henry 1872, *Letters of Mary Russell Mitford*, 2nd series, 2 vols., London: Richard Bentley.

Corbett, Mary Jean 1992, *Representing Femininity. Middle-Class Subjectivity in Victorian and Edwardian Women's Autobiographies*, New York and Oxford: Oxford University Press.

Curran, Stuart 1993, "Women Readers, Women Writers," *The Cambridge Companion to Romanticism*, ed. Stuart Curran, Cambridge: Cambridge University Press.

Davis, Gwenn, and Beverly A. Joyce 1992, *Drama by Women to 1900: A Bibliography of American and British Writers*, Toronto and Buffalo: University of Toronto Press.

Drama; or, Theatrical Magazine, December 1823.

Era, 21 September 1895.

Gore, Catherine n.d., *Quid Pro Quo; or, The Day of Dupes*, London: National Acting Drama Office; also facsimile edition CD-ROM *Nineteenth Century Theatre* 26.2 (winter 1998).

Hemans, Felicia n.d., *Poetical Works*, edited and introduced by W. M. Rossetti, London, New York and Melbourne: Ward, Lock.

Hill, Isabel 1842, *Brian the Probationer: or, The Red Hand. A Tragedy in Five Acts ... To Which is Affixed, a Memoir of the Authoress by Benson Earle Hill, Esq.*, London: W. R. Sams, Royal Library.

Illustrated London News, 1 and 22 June 1844.

Leighton, Angela 1992, *Victorian Women Poets. Writing Against the Heart*, Charlottesville and London: University Press of Virginia.

Lewes, George Henry 1844, "The Prize Comedy and the Prize Committee," *Westminster Review*, 42.1: 105–16.

Moi, Toril 1991, "Appropriating Bourdieu: Feminist Theory and Pierre Bourdieu's Sociology of Culture," *New Literary History* 22.4: 1017–49.

Mullin, Donald (ed.) 1987, *Victorian Plays: A Record of Significant Productions on the London Stage, 1837–1901*, Westport, CT: Greenwood Press.

New Monthly Magazine, August 1832, 1844.

Planché, James Robinson [1872] 1901, *Recollections and Reflections of J. R. Planché*, 2 vols., rev. edn, London: Tinsley Brothers.

"Playbills and Programmes from London Theatres, 1801–1900 in the Theatre Museum, London" 1983, London: Chadwyck-Healey.

Poovey, Mary 1984, *The Proper Lady and the Woman Writer: The Ideology of Style in Mary Wollstonecraft, Jane Austen, and Mary Shelley*, Chicago: University of Chicago Press.

Robinson, Emma 1844, *Richelieu in Love; or, The Youth of Charles I*, London: Henry Colburn.

Spectator, 10 June 1843, 25 May and 22 June 1844.

Sutherland, John 1995, *Victorian Fiction. Writers, Publishers, Readers*, London: Macmillan.

Swindells, Julia 1985, *Victorian Writing and Working Women: The Other Side of Silence*, Cambridge, MA: Polity Press.

Thompson, Nicola Diane 1996, *Reviewing Sex: Gender and the Reception of Victorian Novels*, London: Macmillan.

The Times, 12 December 1823, 12 October 1824, 20 June 1834, 21–24 May 1844.

Wyndham, Henry Saxe 1906, *The Annals of Covent Garden Theatre, from 1732 to 1837*, London: Chatto and Windus.

PART 4

Genre trouble

CHAPTER 10

Genre trouble

Joanna Baillie, Elizabeth Polack – tragic subjects, melodramatic subjects

Susan Bennett

Ye Men, be candid to a Virgin Muse, –
To move you more, – Perhaps a Woman Sues:
Let her Dramatic Saplin 'scape your Rage,
And Spare this tender Scyon of the Stage –
Support the infant Tree, ye pitying fair
Protect its blossoms from the blighting air, –
So may its leaves move gently with your sighs,
The Branches flourish water'd by your Eyes. –

(Baillie, prologue to *De Monfort*, in Cox 1992: 234)

I am interested to write against the rigor with which generic forms have been applied as containers for types of dramatic practice, a rigor which has consistently, if differently, served to judge women's dramatic writings and, for the most part, to find their writings less accomplished than those of their male counterparts. So, on the one hand, I am interested in theories of genre as they pertain to the dramatic arts and to understand their limits and operations as historically fixed and ideologically determined. On the other hand, I am more interested to surface those unruly elements which exceeded or disobeyed those same categories of designation, and to bring back into the critical spotlight those women whose theatrical product engaged audiences in every age of English-speaking dramatic art. I raise these points not simply because they are (I hope) interesting as sites of academic speculation, but because they have a crucial relationship to the increasingly energetic project of archival work. Moreover, the archive, as Michel Foucault has told us, is not simply the library of all libraries (which would presumably house women's dramatic texts on some dark stage, in some inaccessible corner), but more than this it is "the general system of the formation and transformation of statement" situated, as Foucault puts it, "between tradition and oblivion, it reveals the rules of a practice that enables

statements both to survive and to undergo regular modification"
(1972: 130). If we can productively imagine the extent of such an
archive, then we can perhaps understand the complexity of relationships in a system of "accumulation, historicity, and disappearance"
(130). In this way, it can be argued that much of the dramatic writing
by women (in the nineteenth century or any other so-called
"period") that is retrieved, either by way of scholarly edition or
production, is not properly usable if we cannot, or do not, better
understand the categorizations through which they were and are
received. As Susan Stewart has said, it is not just that "the literary
genre determines the shape and progress of its material; but [that] at
the same time, the genre itself is determined by the social formations
from which it arises" (1984: 7).

Questions of social formation are, certainly, marked in particular
ways when the overarching genre is that of theatre. If the archive
has not paid diligent attention to women's dramatic writing, it is
important to understand that fact in the context of the particular
medium. As Julie Carlson has argued for the Romantic period (at
least as far as its male poets/critics were concerned), theatre was a
cultural feminine, in need of surveillance as a vulgar display.
Carlson's argument points to a heightened effect when the authorial
presence behind the "display" was explicitly female; she makes the
crucial observation that theatre "foregrounded active women and
their visible influence in the nation" (1994: 211). If the medium is
always already a feminized participant in the sociocultural real of
the British Romantic period, then the performativity of gender for
the woman playwright is, to say the least, loaded. On the one hand,
gender is foregrounded in that very act of display; on the other, it is
masked by a general cultural opprobrium for the public nature of
the theatrical event. How and on what terms, then, does the woman
playwright intervene in a broadly conceived (which is to say, male)
horizon of expectations for the various genres that constituted
theatrical performances? Analyses of particular genres have
behaved as if "the features of a particular cultural form selected as
sui generis were fixed and immutable" (Pistotnik 1985: 680); here,
instead, I am concerned with relationality – how certain plays by
women rework such "features" to make specific interventions in
their chosen form and claim, for their audiences, a particular place
for women.

Of all the attention to "serious" women playwrights in the

nineteenth century, most has, recently, accrued to Joanna Baillie. Jeffrey Cox, for example, introduces his section on Baillie with the following apparent praise: "From 1789 to 1851 – for over half a century – Joanna Baillie was the most respected and arguably the most important playwright in England" (1992: 50). Baillie came to the critical attention of a contemporary literary/theatrical community after the anonymous publication of her *A Series of Plays: in which it is attempted to delineate the stronger passions of the mind, each passion being the subject of a tragedy and a comedy* (more popularly known as *Plays on the Passions*) in 1798, a collection of play texts prefaced by a long essay theorizing the categories of tragedy and comedy – and how each would best serve "man" in Baillie's own historical moment. Once her identity was revealed (that is, the author being a woman), both the plays and the theory found themselves far less in favor (see Donkin 1995: 159–66). Anne Mellor, pursuing an argument which situates women authors between 1780 and 1820 as producers of a "'counter' public sphere," suggests that Baillie "consciously used the theater to re-stage and revise the social construction of gender" (1994: 560–61). A crucial dimension of that work is, I argue, the disarticulation of genre convention. As illustration of Baillie's contestatory engagement with a received notion of tragedy, I want first to look at her play *The Family Legend* (1810) and, briefly, its critical reception in the first productions. Tragedy in the early nineteeth century was, of course, defined both by dramatic critics, who looked to Shakespeare and other precedents for a model of universalized morality (for example, Hazlitt's claim that tragedy "substitutes imaginary sympathy for mere selfishness. It gives us a high and permanent interest beyond ourselves, in humanity as such" (1930–34: vol. IV, 200), and by the male Romantic writers, perhaps especially Coleridge, who turned to tragedies "in the service of a nationalist polemic" (Carlson 1994: 46).

The Family Legend is a resolutely Scottish play. A tragedy in five acts, it is set on the Isle of Mull and animates the bitter rivalry between the family of the Earl of Argyll and the Maclean clan. The plot makes clear that the marriage of Helen (daughter of Argyll) to Maclean was pragmatic, a means of instituting peace between two warring clans. The play eschews any deliberation of generalized human passions and instead foregrounds the political expediency which can be assured best through an exchange of the reproductive body. While *The Family Legend* offers much of the heroic sentiment and proud declamation that might be expected of a "tartan" tragedy (Alasdair Cameron, in his essay on Scottish drama in the nineteenth century, notes how Sir Walter Scott insisted on authentic tartans being used in the play's premiere production [1988: 430]), it also takes very seriously the fate of the central female character, Helen, daughter of Argyll and wife of Maclean and thus the epitome of the dramatic conflict. Baillie takes great pains through the first scenes to establish Helen as torn between her loyalty to and love for her family, and her commitment to her husband as well as adoration for and duty to their infant son. Moreover, in the play's second scene, Baillie constructs a scene where Helen directly engages the very men who will plot her downfall. In this scene, Maclean's clansmen entreat their leader for the pardon of Allen of Jura. Maclean at first angrily refuses their request ("The man for whom thou pleadest is most unworthy" [13]) but eventually gives in to his wife's pleading: "[*Hanging on him with looks of entreaty, till, seeing him relent, she then turns joyfully to* BENLORA] Bid your wanderer / Safe with his aged mother still remain" (Act 1 Scene 2, 14).

It would be possible to read this intervention by Helen as her shamelessly trying to win over the clansmen of her husband and, in this way, demonstrating the weak will of Maclean that might be said to cause his own downfall (in that sense, a fatal flaw in Maclean's psychology). The scene also, obviously, stages an idealization of motherhood (especially the mother/son relationship which is so central to Helen's destiny in *The Family Legend*) that is both predictable and conventional in a play of this period. But Baillie's representation of Helen is, I think, much more complex, much more attuned to the kinds of negotiation that any woman might be expected to make in order to meet the requirements of her social role. She tells her brother (Lord of Lorne):

> I would myself, while by my side in arms
> One valiant clan's-man stood, against his powers,
> To the last push, with desperate opposition,
> This castle hold.   (Act 2 Scene 1)

Specifically, then, she portrays Helen as a woman who has an all too perspicacious grasp of the homosocial world of the Scottish clans. Helen is self-aware in her choices throughout *The Family Legend*, at the same time as Baillie ably sketches the psychological costs this involves for her female protagonist; the marriage, for example, is described as "Constrained, unblessed and joyless" (Act 2 Scene 1, 22).

Beyond very minor roles for Rosa (as Helen's maid and confidante, allowing, as it were, the female confessional) and a fisherman's wife, Helen is alone in a world of men; those men use her as the very ground on which their battles are enacted. Helen's performance, which is to say the performance of "woman," is inextricably tied to an assertion of masculine identity. "Woman," thus, functions as a fetish object that Luce Irigaray has outlined "inasmuch as, in exchanges, they are the manifestation and the circulation of a power of the Phallus, establishing relationships of men with each other" (1985: 183). At the heart of *The Family Legend*, then, is Baillie's Helen, whose primary function is to show how received expectations of "woman" (including, among others, the idealized mother, the pleading lover and the fickle wife) secure through the very exchange of the sign that is "woman" the imperative of masculine identity. That, it might be said, is the tragedy of *The Family Legend*.

Here, then, it is useful to insert some of Baillie's own theorizing on the goals she envisaged for a tragedy that would speak to her circumstances. She makes a fervent claim for the utility of tragic drama:

but representing the passions, brings before us the operation of a tempest that rages out its time and passes away. We cannot, it is true, amidst its wild uproar, listen to the voice of reason, and save ourselves from destruction; but we can foresee its coming, we can mark its rising signs, we can know the situations that will most expose us to its rage, and we can shelter our heads from the coming blast. To change a certain disposition of mind which makes us view objects in a particular light, and thereby, oftentimes, unknown to ourselves, influences our conduct and manners, is almost impossible; but in checking and subduing those visitations of the soul, whose causes and effects we are aware of, every one may make considerable progress, if he proves not entirely successful. ([1851]1976a: 11)

Notwithstanding the gendered pronoun at the end of this quotation, all other references ("we," "us," "every one," etc.) offer a non-gender specific account – the universalizing convention – but which subliminally at least suggests that Baillie might see (as she does in the character of Helen) a "tempest" that rages in particular ways for women. Hazlitt, in his essay "On the Living Poets," suggests, too, that he found a contradiction between the claims of her 1798 "Introductory Discourse" and the materiality of her plays. He writes of her characters, "they talk virtues and act vices," and describes Baillie's *Plays on the Passions* as "heresies in the dramatic art" (1910: 147). The misogyny of Hazlitt's assessment of female poets is breathtaking and it is in his perceived failure of Baillie to meet the expectations of dramatic art that this hatred is utterly visible.[1]

Furthermore, it must be remembered that this positioning of a central female role is contextualized by a national history which, too, is situated along a narrative characterized by oppression and subjugation. In others, like the category "woman," "Scotland" must stand for lesser, indeed England's femininized other. Should this claim need any substantiation, I might point to George Sampson's remark in *The Concise Cambridge History of English Literature* that Joanna Baillie belongs to the category of "Scottish poets, rather than great poets" (1970: 497). To see how Baillie's tragedies bring a gender and ethnic specificity to the genre, production history is helpful. In an account of Baillie's life included as a preface to her collected works, the anonymous author, strangely replicating Baillie's gesture in the first publication of *Plays on the Passions*, offers the following history for *The Family Legend*:

At the beginning of the year 1810 Joanna's play of the Family Legend was brought upon the Edinburgh stage with considerable effect. Mr. Henry Siddons had become the manager of the theatre, whilst Scott was a shareholder and one of the acting trustees for the general body of the proprietors. The first play produced under this management was Joanna's drama; and Walter Scott, ever warmly interested in the success of a friend, exerted himself in the cause ... The play had a run of fourteen nights continuously, and was acted on subsequent occasions. ("Life of Joanna Baillie" [1851]1976a: xv)

A footnote follows the last sentence of the above quotation and reads: "The Family Legend was performed for the benefit of Mrs. Bartley at Drury Lane Theatre in 1815, and De Monfort was revived by Mr. Kean on the same stage in 1821; but neither play had success" (xv). Here, then, we see the intrinsic appeal of *The Family Legend* within a performance location in which the political content had an immediate recognition – not simply as "Scottish," but in its representation of conflicts which produced and reproduced those fissures internal to the experience of Scottish identity. In London, it was easier to dismiss *The Family Legend* as dealing with romanticized details of lives of Scottish brigands in the remote historical past. In Edinburgh, that same past is literally behind the social constituency of the theatregoing public. There, the account of clan organization would have functioned both nostalgically (in the face of the increasing problems of a rapidly growing urban environment) and as a facet contributing to a specifically Scottish public culture which worked both to recognize and retain elements of traditional Scottish social organization as well as to promote the values of Enlightenment internationalism.[2] Success, then, as a geographically specific tragedy was dependent on a shared recognition of a nationalist and middle-class identity – *The Family Legend* works against the agenda for universality claimed by and for the genre of tragedy and instead posits an identity that is very much about the particularities of social circumstances.

From a shared geography, Baillie is able to mark conduct within that representational frame as particularly gendered. Might it not be possible to extend that equation of shared national identity to indicate a perspective which engaged a female reader or spectator in a way that ignored a hegemonic male gaze invested only and specifically in the homosocial bonds of the majority of the characters in *The Family Legend*? If this is so, Baillie's tragedy does indeed turn away from "the voice of reason" and instead "makes us view objects [that is, in the case of this particular play, Helen, an object here *par excellence*] in a particular light." That light, I would argue, is one with a specifically gendered and national glow and one which illuminates tragedy with different spectatorial ambitions. Put another way, Hazlitt's claim that tragedy enabled "man" as "a partaker with his kind" (1930: vol. iv, 200) plays out in the reception history of *The Family Legend* to suggest that coincidences of positionality gave very local spins to the understanding of the genre.

I will return to Baillie's œuvre with a discussion of *Witchcraft*, a play that Scullion describes as "most unusual, notable for a distinctive and sustained attempt at linguistic realism . . . Although ponderously plotted it is unexpectedly intriguing, something of a psychological thriller set against a backdrop of religious intolerance" (Scullion 1996: lviii). For now, however, I want to look at Elizabeth Polack, a dramatist far less visible than Baillie and her known dramatic production much less extensive; her two "known" plays, however, *Esther, The Royal Jewess* (first produced in 1835 at the Pavilion Theatre) and *St. Clair of the Isles* (first produced in 1838 at the [Royal] Victoria Theatre) might both be seen as challenging the conventional scope of melodramatic form. John Franceschina, in whose wittily entitled *Sisters of Gore: Seven Gothic Melodramas by British Women, 1790–1843*[3] *St. Clair of the Isles* appears, attaches the nomination "the first Jewish woman melodramatist in England" to his introduction of Polack and the play (Franceschina 1997: 227).[4]

Franceschina goes on to point out that almost nothing is known of Polack's life and that two of her five known plays are lost. In itself, this information brings into focus Polack's outsider status, a fact that is surely underscored by the marking of her Jewish identity. *Esther, the Royal Jewess* was produced in March 1835 at the Pavilion Theatre in the East End of London, an important theatre for melodrama and one which drew a predominantly local audience; it was also the neighborhood in which the Polack family lived. This, like the performance of *The Family Legend* for Edinburgh audiences, gives Polack's play purchase on a specificity of viewing public, an intimate local knowledge. Moreover, as Franceschina points out, Polack modifies the genre of "Eastern melodrama" in two significant ways:

Two facts set *Esther* apart from other Eastern melodramas: the heroine is, in fact, the hero of the piece, and the exoticism is Jewish rather than Turkish. Both these issues culminate in the final speech of the play (usually reserved for the male hero or masculine symbol of restored order) where Esther exalts her victory as well as her people: "Blessed be this hour! happy be my king! and prosperous be the Jews of every land and clime! May the sacred tree of liberty never lose a branch in contending for religious superiority; but all be free to worship as he pleases. Let that man be forever despised who dares interfere between his fellow man and his creed. Oh, people of my nation, may the heart promised home you've sighed for present you golden hours of freedom; and down to posterity may the sons of Judah in every clime celebrate this time in happy Purim!" (1997: 229)

Esther's reference to "Jews of every land and clime" indicates a consciousness of the *actual* experience of at least some of her spectatorship (Jewish communities lived close by the Pavilion) as well as an appetency for that experience to be one that is less marginalized and criticized, a response perhaps to a tradition of nonconformism in that part of London. Moreover, notwithstanding the religious specificity of Esther's speech, her heroism in the play as a whole offers not a little irony in her claims for "the *sons* of Judah" (my emphasis) and, as such, an irony that would be underscored by her own corporeal presence front and center stage in the play's denouement. While *Esther* makes gender explicit through the play's

eponymous hero(ine), *St. Clair of the Isles* redistributes similar questions through three particular appearances of "woman" in the
geographical context of Scotland.

If the triumphant Esther characterized Polack's earlier play, in *St.
Clair of the Isles* the playwright attempts to work from the other end of
the melodramatic scale: to craft a thoroughly wicked villainess who
controls the action of the plot. While Polack had already shifted
genre for her adaptation of Elizabeth Helme's romance novel of the
same name, she also regendered typical characters in melodrama.
Beyond making the villain a villainess (and one, incidentally, far more
wicked than the novel's original), *St. Clair of the Isles* involves two other
female bodies: one, the character of Ambrosine, whose first appearances in the play are in cross-gender dress but who will eventually
appear as St. Clair's wife; the other, the key figure of Randolph
(supposedly the son of St. Clair, the revelation of whose "true"
identity forms the climax of the play), who was in the premiere
performance played by a woman (Mrs. Loveday). As Franceschina
suggests in a rather understated way: "As even a cursory reading of
the play will indicate, *St. Clair of the Isles* is not a typical 'tortured
heroine' melodrama" (1997: 230). Women, here, are subjects and not
objects of the situation presented.

From the play's opening moment, the resolute villainy of Lady
Roskelyn is palpable – as is her "inappropriate" command of her
husband, as well as her refusal of what is naturally right by way of a
politically wrought justification of her pathological contempt for St.
Clair:

LORD ROSKELYN: Lady of Roskelyn, I once more advise you to cease this
    persecution of the outlaw, St. Clair Monteith; the time is arrived for
    the payment of his demand on our agent and though it has pleased
    James of Scotland to proscribe him and his companions; we have no
    right to refuse his claim to his own property; you will therefore order
    Carnegie to satisfy St. Clair's demand.
LADY ROSKELYN: Never, my lord; the estate and property devolve to us by
    the king's will, and till he commands, they shall not be restored. If St.
    Clair of Monteith dare impugn the mandate of King James, I shall
    find means to silence him.   (Act i Scene i)

The plot of *St. Clair of the Isles* is thus concentrated on those very
means by which Lady Roskelyn endeavors to effect her politically
sanctioned but intrinsically wrong actions. Polack's construction of
such a resolute and unabashed villain is impressively determined:

she exceeds in both quantity and quality the kinds of villainy typical for male scoundrel of contemporary melodrama. Lady Roskelyn is never for a moment a sympathetic character, nor do we ever get more than a glimpse of self-doubt or repentance. Even when, in the play's penultimate scene, she is finally rejected by her husband, the sorrow she claims lasts but a fleeting second until she is once again caught up in her revenge plot:

LADY ROSKELYN: But may I not behold my boy [Randolph] once more?
LORD ROSKELYN: It cannot be – I would not have him know his mother's crimes. I have burst the trammels that made me thy slave so long, and he shall never be another victim. Lady of Roskelyn, farewell, for now we part for ever. [*Exit*]
LADY ROSKELYN: I have deserved all this, and yet the blow falls heavily upon me. It was St. Clair who bore away the child, and had he not a right to injure them who injured him? have I not been his most inveterate foe – and dare I murmur that he has taken vengeance for his wrongs? [*Enter* BRIDGET]
BRIDGET: The lady Ambrosine craves an audience of your ladyship.
LADY ROSKELYN: 'Tis St. Clair's wife, why comes she here? No matter, I will see her. [*Exit* BRIDGET] Perhaps she will ask his life, but she has come in vain. (Act 3 Scene 2)

The fierce exchange between the two women (Lady Roskelyn refusing Ambrosine's plea) constitutes Lady Roskelyn's last appearance on stage. The final scene turns away from her effective engineering of the plot to offer a conventionally melodramatic conclusion to the play. In this last scene, where St. Clair is awaiting execution, we encounter Lord Roskelyn's reconciliation with St. Clair as well as his expressed hope that St. Clair might be saved. At this point the revelation of Randolph's true identity is made as he intervenes in the execution and takes the bullet intended for St. Clair. The tragedy of the story is cemented by the royal declaration that arrives too late to save Roskelyn's son and which restores title and properties to St. Clair. Notwithstanding the conventionality of this ending, I wonder what effect is produced by the physical fact of Randolph "as a" woman. Polack's play, I would suggest, oscillates between seeing and believing. This, of course, is literalized in the crux of her plot: Randolph is identifiable *only* through recourse to a birthmark on his right arm. What Polack achieves is an elaboration of that principle through the performance of gender more generally in her text, where received generic expectations are reversed and problematized. There is, I think, some difficulty in believing what we see in this play – a customary reliance on the "truth" of the visual is steadily undermined by what actually happens.

Once again, however, performance history is a telling counterpart to the potentialities of the playwright's script. Like Baillie's *The Family Legend* in the hands of Sir Walter Scott, *St. Clair of the Isles* recognizes the dramatic appeal of Scotland and is at pains to offer its London audience the full tartan spectacle. Costume notes offer much detail of plaids and tartans as well as several costume changes for St. Clair, Lord Roskelyn, and Ambrosine. Yet, according to the account published as "Remarks" that appears just before the script itself, the Victoria Theatre performance was far from a success:

> We are free to confess that we anticipated a milk and water concern, but Miss Polack, the fair authoress of *St. Clair of the Isles*, agreeably disappointed us. – The present production does her infinite credit, and although palpably taken from the novel of the same name, the incidents are so well strung together, and the interest so well preserved, that, not to award our mite of approbation to the lady would be as ungallant, as unjust. Out of consideration to her feelings, we will not criticize the performers who played in the piece, for ... the performers introduced into this melodrama, would have disgraced a barn. By the way the bills of the night announced a grand Tournament! All we can say, is, if there was one introduced on the stage, the filth and dirt of the scenery, obscured it from our vision – for we saw none. The manner in which this piece was gotten up must have sorely grieved Miss Polack, but, we believe blue stocking ladies care little about the "appliances to boot." (Franceschina 1997: 237)

I quote this passage at some length because it gives a remarkable account of an apparent gap between the potentialities of script and the realities of that script's performance. Whatever the actual conditions of performance, this critic's dismissal of Polack's interest in the mechanics prejudges her ability to be an active participant in its realization.

Polack's recourse to a Scottish setting gave her access to a world always already outside the hegemony of English cultural production, to a site of danger/threat which acts, as Franceschina has indicated, as a displacement of her own outsider identity as a Jew (1997: 230). Multiplication of gender dissonance within the action of *St. Clair of the Isles* enacts a doubling of that outsider status, to place gender on a par with ethnicity. Cross-dressing (masquerade) and cross-gender casting had, of course, an already well-established theatrical history in the context of the comic and the burlesque, as well as in emphasizing heroism in tragedy; Polack, however, spins the convention to effect an intensity of wickedness. The final scene, despite the pathos of Randolph's death, is almost anticlimactic without the considerable presence of the villainess – it is as if Polack refused Lady Roskelyn's containment by the events of the plot and left her, somewhere outside the action, as an out of control object whose existence might yet surface to undo St. Clair's restitution.

Notwithstanding the subtleties of Polack's revisionist melodrama, it is more important to record what happened after her authoring of *St. Clair of the Isles*. Nothing. Polack wrote no other plays and disappeared from any record of involvement in the theatre. Franceschina writes: "Nothing is known about Miss Polack after the presentation of this play. Perhaps she married, came into money, or was forced to assume familial responsibilities due to the death of a relative. All we know is that no play bearing her name was produced in London after *St. Clair* in 1838" (1997: 232). Or was it the nasty and damning rhetoric of at least one reviewer, determined to find failure in the public display of her script, that persuaded Polack to stay away from future ventures? In *Esther* and *St. Clair*, Polack crafted strong and unmistakable representations of what it means to appear according to one's regulated identity. Whatever the reason(s) for her departure from the theatre, it seems symptomatic of the critical fate of women dramatic writers generally that Polack's disappearance should be so complete.

The condition is reproduced in Joanna Baillie's career. The sparse if often quoted praise from Byron who wrote "Women (saving Joanna Baillie) cannot write tragedy" (Webb 1986: 41) suggests how hard it was to be taken seriously as a woman playwright. The lack of success of Baillie's plays after *De Monfort* suggests that Gwenn Davis and Beverly Joyce's assertion that she was one of the "literary aristocracy" (1992: xii) is perhaps overstated. Nonetheless, the striation of gender with class positionality is important: rather as Polack was simultaneously limited and criticized as a "blue-stocking," Baillie is "elevated" into a literary aristocracy under terms and conditions which she was bound, at least biologically, to fail. Even more pertinent are Baillie's own claims about her chosen profession, made in the "Introductory Discourse." Her commentary seems uncannily prescient of the actual unfolding of her own dramatic career:

It may, perhaps, be supposed, from my publishing these plays, that I have written them for the closet rather than the stage. If, upon perusing them with attention, the reader is disposed to think they are better calculated for the first than the last, let him impute it to want of skill in the author, and not to any previous design. A play but of small poetical merit, that is suited to strike and interest the spectator, to catch the attention of him who will not, and of him who cannot read, is a more valuable and useful production than one whose elegant and harmonious pages are admired in the libraries of the tasteful and refined. To have received approbation from an audience of my countrymen, would have been more pleasing to me than any other praise.

([1851]1976a: 16)

Far from intending her work for a literary aristocracy, it is evident that Baillie had remarkably populist goals for her dramatic creations. Mellor makes the pertinent observation that populist is for Baillie the "middling and lower class." In other words, to participate in theatre "as a" woman is, not surprisingly, to address the world as a bourgeois subject. What I want to argue, however, is that it is precisely at the intersection of nationality and class that Baillie can best interrogate the effects of gender in the production of genre. It is, as Michael Hays and Anastasia Nikolopoulou argue, the juxta-position of "different 'horizons' of understanding and desire" (1996: xiv) that allows the questioning (but not displacement) of a dominant horizon (here, tragedy; in Hays and Nikolopoulou's study, melo-drama). But, before elucidating the implications of Baillie's desire to present a "popular" theatre, I would like to look briefly at one of Baillie's unproduced dramas, *Witchcraft* (1836).

In very many ways, *Witchcraft* is a startling text, not so much revising the category of tragedy as reinventing it. The scope of Baillie's ambition to do things differently is perhaps no better realized anywhere than in this text. There are many conventional devices: standard settings (here, variously and among others, a moor, a miserable cottage, a cave, a marketplace prepared for execution), offstage renditions of ominous storms, and the frequent citation and rendition of the supernatural. What is different about Baillie's reference to these commonplaces is her perception of the psychology that motivates and performs such a world. It is interesting, too, to note Baillie's impetus for the play, something she explains in a footnote to the play's title. She writes:

The subject of this drama was first suggested to me by reading that very curious and original scene in the "Bride of Lammermuir," when the old women, after the division of largess given at a funeral, are so dissatisfied with their share of it, and wonder that the devil, who helps other wicked people willing to serve him, has never bestowed any power or benefits upon them. It appeared to me that the gifted author had come within one step of accounting for a very extraordinary circumstance, frequently recorded in trials for the crime of witchcraft, – the accused themselves acknowledging the crime, and their having had actual intercourse with Satan and other wicked spirits. This was a confession that was sure to be followed by a cruel death, and the conjectures produced to account for it have never been satisfactory. (Baillie [1836]1976b: 613)

This passage is surely revealing in its implication that *Witchcraft* will take that one step that Scott's novel would not (or could not).[5] Baillie goes on to note that she had tried to persuade Scott to pursue this project and failed. I would argue that while for Scott this scene is one that is primarily interesting insofar as it serves the course of his novel, for Baillie this is a springboard into a consideration of the brute events of history (women did get put to death as witches) and the psychological circumstances which underpin such events. Her project, it might be said, is grounded not in the Gothic supernatural but in a historical reality that has had particular consequences for women.

Baillie creates an impressive range of women characters in *Witchcraft*, including the aristocratic Lady Dungarren, the villainous Annabella, and three "reputed witches," Grizeld Bane, Mary Macmurren, and Elspy Low. The energy of much of their transgressive behavior carries an otherwise laborious plot to startling and provocative moments. It is hard to find any place of sympathy, far less empathy. In their stead there is a relentless pursuit of the play's subject under which the various schemes of the plot might be stage-managed (so to speak). Moreover, Baillie demarcates her characters very specifically, through linguistic competence. Unlike verse tragedies such as *The Family Legend*, this play is constructed as a prose tragedy and Baillie takes great pains to develop a hierarchy of voice through both vocabulary and accent which renders an accurate portrayal of the social behavior of her geographical setting, Renfrewshire in Scotland. Baillie writes:

The language made use of, both as regards the lower and higher characters, is pretty nearly that which prevailed in the West of Scotland about the period assigned to the event, or at least soon after it; and that the principal witch spoke differently from the other two, is rendered probable from her being a stranger, and her rank in life unknown. Even in those days the well-educated classes were distinguished from their neighbours on the south side of the Tweed, by their accent and pronunciation, rather than any actual difference of words. (Baillie [1836] 1976b: 613)

What Baillie is claiming here is a realism for her characters' voices, one which might give an authenticity to the experiences presented in her play. She eschews the received sensibilities of dramatic speech in favor of a mode which she believes can more accurately give insight into the lives and beliefs of her subject characters. This, it seems to me, is radical in a way that the early (male) European proponents of naturalism have been claimed to be. Baillie's drama – while retaining a surface of conventions that would ally her writing to predominant modes of early nineteenth-century England – is inventing a new articulation of experiences which has, like, for example, Gerhard Hauptmann's *The Weavers* (1892), a particular claim on the significance of "the real."[6] *Witchcraft* locates subjectivity in the very social formation of community, and while Mellor is in many ways right to see Baillie's concern with the middle to lower classes, what needs to be stressed here is Baillie's consciousness of delineation among those social groups. Moreover, it is a delineation that is always aware of gender. Once again, unlike the observed unities and goals of universality in traditional tragic drama, Baillie manipulates the genre to spotlight particularities and differences.

In *Witchcraft*, no one character dominates the action. Instead, the play accumulates voices until a cacophonous denouement in which almost everyone's voice is struggling to be heard above another's and the vindictive crowd encircle the stake where purported witch Mary Macmurren is tethered. The Sheriff's concluding address seems both unconvincing and irrelevant given the heightened expression of passion that has been witnessed on stage immediately before: the death of Annabella, the seizing of Grizeld Bane, the revelation of Murrey and the emotional reconciliation with Dungarren. He says: "Good people, be pacified; and instead of the burning of a witch, ye shall have six hogsheads of ale set abroach at the cross, to drink the health of Violet Murrey, and a grand funeral into the bargain" (Act 5 Scene 2, Baillie[1836]1976b: 642–43). The play's remaining lines go to Dungarren who, it might be said, explicitly articulates the very trajectory that the play itself has followed, its very unsuitability to appear on stage at all: "Forbear, sheriff: the body of this unhappy lady [Annabella] is no subject for pageantry. She shall be interred with decent privacy; and those who

have felt the tyranny of uncontrolled passions will think, with
conscious awe, of her end" (Act 5 Scene 2: 643).

It is easy in the case of *Witchcraft* to concur with Jeffrey Cox's claim
that Baillie's plays "explore the power that literary representations –
and particularly dramatic ones – have to fix women within a particular
cultural gaze. Her plays do not merely offer alternative images of
women; they offer a critique of various conventional modes of drama-
tizing women" (Cox 1992: 52–53). It seems to me that it is precisely
because Baillie's women are to be dramatized, that is embodied, that
they so challenge the conventions of genre and the nature of
spectacle. In effect, they do precisely what Hazlitt says: they speak
virtue and act vice (although not at all in the manner that he means).

Davis and Joyce write that nineteenth-century theatre "Audiences
loved happy endings, the marriage of comedy, the perils narrowly
averted of melodrama, the remote sacrifices of historical tragedy. It
was not a place for advocacy, but women writers did use it to express
their major concerns" (1992: xviii). Through the texts cited here, I
argue that Baillie and Polack rely on "generic mutability" (Hays and
Nikolopoulou 1996: xiv) – that is, their genre trouble determinedly
refers to the ideological and historical bases on which the production
of theatre was, at specific cultural moments and in specific geographical locations, made possible. This suggests that women playwrights made attempts to challenge in public the representation of
hegemonic cultural codes expressed in those genres which had
hitherto been claimed by men for their own (serious) concerns.
Otherwise the production methodologies and repertory commitments of male theatre managers provided an often less than
satisfactory life for these women's texts.

The samples given here from the œuvres of Joanna Baillie and
Elizabeth Polack are intended to suggest some of the grounds on
which these women troubled genre. These playwrights put the
spotlight on specific, localized concerns, those borne by a body and
voice marked by ethnicity and gender. To return to Baillie's epigraph
to *De Monfort* which opened this chapter – specifically its hope that
men would let a woman's "Dramatic Saplin 'scape your Rage"
(quoted in Cox 1992: 234) – it would seem that the theatre did not
provide the necessary husbandry for the hybrid genres that Baillie,
Polack, and other nineteenth-century women developed. Though
their theatre contemporaries apparently could not cope with the

genre trouble these women caused, it is crucial for theatre history that we now apprehend our responsiveness to these women's concerns rather than, one more time, reproducing the straightjacket (or is that corset?) of the categorization of dramatic genres.

NOTES

1 Hazlitt has much to say in praise of Wordsworth and Scott, of course; consider, by constrast, Hannah More, of whom he says merely that she "is another celebrated modern poetess, and I believe still living. She has written a greal deal which I have never read" (1910: 147).

2 Alexander Murdoch and Richard B. Sher's essay on "Literary and Learned Culture" outlines the complexity of Scottish culture in the late eighteenth and early nineteenth centuries. Their discussion of "Scottish cultural confidence and achievement" (1988: 127) points to a productive tension in the very term "Scottish enlightenment," at once recognizing its international ambitions (with English as its lingua franca) along with its resolutely Scottish aspects.

3 The title is a lovely play both on the conventions of the genre he is anthologizing and on Catherine Gore, author of two of the plays in this seven-text volume.

4 *St. Clair of the Isles* is an adaptation of Elizabeth Helme's novel of 1803. Polack's stage play was featured in the repertoire of the Royal Victoria Theatre (now the Old Vic) in London for three weeks in 1838.

5 Anastasia Nikolopoulou suggests that conventions of prose narrative require the plots of Scott's novels to effect closure while adaptations of those same novels (she discusses *The Bride of Lammermoor* and *Guy Mannering*), because of "fragmented structure of the melodrama, contest political realities" (see Hays and Nikolopoulou 1996: xi and 121–43).

6 In passing it is perhaps worth noting that such experiments with language have often characterized women's playwriting and have equally often consigned that same playwriting to a minority interest or, at least, to a received opinion of its limited appeal. One thinks especially of the dismissive critical attitudes towards Augusta (Lady) Gregory's dramatic experiments with Irish language and dialect.

REFERENCES

Baillie, Joanna [1851] 1976a, "Introductory Discourse," in *The Dramatic and Poetical Works of Joanna Baillie*, Hildesheim: Georg Olms, 1–17.
Baillie, Joanna [1836] 1976b, *Witchcraft, in The Dramatic and Poetical Works of Joanna Baillie* (1851), Hildesheim: Georg Olms, 613–42.
Baillie, Joanna [1810] 1996, *The Family Legend*, in Scullion 1996, 3–74.
Cameron, Alasdair 1988, "Scottish Drama in the Nineteenth Century," *The*

History of Scottish Literature, vol. IV, *The Nineteenth Century*, ed. Douglas Gifford, Aberdeen: Aberdeen University Press.

Carlson, Julie A. 1994, *In the Theatre of Romanticism: Coleridge, Nationalism, Women*, Cambridge: Cambridge University Press.

Cox, Jeffrey N. (ed.) 1992, *Seven Gothic Dramas 1789–1825*, Athens, OH: Ohio University Press.

Davis, Gwenn, and Beverly A. Joyce 1992, *Drama by Women to 1900: A Bibliography of American and British Writers*, Toronto and Buffalo: University of Toronto Press.

Donkin, Ellen 1995, *Getting into the Act: Women Playwrights in London 1776–1829*, London and New York: Routledge.

Foucault, Michel 1972, *The Archaelogy of Knowledge and The Discourse of Language*, trans. A. M. Sheridan Smith, New York: Pantheon.

Franceschina, John (ed.) 1997, *Sisters of Gore: Seven Gothic Melodramas by British Women, 1790–1843*, New York and London: Garland.

Hays, Michael, and Anastasia Nikolopoulou (eds.) 1996, *Melodrama: The Cultural Emergence of a Genre*, New York: St. Martin's Press.

Hazlitt, William 1910, *Lectures on English Poets: The Spirit of the Age*, London: J. M. Dent.

Hazlitt, William 1930–34, *Collected Works*, ed. P. P. Howe, 21 vols., London: J. M. Dent.

Helme, Elizabeth [1803] 1867, *St. Clair of the Isles*. London: Frederick Warne.

Irigaray, Luce 1985, *Speculum of the Other Woman*, trans. Gillian Gill, Ithaca, NY: Cornell University Press.

"Life of Joanna Baillie" [1851] 1976, preface to *The Dramatic and Poetical Works of Joanna Baillie*, Hildesheim and New York: Georg Olms, i–xx.

Mellor, Anne K. 1994, "Joanna Baillie and the Counter-Public Sphere," *Studies in Romanticism*, 33.4: 559–67.

Murdoch, Alexander, and Richard B. Sher 1988, "Literary and Learned Culture," *People and Society in Scotland*, ed. T. M. Devine and Rosalind Mitchison, Edinburgh: John Donald, 127–42.

Pistotnik, Vesna 1985, "Towards a Redefinition of Dramatic Genre and Stage History," *Modern Drama*, 28.4 (December): 677–87.

Polack, Elizabeth [1835?], *Esther, the Royal Jewess*, London: Dancombe.

Polack, Elizabeth [1840?]1997, *St. Clair of the Isles*, in Franceschina 1997, 225–84.

Sampson, George 1970, *The Concise Cambridge History of English Literature*, Cambridge: Cambridge University Press.

Scullion, Adrienne (ed.) 1996, *Female Playwrights of the Nineteenth Century*, London: Everyman.

Stewart, Susan 1984, *On Longing: Narratives of the Miniature, the Gigantic, the Souvenir, the Collection*, Baltimore: Johns Hopkins University Press.

Webb, Timothy 1986, "The Romantic Poet and the Stage: A Short, Sad History," *The Romantic Theatre: An International Symposium*, ed. Richard Allen Cave, Gerrards Cross, Bucks: Colin Smythe, 9–46.

CHAPTER 11

Sappho in the closet

Denise A. Walen

The nineteenth century witnessed a swell of performative texts which presented the character of Sappho, with many written as closet dramas by women authors.[1] These writers were poets and translators who appropriated the dramatic genre, but whose primary obligation was to a reader, not to performance. Catherine Godwin's play was published posthumously, though a brief version appeared in print before her death. Lucy Cumming translated plays and, though she wrote essays and poetry, wrote no original dramas of her own. Estelle Lewis published poetry and essays as well as two plays, and although her *Sappho* was thought to be stage-worthy no evidence exists that it was acted in England (Lewis 1876: afterword 1–8). Actually, a clear distinction between plays meant for performance and those meant for publication is difficult to make in regard to nineteenth-century drama, since there was easy and accepted slippage between what poetic or lyric drama would and would not appear on the stage (Nicoll 1955: vol. IV, 191). However, in the case of some women it seems that self-censorship was one reason they did not write for the theatres. Godwin is self-deprecating in her emphasis that her work is merely a dramatic "sketch" (Godwin 1854: 3), while Cumming's biographer makes it clear that no woman of good breeding would entertain "literary ambitions" or engage in a "conscious self-display" (Merriam 1890: vi). In reading these Sappho plays I was intrigued that texts in which I saw potentially subversive sexual representations would also subvert the readerly expectations of their audience. I began to theorize a project supporting illicit pleasure cloaked in genteel respectability; more specifically, I began to wonder about the signs of sexual transgression embedded in the texts.

These plays, as was the convention of closet drama in general, focus on the "passions" of the title character (Nicoll 1955: vol. IV,

193; Burroughs 1997: 86–89; Richardson 1988: 1–19). An individual was meant to quietly immerse her or himself in a careful contemplation of the main character's psychological struggle. The dramatic emphasis for plays dealing with Sappho rested on the internal conflict between love and fame which the character endured. Focusing on the thematic elements of the drama, specifically love, brings to light the transgressive potential of these texts. A thematic approach uncovers how the conventional heterosexual pairings get subverted when a nonheterosexual subject position is introduced into the narrative. This strategy also seems appropriate since the form of closet drama encouraged studied consideration of the text.

Identification of these Sappho plays as closet drama has a significant bearing on the potential to read homoerotic characters in the playwrights' projects. Shuo-Ren Wang, in his *Theatre of the Mind*, defines closet drama as a form that uses language rather than visual representation to communicate ideas, and which relies on the reader's imagination for its full appreciation (1990: xxiii). He goes on to express his belief that closet drama exceeds the practical restrictions of the physical theatre and can present the theatrically unfeasible (xxiii). Closet drama, according to Wang, has the potential to express what is physically impossible to present on the actual stage. The lesbian subject has often been rendered invisible in drama, and is, if not impossible, at least extremely difficult to represent on stage, given the infrequency with which she appears in the great breadth of the drama. Closet drama, then, becomes an obvious choice for women playwrights seeking to surmount the restraints of the traditional theatre. As a transgressive practice, it is theorized by Catherine Burroughs in her *Closet Stages* (1997: 10). Burroughs sees female playwrights as more comfortable with the theatrical potential of their closet dramas and less inclined to distinguish between the closet and the stage. However, she does specifically mention Joanna Baillie's use of closet drama as a literal space in which to work out issues of gender and sexuality (16). Burroughs also draws specific connections between the practice of closet drama and the contemporary associations of the word *closet* with queer theory (106–9).

The closet for the playwright, as well as the closet for the reader, becomes a private, intimate space in which the complexities of gender and sexuality might be explored in the safety of the imagination. Of course, women playwrights who wrote closet dramas, like Lord Byron, might have been engaging in a literary pursuit as a project to distance themselves from what they perceived as vulgar theatre audiences (Wang 1990: 1–7). Writing closet drama may have been a choice by these women to write themselves into a literary rather than a theatrical tradition. Or, seeing the stage filled with comedies and melodramas, women desiring to write tragedy may have turned to closet drama out of necessity. Most of the chapters in this book discuss women playwrights writing comedies, melodramas, burlesques, and extravaganzas for the theatre. Women who wrote tragedy seem to have preferred the genre of closet drama, although many women playwrights, like Baillie, may have intended their plays for production (Burroughs 1997: 8–17). Of course, it may be that women who could not, or did not care to, struggle within the male dominant theatre system of nineteenth-century England utilized closet drama as an option to writing for the stage. Alternately, as Burroughs suggests, closet drama may not refer to unacted play scripts, but, as Joanna Baillie theorized, to plays which required intimate theatrical spaces, and naturalistic acting techniques to appropriately depict the intense personal emotions of an individual character's private life (86–91). Women writers may have turned to closet drama in nineteenth-century England for any combination of reasons, none of which preclude them from exploring transgressive gender and sexuality within their texts.

This chapter looks at instances of female homoerotic desire in dramatically based texts about Sappho (re)constructed by female writers during the nineteenth century. I define lesbian desire as a woman's longing for intimacy with another woman, combining various levels of emotional, physical, psychical and carnal impulses.[2] In these texts especially, acknowledging desire is paramount since the heterosexual imperative which drives dominant narratives denies realization outside a heterosexual dynamic. Unconsummated desire is all that is possible since the lesbian is always erased; Sappho always jumps from the Leucadian promontory to her death. The site of lesbian transgression in these texts is decentered. Lesbian desire exists on the margins of (sub)plots/(sub)texts, in latent characters and barely repressed liminal situations. Terry Castle, in *The Apparitional Lesbian*, theorizes the difficulty of "seeing" the lesbian subject. The lesbian, who Castle believes existed in premodern literature, is an intangible phantom whose identity emerges from suggestion and implication, although even when she is patently visible she is neglected and unrecognized by the viewing audience (1993: 1–19).

The work of Marilyn R. Farwell has demonstrated the possibility of reading lesbian subtexts in otherwise heterosexual plots (1990: 91–103). Farwell's theory in *Heterosexual Plots and Lesbian Narratives* is that a lesbian subject becomes the center of a lesbian narrative which disrupts the central narrative of the dominant heterosexual plot (1996: 23–24). Similarly, Lillian Faderman calls for the expansion of the lesbian literary canon to include texts, even premodern texts, that encode lesbian subject matter, whether or not centrally located in the text (1995: 49–59). A project that identifies how women writers, whether consciously or not, subverted dominant ideologies regarding gender and sexuality, even though the dominant discourse has positioned itself centrally in the narrative fiction of the past, privileges a lesbian reading; it evokes a suppressed longing. Reading the lesbian desire, working to make it visible, resists the effacement of that desire by the larger readerly audience.

The plots of these Sappho plays revolve around the Sappho and Phaon myth popularized by Ovid in epistle 15 of *Heroides*. Ovid's myth takes the form of a letter which Sappho writes to Phaon in which she acknowledges her love for this younger man, and whose affection she considers more important than her poetry, who has, in fact, made her forget all the women she previously desired. The letter identifies the two as past lovers, and confesses Phaon's rejection of Sappho and his flight to Sicily to pursue other women. The letter ends with Sappho's promise to jump from the Leucadian cliff tops if Phaon does not return to her. This myth was taken by many, during the early and mid-nineteenth century for historical fact.[3] However, the Phaon story was much debated, and by the end of the nineteenth century the story of Sappho's ruinous heterosexual passion was discarded.[4] Still, nineteenth-century women writers privileged the Phaon story, constructing various versions that read either more or less homoerotically.

The character of Sappho was connected with homosexual or homophilic desire in England during both the eighteenth and nineteenth centuries. Alexander Pope's 1707 translation of Ovid's epistle mentions Sappho's "guilty love" for the women of Lesbos (quoted in Wharton 1885: 164). Pierre Bayle, in the 1738 English translation of his *Dictionary Historical and Critical*, which was often reissued, states that Sappho's "amorous passion extended even to the persons of her own sex, and this is that for which she was most cried down" ([1738] 1984: 45). Bayle cites Pope's translation of Ovid for proof of her lesbian desire, and he identifies her as a "tribade," though he credits the Phaon myth (45–46). Emma Donoghue, in her exhaustive study of lesbian culture in Britain during the seventeenth and eighteenth centuries, identifies *Sappho* as a term applied to women who desired other women (1996: 4, 243–68). She concludes that the educated classes in English society had knowledge of Sappho's sexuality (4). Towards the end of the eighteenth century she sees a shift away from the extensive use of variants of Sappho to identify lesbian desire, to a more refined, if repressive, conception of the character and veiled allusions to lesbian practice (262). However, during the mid-nineteenth century, in his dictionary of Greek and Roman biography, William Smith could question, with obvious concern, "the relations of Sappho to those of her own sex" (1849: 708). He identifies that the nature of those relations cannot be ascertained, but he raises the specter of female same-sex sexual activity. William Mure, also at mid-century, in the third of his five-volume work on the *History of the Language and Literature of Antient [sic] Greece,* believed that contemporary scholarship on Sappho was attempting to conceal her homosexuality (1854: 315–18). In a section discussing Sappho's "relations to her female associates" he identifies female homosexuality as "the Lesbian vice," and cites Sappho's poetry as evidence of her sexual attraction to women (315–18). Further, a homoerotic image of Sappho was envisioned by at least one artist of the nineteenth century known to inhabit the homosexual sphere of 1860s Oxford. Simeon Solomon's 1864 painting, *Sappho and Erinna in the Garden Mytelene,* images a patently homoerotic scene of Sappho embracing another woman (see Stein 1981: 296; DeJean 1989: 225).[5] Finally, and perhaps not surprisingly, "The Loves of Sappho" is the title of a pornographic serial essay which appeared in the London weekly *Exquisite* during 1842. Starting with a history of Sappho, the work depicts heterosexual fantasies of sex between women (see Norton 1992: 249).

Sappho seems to have always been associated with transgressive desire for her own sex. In "The Seven Ages of Sappho," Linda Semple examines chronologically the constructions of Sappho from ancient Greece to contemporary times. She reads the nineteenth century as a period where Sappho's identity was hotly contested. Though her poetry was almost universally applauded, her character was either questioned, canonized, or accepted by a small group for its sexual transgressiveness (Semple 1994: 23–28; Jay and Lewis

1996: 11). In fact, the nineteenth century saw a vigorous debate concerning the sexual morality of Sappho (Wharton 1885: 1–44; Foster 1985: 21). Attempts were made to purify the poet's image through careful heterosexual bowdlerizations of her poetry and mythic reconstructions of her life. Typical of the Victorian restoration effort on Sappho's behalf is the biographical entry by Mary Cowden Clarke in her *World Noted Women*, which discredits the historical accuracy of the Phaon narrative. Clarke chastises the translators and commentators who have "construed into vilest meaning" Sappho's poems, and used them as "the ground of the most odious imputations" against Sappho (1858: 15). Clarke concludes her biographical sketch by asserting that "Sappho is a shining exemplar of glowing womanhood" (21). Despite such efforts to sanctify Sappho's reputation, as Ruth Vanita argues in *Sappho and the Virgin Mary; Same-Sex Love and the English Literary Imagination*, since her lesbian desire was an identifiable passion in eighteenth-century England, it was accessible in the nineteenth century (1997: 41–50). By the end of the nineteenth century, critics could acknowledge the debate regarding Sappho, but still had no clear image of Sappho's moral character (Thompson 1894: 368).[6]

In most recent criticism, the debate regarding Sappho and her constructions remains. Joan DeJean, in her admirable study of Sappho in France, perceives the nineteenth century as an era which liberated Sappho from the disrespect of previous generations, and constructed her as chaste and pure (1989: 201, 210, 230). She writes specifically that Sappho was interpreted as virginal in England by the end of the nineteenth century (210). However, in discussing the reconstructions of Sappho in England during the period, the only examples she offers are from representations that posit Sappho's homosexuality (222–27). Sappho's image appears, more appropriately, to have been in flux in England, moving simultaneously through the disrepute of promiscuity and sexual transgression to chaste purity. As Susan Brown writes in her study of Sappho in Victorian women's poetry, England witnessed a range of texts representing various moral constructions of Sappho, and by the end of the nineteenth century Sappho was being represented in England as homosexual (1994: 217–18). At least one commentator blames the theories of sexologists such as Richard von Krafft-Ebbing and Havelock Ellis for the negative associations ascribed to Sappho's character by the end of the nineteenth century (Reynolds 1996: 306n).

The nineteenth century was an era when women could express and respond to homoerotically charged literary allusions. The work of Lillian Faderman and Carroll Smith-Rosenberg, though identifying emotional connections between women, has glossed those connections as "romantic," or roughly platonic (Smith-Rosenberg 1989: 269–70; Smith-Rosenberg 1985: 74–76; Faderman 1981: 145–277). However, Lisa Moore has written a compelling argument refuting Faderman and Smith-Rosenberg that identifies the erotic and sexual potential of nineteenth-century romantic friendship. Her article, " 'Something More Tender Still Than Friendship': Romantic Friendship in Early-Nineteenth-Century England," offers a reading of several diverse texts which support the existence of conscious female homosexual desire and the potential threat to heterosexuality implicit in that desire (1992: 499–520). Fictionalized texts about the Greek poet Sappho offered an excellent narrative position from which to fashion a lesbian subtext in dramatic form through the desire of female characters.

It is impossible to know which constructions of Sappho's character influenced the authors or readers of the following plays, though Estelle Lewis at least had read Bayle (xi), and both Catherine Godwin and Lewis mention researching the character (Lewis 1876: v–xi; Godwin 1854: 3). The image of the female writer sitting alone in her closet, translating or composing a play about Sappho and grappling with the variable constructions of the character available to her in nineteenth-century England, lends itself to the belief that she could, consciously or not, script a homoerotic subtext. Since the reader supplies her own visual image, becoming the director of her own mentally staged version of the text, the various constructions of Sappho's character must have also influenced her reading of the plays, and supports the potential for her reception of a homoerotically charged subtext. The intimacy of the closet and the imaginative capacity of closet drama provide a literal and figurative space for the representation and reception of lesbian desire.

The 1818 interpretation of the Sappho legend by the popular German playwright Franz Grillparzer, only the second of his many plays, was a favorite text for women to translate. Americans Eliza Buckminster Lee (1846), Edda Middleton (1858), and Ellen Frothingham (1876) rendered versions of Grillparzer's play into English. Lucy Caroline Cumming (later Smith) prepared a version of the script in England at mid-century. These translations are almost indistinguishable from each other save for minor points of wording. Prepared during the mid- to late nineteenth century, the translators generally meant the scripts as closet dramas to be read for their literary merit, not performed on the popular stage.[7] Lucy Cumming translated both French and German texts on occasion and turned to translation for an income out of economic necessity in 1854 when the family finances were ruined. At the age of thirty-six she moved with her family from Wales to Scotland, where she found steady work with the publisher Thomas Constable, who was the Scottish publisher to Victoria. He published her translation of Grillparzer's *Sappho* in 1855 (Merriam 1890: 150–71, 220–21).

The plot structure of these translations of Grillparzer is extremely simple. Sappho, accompanied by Phaon, a simple shepherd, returns triumphantly to Lesbos/Mytilene from poetic competition at the Olympia. Her talent and fame have overwhelmed Phaon, while his physical appearance and adoration captivate Sappho. Immediately upon seeing Phaon, Melitta, Sappho's favored young domestic slave, is also attracted to him. The developing relationship between Melitta and Phaon angers Sappho, who alternately attempts to murder Melitta and exile her. The play concludes when Sappho, after an almost instantaneous reversal, sanctions the union of Melitta and Phaon, and throws herself from a cliff into the sea.

The Grillparzer version is written in iambic pentameter, with love as the emotion that furthers the dramatic action of the plot. The supertextual message in these scripts is the dichotomy between fame and love. Early in Act 1 Sappho exclaims that in bringing Phaon with her she is "Gladly the laurel for the myrtle changing" (1.2.54).[8] She loses herself in her passion for Phaon and is only capable of recovering her identity through death, which is union with the gods. Sappho, in Grillparzer's play, though the heroine, incurs criticism for denying her talents and casting aside literature in favor of base love wasted in an unworthy affection.

Despite being constructed as a heterosexual plot, Grillparzer's text has homoerotic undertones. Phaon is the clear object of Sappho's physical desire, but her passionate affectional preference for Melitta complicates the lovers' triangle. Castle's *Apparitional Lesbian* has demonstrated how this kind of triangulated relationship involving two women and a man allows for a reading of lesbian desire between the two female characters (1993: 72–74). Melitta is Sappho's slave/ servant, who, orphaned and apparently sexually abused as a child, was purchased at a young age (2.3, 2.4.1–83). In the power dynamic that informs their relationship, desire is constructed oppositionally, with Sappho in a position of dominance over Melitta. Twice the text informs the reader that in dealing with Melitta, Sappho is both cruel and kind (1.5.26–40; 2.4.82–83). At first, Sappho offers this information herself, then Melitta validates the report, both establishing its credibility and indicating Sappho's potential to violent outburst. They relate to each other in the context of an oppressive system, and are able to negotiate that system only through emotionally dysfunctional, almost sadomasochistic practices.

Melitta is, throughout the play, the perfect submissive servant. She acquiesces to all of Sappho's commands and excuses any abuse she receives at Sappho's hands, continually searching for Sappho's acceptance. Melitta is controlled emotionally by Sappho throughout the play. At the end of Act 3, after Phaon has prevented Sappho from stabbing Melitta, Sappho is moved to tears. As Phaon attempts to remove Melitta from the scene, the young servant refuses to leave Sappho in distress:

MELITTA: Shall I my much-loved lady suffering see?
PHAON: Her spells work on me too. Away – away!
  Before her coils be further round thee cast.   *[Leading her away]*
  ...
MELITTA: [*returning and embracing her [Sappho's] knees*]:
  Look on me, Sappho! Take the rose – 'tis here;
  Take it, and take my life. Where is thy steel?   (3.4.164–69)

The connection between the two women is such that Melitta would exchange both lover and life to console Sappho. Melitta's willingness to die at her mistress's hand signifies the sadomasochism of their relationship. Melitta's desire to please and comfort Sappho continually subverts her passion for Phaon. When he determines to take her off the island she displays extreme reluctance to leave with him. By the end of the play Melitta is completely contrite and deferential, speaking more of her feelings for Sappho than of her love for Phaon. Kneeling to Sappho, Melitta says of her,

  If she thinks right, why, let me punish'd be;
  I will not even murmur 'gainst her will
  ...
  I only love her gifts
  ...
  Here will I kneel, till one dear gentle look,

One gracious word, bespeaks forgiveness mine.
How often have I lain here at her feet

...
I cannot live on if condemned by her.   (5.3.165–92)

Melitta finally gives up Phaon for Sappho, declaring, "Fallen the
darkness from mine eyes away. / Oh! let me be again thy child – thy
slave; / That which is thine possess it, and forgive" (5.6.2–4). The
homoerotic connection with Sappho displaces the heterosexual love.
Sappho emotionally manipulates Melitta, and the girl's affection is
so controlled by Sappho that Melitta relinquishes her agency and
mortality to Sappho. An attraction or affection exists between
Melitta and Sappho that frustrates the union Phaon attempts to
create with Melitta.

Sappho's attraction to Melitta is displayed in several instances in
the text. In the first, Sappho sexually taunts Melitta about her
attraction to Phaon. In Act 2, Eucharis, another servant, relates the
following story to Melitta:

> Wherefore at the feast
> Did Sappho with arch smile upon her lips
> Look towards thee and then cast down her eyes?
> Oft as she did so I could mark thee blush,
> And trembling with confusion and distress,
> Forget thy service at the festal board.   (2.2.14–19)

Sappho apparently takes great pleasure in Melitta's growing sexual
awareness, laughing when Melitta drops a cup of wine out of
awkward confusion. Phaon is an agent for Melitta's sexual arousal,
which Sappho voyeuristically enjoys. However, Phaon is a nonactive
member of the narrated scene, as the two women communicate the
sexual message between themselves. Sappho admits that of all the
female servants, "None has been better lov'd than she, Melitta"
(2.6.36). Later in the play, Sappho convinces herself that Melitta is
guileless in the relationship with Phaon and assuages any doubts she
has with a heartfelt speech to Melitta:

> come hither to my breast – come hither;
> I knew it well thou couldst not me betray –
> Not knowingly – not willingly betray.
> Oh! let our hearts upon each other beat,
> Our eyes be fixed upon a sister's eyes,
> Our very words be blended as our breath.   (3.4.56–61)

The language of the speech is impassioned and seductive. Sappho's affection for Melitta throughout the play is alternately mothering and amatory, suggesting an incestuous maternal affection. In the love triangle which Grillparzer constructs, Sappho demonstrates almost as much desire and affection for Melitta as she does for Phaon, and Melitta's confused attraction to Phaon is surpassed by her disturbing desire for Sappho.

The text also provides physical evidence to support the erotic connection between Sappho and Melitta. Throughout the play, the stage directions never identify Sappho and Phaon kissing or exchanging physical intimacies, rather Melitta is the object of physical expressions from both Phaon and Sappho. In Act 2 Scene 4, Phaon touches Melitta's shoulder, places a flower in her bosom, catches her during a fall, embraces her, and finally kisses her. The only other physical contact recorded in the stage directions occurs between Sappho and Melitta. During an exchange in Act 1 Scene 5, Sappho kisses Melitta, surveys her physical appearance and then kisses her again. The physical intimacies exchanged between the heterosexual couple, represented by Phaon and Melitta, are paralleled by the homoerotic physicality of Sappho and Melitta.

Whether female playwrights were drawn to Grillparzer's play because of its homoeroticism is indiscernible. Allardyce Nicoll remarks on the popularity of closet dramas from German translations (1952: vol. III, 218), and Grillparzer was one of the most popular playwrights of the nineteenth century, making him an obvious source for writers. Both Frothingham and Lee were translators of other German authors, though neither ventured on to other Grillparzer dramas. The play's sentimentality, its central female character, Sappho's literary identity and fame, all make Grillparzer's text an obvious choice for translation by women. By scripting the story of Sappho, female writers figure themselves into her literary heritage, identifying themselves as exceptional women writers in the tradition of Sappho (Brown 1994: 205–7). However, as Margaret Reynolds has shown, comparison with the emotional, passionate, and self-destructive Sappho could be disadvantageous for women writers (1996: 278–79).

Estelle Lewis's version of the Sappho legend, which follows in certain details Grillparzer's text, was an extremely popular version of the play that deemphasized the homoerotic potential of the narrative. By the time of her death in 1880 it had reached six editions. Lewis was born in Baltimore, Maryland in 1824 and began her literary career at an early age. In 1841, at the age of seventeen, she married Sylvanus Lewis, a Brooklyn lawyer, and lived with him there until they divorced in 1858. Edgar Allen Poe, a friend of the family, highly praised her literary work, though Poe may very well have supplied the acclamation for his own financial gain from the family (Bowerman 1933: 212). After Lewis divorced, she lived primarily in Europe and settled for the last twenty years of her life in London, where she wrote and published *Sappho, A Tragedy in Five Acts* in 1875. The play is written in verse and the author's intention for the work is unclear. It was not acted in England, though it was apparently considered for the stage (Lewis 1876: afterword 5), and it was translated into modern Greek and was performed in Athens (Phillips 1980: 571–73).

Lewis's Sappho is proud, passionate, sensitive, and highly emotional; she is almost primitive in nature, though at the same time she is graceful and intelligent. This is a woman who, deeply hurt when she overhears her students complain of their training at her hands, imperiously directs them each to write "an ode on slander" (1.1.79).[9] Her fascination with Phaon slips into an obsessive psychosis, as she threatens to kill both Cleone and Phaon more than once, attempts to stab to Pisistratus, and in her jealousy burns Athens to the ground. The play represents twenty-nine characters, including six of Sappho's pupils: in contrast, the Grillparzer translations do not mention Sappho's poetic teaching. The narrative also offers several events and plot complications not imagined by Grillparzer. For example, Lewis includes the competition at the Dionysia. She attaches subplots of Alcaeus' love for Sappho, and the obsession with Sappho of Pisistratus, king of Athens. And, although the main action again concerns Phaon's awe of the poet that she takes for love, his abandonment in favor of her slave, (here called Cleone), and Sappho's eventual suicide, this play ends with enough deaths to resemble a Jacobean revenge tragedy. Before Sappho's suicide, Alcaeus kills Phaon, and the Eumenides (though not listed in the dramatis personae) murder Cleone. In the play's concluding action, Alcaeus stabs himself to be with Sappho. More interesting, near the end of Act 3 we hear that Erinna, one of Sappho's pupils, has died, apparently due to Sappho's unrequited love.

The heterosexual imperative is stronger in this play than in the Grillparzer translations; however, in the character of Erinna a homoerotic subtext is identifiable, although Sappho demonstrates little interest in the female characters in the text. Lewis exhibits Sappho's female literary salon as a group of plaintive malcontents, except for Erinna, who functions as the play's confidante, revealing Sappho's inner thoughts. In her capacity as intimate associate, Erinna's love for Sappho is apparent. Erinna defends Sappho against the criticism of the other students. In a dialogue with Sappho, as the poet deplores her solitude, Erinna hopefully inquires, "Erinna loves thee – is not this enough?" To which Sappho responds, "Sweet, artless child! Thy love to Sappho's heart / Comes like the perfume of a vernal flower – / It soothes and calms, but does not nourish it" (1.1.120–23). The vital indication of Erinna's love for Sappho occurs during the climactic scenes of Act 3. After discovering Phaon embracing Cleone, Sappho is inconsolable. In her grief she rejects Erinna's empathetic efforts at solace and, in a rage, expels Erinna from her presence. Erinna's reaction is extreme; she faints and Alcaeus carries her off the stage. In the succeeding scene, Alcaeus reveals that Erinna is dead. Apparently, Erinna's death resulted from Sappho's rejection. Alcaeus' report is simple: "The young Erinna's dead – slain by thy woes, / And sudden changéd love" (3.5.120–21). Erinna's sudden death signifies the strength of her emotional and psychical connection to Sappho, though Erinna's love for Sappho is wholly unrequited, minimized by her character's marginality and early exit from the text, and inferior to the consuming heterosexual passions displayed by the other characters.

In a lesbian reading of the text, Lewis has little to offer her female audience. The relationship between Sappho and her pupil Erinna is minor. The homoerotic connection in the Grillparzer text between the slave Melitta and Sappho does not exist in Lewis's version. Here the Melitta character, Cleone, is depicted as simply fearing Sappho. However, Lewis's almost hysterical Sappho would have probably appealed to a male spectatorship flattered that a woman would resort to such extremes for the love of a man, even one as unworthy as Phaon. It is not surprising that literary critics in both England and America highly regarded the play (Lewis 1876: afterword 1–8).

Catherine Godwin's dramatic sketch, *Sappho*, is a text wonderfully rich in homoerotic possibilities. Godwin was born in 1798 in Glasgow. Her mother died at her birth, and her father shortly thereafter. She and an older sister were raised by a Miss Worboys, described by one biographer as "her mother's intimate friend" (see

DNB). Worboys and the girls lived in Westmoreland, where Godwin stayed after her marriage to Thomas Godwin, a businessman with the East India Company. A short biographical sketch prefaced to Godwin's collected works establishes Worboys, who outlived Godwin, as a constant and visceral presence in Godwin's life. They were rarely separated and are buried together, along with Godwin's husband, near their Westmoreland residence (Godwin 1854: i–viii). Godwin was a poet, author of children's stories, and miniature portrait painter, whose verse attracted the attention of Joanna Baillie, William Wordsworth, and Robert Southey (Godwin 1854: iv). In 1824, she first published a shorter version of *Sappho*, and the entire text appears in the 1854 version of her collected works, published posthumously. This is an episodic poetic closet drama written in iambic pentameter with twelve scenes and no act breaks.

Godwin's version of the Sappho story is significantly different from the texts already discussed. Phaon is not a character represented in the script, though he is a part of the narrative, and the plot does not illustrate a love triangle. When the play opens, Phaon has already rejected Sappho, who is a widow with a young child, though she hopes for a reconciliation. She is shortly exiled from Lesbos for her involvement in a political intrigue, and follows Phaon to Sicily. There, in descriptive passages related by a third character, the audience learns she is twice more rejected by Phaon. A chance meeting with a hermit motivates her contemplation of suicide. The last four scenes, a quarter of the text, depict her preparations for, and the aftermath of, her suicide.

Godwin's Sappho is generous and compassionate. Her death comes after she realizes that in experiencing sexual desire for Phaon she has debased her literary fame (8.66–79).[10] In death, Sappho seeks an immortal metaphysical existence, where her mind will flourish separate from the degrading cares of her body (11.8–11; 11.62–76). This Sappho despairs the unrequited love of Phaon; however, her response, unlike the malicious vengefulness of the Grillparzer and the Lewis Sapphos, is transcendent introspection which leads her to disavow material existence. As with all these texts, this version is sentimental with elaborate language and affected emotions. It portrays the collapse of a strained, refined personality. At one point, Sappho stands at the brink of mount AEtna amidst the erupting volcano, like a literary counterpart to a Romantic painting.

The homoerotically desiring subject in this play is again a student

Scene First.

On the Island of Lesbos. Time, Evening.

Plate 10. Illustration of the island of Lesbos from *Sappho, a Dramatic Sketch,* in the *Poetical Works of the Late Catherine Grace Godwin.*

of Sappho's, named Atthis. At the play's opening, Atthis and other students discuss Sappho's emotional state. Atthis believes that Sappho's love for Phaon has displaced her own position in Sappho's affections. However, she is informed that Phaon has left the island and is encouraged by the other women, as Sappho's favorite, to console the grieving poet (1.72–89). Atthis' attempt is deflected by Sappho, who maintains that she is unaffected by Phaon. During this exchange the reader is given a measure of the bond between Sappho and Atthis. Confronted by her student with her weakening physical state, Sappho responds to Atthis,

> Fear is love's offspring,
> And doth mislead thee. If my cheek is blanched,
> Dear Atthis! it in sympathy grows pale.
> For as my heart responds, fond girl, to thine,
> So also doth my aspect shew thee now
> Thy woeful looks reflected.   (3.57–62)

Atthis is Sappho's confidant and loving companion. She is among the women who accompany Sappho to Sicily and attempt to shelter her from disappointment. The reader hears that of the women who surround Sappho, Atthis is the most loved (1.72–79; 4.21–23). The domestic vision that Godwin creates signifies a female enclave with Sappho as its center, adored by the women around her. The intrusive male presence of Phaon disrupts their structured harmony.

Atthis is the character who counsels Sappho near her death and attempts to dissuade Sappho from her course by reason and appeals to emotion. Twice is Atthis described by other characters in impulsive, fervent situations. The first event occurs when Sappho seeks out the high priests of the temple of Apollo Leucadius. Atthis is portrayed as "a pale, beauteous maiden / Who clung to her [Sappho], hiding her weeping eyes / In Sappho's bosom." The high priest goes on to consider,

> Methinks I never looked upon such eyes
> As hers, when fixed upon the face of Sappho;
> Their tremulous blue was like the twilight heavens,
> Meeting and mourning o'er the darkened earth.
> She spoke not, but when Sappho took the oath
> She uttered a faint cry, relaxed her hold,
> And sank down senseless.   (10.15–26)

This passage presents Atthis as a beautiful, passionate woman, distraught at Sappho's decision. She gazes at Sappho, stricken with anguish. The extremity of the emotion elevates the character above the level of friend. Atthis demonstrates an emotional and physical need for Sappho's presence to sustain her. After Sappho's suicide, a bystander recounts how Atthis endeavored to prevent Sappho's leap:

> She came where Sappho stood,
> And laying on her robe a hand as white
> And cold as Parian marble, cried to her,
> "Yet once again! Ah, hear me once again,
> "Or perish both" ...

Sappho turned,
And the inspired light which late had played
Over her features, vanished as a dream,
And tears fell glittering midst the long fair tresses
Shading the maiden's brow; and in a voice
Choked by emotion, she replied to her,
"Would thou hadst spared me this!" But she who knelt
Low at her feet heard not.

(12.42–57)

In these two passages the gaze becomes a sexual exchange, as suggestive looks by knowing participants transmit longing and desire. Atthis is constructed as the desiring subject in the text. Her passion toward Sappho elicits a sympathetic response from the reader. However, her gender and her position as a desiring individual focused on the central female object of the text identifies Atthis as more than a dramatic convention. The character is erotically connected to the figure of Sappho in the text, which opens her to a homoerotic reading.

In the middle of the play, Godwin develops a peculiar interaction between Sappho and a misanthrope named Hipparchus. The encounter sustains the dramatic action, since this meeting inspires Sappho's thoughts of suicide; however, the character of Hipparchus is intriguing for his homoerotic tendencies. He relates to Sappho a mawkish story of failed friendship, lost love, and inexorable grief:

I had a friend – what say I? was he not
One whom I cherished more than mine own life?
We were the same in country and estate –
In years, vocation, and, I thought, in heart;
We fought beneath one buckler; that hard couch,
The war cloak, spread upon the ensanguined field,
Served us alike. We drank from out one cup. . . ,
            So complete our friendship,
It soon became a proverb in the land
To love as Diocles and Hipparchus loved.

(8.111–23)

This friend disappoints Hipparchus, who spends his time secluded from the world. The speech is erotically charged, for in the description of Diocles is a comparison to the unrequited love of Phaon. As Sappho loved Phaon and was wronged by him, so Hipparchus loved Diocles with the same result. Besides advancing the narrative of the story toward Sappho's death, this experience supports a homoerotic reading in the drama.

Scene Third.

A Grove in the Island of Lesbos. A small Grecian Temple in the back ground. SAPPHO, ATTHIS, IOLE, *and* TELESIPHE *are discovered; the former pensively reclining, while her three companions or pupils touch each a lyre which they hold in their hands, in celebration of the birth of* AURORA. *Time, early Morning.*

Plate 11. Sappho listens to her companions singing a hymn to Aurora.
Illustrated in the *Poetical Works of the Late Catherine Grace Godwin.*

Godwin's text presents the reader with a Sappho who not only attracts homoerotic affection, but is conscious of that affect. Her concluding scene with Atthis demonstrates her knowledge of the other woman's desire. Sappho opens the eleventh scene on a mountain summit with Atthis where she envisions the freedom her death will bring. During her opening speech she declares to Atthis, "And thou, twin sister of my soul! may'st see / The spirit dear to thee crossing thy path / In some fair shape, and challenging thy love / Ev'n as I claim it now" (11.12–15). These words are followed by a line break, which presumes that Sappho claims Atthis' love with some physical manifestation, either by an embrace or a kiss, or both. Sappho is aware that Atthis loves her. Godwin acknowledges that love and provides an opportunity for a physical expression between the characters. A few lines later, Sappho recognizes the extent of Atthis' attraction when she compares it to her own unrequited passion for Phaon. Sappho says,

> Where'er hearts trust, they're broken – wheresoe'er
> There is devoted love, it is betrayed
> . . .
> The love I would requite meets but the boon
> Of withering sorrow that consumes my breast.
> Such have I been to thee sweet friend, for thou,
> With tenderness surpassing human love,
> Hast clung to me through every change of fortune,
> Faithful to the last. (11.36–45)

Sappho has not been insensible to Atthis' love, she identifies it as similar to her own, though it surpasses "human love." Still, in the desire which passes between two emotionally connected characters exists an erotic element, which Sappho identifies.

Given Phaon's physical absence from the text, Sappho and Atthis present the only identifiable couple in a sentimental, clearly romanticized drama. Godwin's text, more than the other versions of the story, privileges the female attachment of the women in Sappho's school, and the location of most of the action is a female-centered space where women live in harmony. The disruptive effects of an incorporeal male presence on this community and the manner in which individuals in the society react to the disruption constitute the action of the play. The absence of Phaon from the dramatis personae of Godwin's play removes a heterosexual couple from the reader/spectator. Atthis represents an alternative to the heterosexual imperative complicit in Sappho's suicide, and perhaps the tragedy of the drama is that Sappho is incapable of choosing her. In the end, Sappho's death is the death of the lesbian potential, which secures the heterosexual norm. However, the female community and the strength of Atthis' desire for Sappho provides the nineteenth-century female reader with an identifiable lesbian subtext. In Godwin's play, the heterosexual plot allows for a significant lesbian subtext, especially taking into consideration the nineteenth-century conception of romantic love between women and the homosexual potential of those relationships as discussed by Moore (1992: 499–503). Here, as Carolyn Woodward has suggested for another genre, the lesbian subtext critiques the patriarchal narrative but does not ultimately subvert the dominant fiction (1993: 858).

This closet drama offered a site to question narrowly defined identities of sexuality and love, which Donoghue identifies as a potential for all poetry (1997: xxiii). Broadening the lesbian literary canon, as Faderman suggests (1995: 57), makes it imperative that the reader perceives, in the construction of Sappho and her partners, the lesbian subject assuming a lesbian narrative space in the dominant plot structure. These plays belong to what Brown calls "a lost or repressed lesbian literary tradition" (1994: 219), and are part of the history of representations of lesbianism which Moore has begun to uncover (1992: 499). The lesbian desire in these closet dramas has itself, like women's drama in general, been closeted. These plays have been marginalized from the scope of dramatic history by form and content, as well as by the gender of their authors. The metaphor of the closet, on the one hand, implying intimacy, privacy, and comfort, can become isolating, confining, and sterile. Releasing from closeted spaces the identities and works of female playwrights has the potential to uncover multiple marginalities, such as the potential of closet drama to represent lesbian desire in premodern texts.

NOTES

1 Besides the texts discussed in this chapter, I have also found references to nineteenth-century tragedies and operas about Sappho by Jessie Norton, Mary Wellesley Sterling, J. Bramsen, Francis Cowley Burnand and William Brough, George Gervase Collingham, James Dryden Hosken, Harry Lobb, Thomas James Serle, William Gorman Wills, William Nelson, Robert Sherman, Nelson Compston, Jacob Gordin, William Mason, Clyde Fitch, Alphonse Daudet, Charles Gounod, an opera by Jules Massenet with libretto by Henri Cain and Arthur Bernede, and an opera by Giovanni Pacini.

2 It is important to explain my use of the term *lesbian* in regard to constructionist theories of sexuality. Though I agree that our contemporary understanding of female homosexuality maintains a historical and cultural specificity, I also agree with Martha Vicinus that "same-sex erotic attraction appears to be transhistorical and transcultural" (1992: 469; see also Donoghue 1996: 2–24). The plays I discuss belong to the

evolution of contemporary lesbian identity, with all its variable expressions.

3   For contemporary nineteenth-century biographies of Sappho see, for example, Hale 1870: 56–57. Estelle Lewis (1876: v) assumes the Phaon story to be a historical fact. By 1899, T. G. Johnson declared the Phaon story and Sappho's suicide "myths and of purely legendary origin" (1899: 50).

4   William Smith, at mid-century, questioned the Phaon story (1849: 708). By the end of the century, Henry Wharton questioned the historical validity of the Phaon myth, translated Sappho's poems with female pronouns, and was very aware of Sappho's affection for women (1885: 13).

5   Stein discusses multiple homoerotic representations of Sappho in both text and paintings in the final chapter of her work, though she finds these representations to be the exception to constructions of Sappho as heterosexual lover or solitary voluptuary (1981: 254–306).

6   In contradiction to Thompson, Johnson states categorically that Sappho's character has been irrevocably restored by the turn of the century in both England and Germany (1899: 51).

7   Allardyce Nicoll discusses the unsuitability of translations of German plays for the English stage (1952: vol. iii, 64–69).

8   All quotations from the Grillparzer translations are from *Sappho, A Tragedy* (Cumming 1855). My thanks to Mona Kratzert from the California State University Library at Fullerton for her help in acquiring the full text of this play.

9   See Lewis 1876: 5. All subsequent quotations from this play will be taken from this version of the script.

10 See Godwin 1854: 38. All subsequent quotations from this play will be taken from this version of the script.

REFERENCES

Bayle, Pierre [1738] 1984, *The Dictionary Historical and Critical of Mr. Peter Bayle*, 2nd edn, vol. v, New York and London: Garland.

Bowerman, Sarah G. 1933, *Dictionary of American Biography*, vol. ix New York: Scribner's Sons, 212–13.

Brown, Susan 1994, "A Victorian Sappho: Agency, Identity, and the Politics of Poetics," *English Studies in Canada*, 20.2: 205–25.

Burroughs, Catherine B. 1997, *Closet Stages: Joanna Baillie and the Theater Theory of British Romantic Women Writers*, Philadelphia: University of Pennsylvania Press.

Castle, Terry 1993, *The Apparitional Lesbian, Female Homosexuality and Modern Culture*, New York: Columbia University Press.

Clarke, Mary Cowden 1858, *World Noted Women; or, Types of Womanly Attributes of all Lands and Ages*, New York: D. Appleton.

Cumming, Lucy Caroline (trans.) 1855, *Sappho, A Tragedy*, by Franz Grill-parzer, Edinburgh: Thomas Constable.

DeJean, Joan 1989, *Fictions of Sappho, 1546–1937*, Chicago: University of Chicago Press.

Donoghue, Emma 1996, *Passions Between Women: British Lesbian Culture, 1668–1801*, New York: HarperPerennial.

Donoghue, Emma 1997, *Poems Between Women: Four Centuries of Love, Romantic Friendship, and Desire*, New York: Columbia University Press.

Faderman, Lillian 1981, *Surpassing the Love of Men: Romantic Friendship and Love Between Women from the Renaissance to the Present*, New York: William Morrow.

Faderman, Lillian 1995, "What is Lesbian Literature? Forming a Historical Canon," *Professions of Desire: Lesbian and Gay Studies in Literature*, ed. George E. Haggerty and Bonnie Zimmerman, New York: MLA, 49–59.

Farwell, Marilyn R. 1990, "Heterosexual Plots and Lesbian Subtexts: Toward a Theory of Lesbian Narrative Space," *Lesbian Texts and Contexts: Radical Revisions*, ed. Karla Jay and Joanne Glasgow, New York: New York University Press, 91–103.

Farwell, Marilyn R. 1996, *Heterosexual Plots and Lesbian Narratives*, New York: New York University Press.

Foster, Jeannette H. 1985, *Sex Variant Women in Literature*, Florida: Naiad.

Frothingham, Ellen (trans.) 1876, *Sappho, a Tragedy in Five Acts*, by Franz Grillparzer, Boston: Roberts Brothers.

Godwin, Catherine Grace 1854, *The Poetical Works of the Late Catherine Grace Godwin*, ed. A. Cleveland Wigan, London: Chapman and Hall.

Hale, Mrs. 1870, *Woman's Record; or, Sketches of all Distinguished Women*, New York: Harper.

Jay, Peter and Caroline Lewis (eds.), 1996, *Sappho, Through English Poetry*, London: Anvil Press Poetry.

Johnson, T. G. 1899, *Sappho the Lesbian; A Monograph*, London: Williams and Norgate.

Lee, Eliza Buckminster (trans.) 1846, *Sappho*, by Franz Grillparzer, in *Correggio: A Tragedy, by Oehlenschlager*, Boston: Phillips and Sampson, 176–303.

[Lewis, Estelle], Stella 1876, *Sappho, a Tragedy in Five Acts*, 2nd edn, London: Trubner.

Merriam, George S. (ed.) 1890, *The Story of William and Lucy Smith*, Boston: Houghton Mifflin.

Middleton, Edda (trans.) 1858, *Sappho, a Tragedy in Five Acts*, by Franz Grillparzer, New York: D. Appleton.

Moore, Lisa 1992, "'Something More Tender Still Than Friendship': Romantic Friendship in Early-Nineteenth-Century England," *Feminist Studies*, 18.3: 499–520.

Mure, William 1854, *A Critical History of the Language and Literature of Antient*

Greece, 2nd edn, vol. III, London: Longman, Brown, Green, and Longman.

Nicoll, Allardyce 1952, *A History of English Drama, 1660–1900*, 3rd edn, vol. III, Cambridge: Cambridge University Press.

Nicoll, Allardyce 1955, *A History of English Drama, 1660–1900*, 3rd edn., vol. IV, Cambridge: Cambridge University Press.

Norton, Rictor 1992, *Mother Clap's Molly House: The Gay Subculture in England, 1700–1830*, London: Gay Men's Press.

Phillips, Elizabeth 1980, *American Women Writers: A Critical Reference Guide from Colonial Times to the Present*, vol. II, ed. Lina Mainiero, New York: Frederick Ungar.

Reynolds, Margaret 1996, "'I lived for art, I lived for love': The Woman Poet Sings Sappho's Last Song," *Victorian Women Poets: A Critical Reader*, ed. Angela Leighton, Cambridge: Basil Blackwell, 277–306.

Richardson, Alan 1988, *A Mental Theatre: Poetic Drama and Consciousness in the Romantic Age*, University Park: Pennsylvania State University Press.

Semple, Linda 1994, "The Seven Ages of Sappho," *Perversions*, 7: 5–41.

Smith, William 1849, *Dictionary of Greek and Roman Biography and Mythology*, vol. III, London: Taylor, Walton, and Maberly and John Murray.

Smith-Rosenberg, Carroll 1985, *Disorderly Conduct: Visions of Gender in Victorian America*, Oxford and New York: Oxford University Press.

Smith-Rosenberg, Carroll 1989, 'Discourses of Sexuality and Subjectivity: The New Woman, 1870–1936,' *Hidden from History: Reclaiming the Gay and Lesbian Past*, ed. Martin Duberman, Martha Vicinus, and George Chauncey, Jr., New York: Meridian, 264–80.

Stein, Judith Ellen 1981, 'The Iconography of Sappho, 1775–1875,' Ph.D. dissertation, University of Pennsylvania.

Thompson, Maurice 1894, "The Sapphic Secret," *Atlantic Monthly*, 73: 365–72.

Vanita, Ruth 1997, *Sappho and the Virgin Mary; Same-Sex Love and the English Literary Imagination*, New York: Columbia University Press.

Vicinus, Martha 1992, "'They Wonder to Which Sex I Belong': The Historical Roots of the Modern Lesbian Identity," *Feminist Studies*, 18.3: 467–97.

Wang, Shou-Ren 1990, *The Theatre of the Mind, A Study of Unacted Drama in Nineteenth-Century England*, New York: St. Martin's Press.

Wharton, Henry Thornton 1885, *Sappho, Memoir, Text, Selected Renderings and a Literal Translation*, London: David Stott.

Woodward, Carolyn 1993, "'My Heart So Wrapt': Lesbian Disruptions in Eighteenth-Century British Fiction," *Signs*, 18.4: 838–65.

CHAPTER 12

Conflicted politics and circumspect comedy
Women's comic playwriting in the 1890s

Susan Carlson

In 1882, Emma Schiff wrote a comic play, *The Rights of Woman*, in which women reject the freedoms of women's rights to embrace traditional notions of the woman's role in marriage. In 1914, Constance Campbell wrote *One of the Old Guard*, a comedy in which a similar debate over women's rights discredits restrictive gender stereotyping and hails a new freedom for women. In Schiff's play, young women are laughable in their flirtation with independence; in Campbell's, traditional notions of womanhood are laughed away. These two plays epitomize the political extremes of the women's rights debate as it manifested itself in comic dramas on the turn-of-the-century English stage.

During the last ten years of the nineteenth century – which are the focus of this chapter – both the triumph of traditional gender typing in Schiff's play and the acceptance of women's new autonomy in Campbell's coexist, often uncomfortably, in the drama written by women. While I began my own study of the decade ready to position these women as the capstone to a century of forgotten theatre work by women, what I have to tell now is a much more ambiguous story of women whose writing is marked by the decentered political communities and ideological contradictions of 1890s gender debates. These playwrights leave us with a complex theatrical legacy in which tidy categories of genre disappear and in which the work of writers from Joanna Baillie to Sarah Lane to Mrs. Gore exhibits multiple resonances.

CONFLICTED POLITICS

In the 1890s, ideological debates over women's rights and roles gained both notoriety and popular recognition. It was an era during which a new generation of women – college-educated, professionally ambitious, and independently propertied – were extending the parameters of acceptable behavior for women. It was, of course, the decade of the "New Woman," a figure both feted and condemned by journalists, novelists, and playwrights.

Much of the language of this debate – specifically the debate over the New Woman and more generally over women's rights and roles – is familiar to late twentieth-century feminists, with its frequent attention to economic conditions and social institutions and its hostility to the patriarchal constructions of women's lives. In a division that continues to resonate, women argued heatedly among themselves over the relative values of "arguments rooted in equality and those based on difference" (Hannam 1995: 226). A notable element in public discussion was the frequent reference to the constructed nature of women's roles. Arguing against the pressure to naturalize women's roles as wife and mother, writers as varied as Edith Simcox and Mona Caird urged the recognition of women's options in personal, professional, and social realms (Simcox 1887: 583–97; Caird 1890: 632). In these familiar debates about the constructed nature of social institutions, equally familiar lacunae appear; as Antoinette Burton succinctly puts it, this largely middle-class Anglo-feminism may have challenged the way women were excluded from power, but did not challenge "all of the structures through which political power itself was constituted in an imperial landscape" (Burton 1994: 21). Most politically progressive women were indeed blind to the aspects of racial and national difference implied in their political campaigning.

No less influential were the generational conflicts which marked women's activism in this decade, for as some women laid claim to an increased public presence – bicycles, jobs, and sexuality – other women reacted in opposition by claiming purity and chastity as core values for women. And some women claimed both simultaneously. As the older generation of mid-Victorian feminists faced what seemed to them the antagonistic autonomy of the new generation of feminists, ideological debates separated women from women. Speaking as an "Old Woman" herself, novelist Sarah Grand argued somewhat sternly that the Old Woman "must go," must give way to the urgency of the New (Grand 1898: 675).

The final decade of the century was an ideologically turbulent time; and the image of the gutsy New Woman masks women's various commitments to social, cultural, and political change. By the

early twentieth century, much of the more radical fomentation
would coalesce in the charged political writing of Cicely Hamilton,
Olive Schreiner, Clementina Black, and others, leading, in turn, to
the disruptive campaigning of the Women's Social and Political
Union (WSPU). But what prevailed in the 1890s was a mixture of
compartmentalized, often circumspect political actions and tenta-
tive, exploratory theorizing of women's rights and roles.

In the campaign for women's votes, for example, the decade saw
the formation of the National Union of Women's Suffrage Societies
(NUWSS) in 1897, overseen by Millicent Garrett Fawcett. While this
organization initiated a new sense of coalition, as it filled the need
for intensified national campaigning, its politics were anything but
radical. Significantly, the union adhered to an image of woman
based first on her domestic duties as a wife and mother; the vote was
seen as a way for women to certify the importance of these roles.
Fawcett herself noted that the "difference between men and women,
instead of being a reason against their enfranchisement, seems to me
the strongest possible reason in favour of it; we want the home and
the domestic side of things to count for more in politics and in the
administration of public affairs than they do at present" ([1887]: 3).
For Fawcett and the NUWSS, a commitment to marriage was the
foundation of women's social and political responsibilities and
rights.

In 1866, Helen Taylor labeled the debate on women "peculiarly
contradictory" (Taylor 1866: 461), and indeed the women who came
of age with her – activists like Frances Power Cobbe, Josephine
Butler, and Eliza Lynn Linton – appear intellectually and emotionally conflicted. Jill Davis notes similar conflations and contradictions
among younger activists; she argues that seemingly progressive
political groups of the time – like the Fabians – reverted from
materialist to essentialist thinking when faced with "the woman
question" (J. Davis 1992: 22). Younger feminists' campaigns for
equality were also compromised by conflicting responses to issues of
gender, class, and race. While working-class women suffragists were
often forced to choose between loyalties to labor or to women,
middle-class suffragists aligned themselves with the cause of the
empire, and argued that the vote would allow them to mobilize on
behalf of native, colonized women (Burton 1994: 18). Yet the over-
riding trope of the empire, of the age, was progress, and it is that
expectant look to the future that allowed – even encouraged – the

politically active women of the late nineteenth century to ignore the
conflicts and compromises of their piecemeal beliefs and practices.

THE POLITICS OF STAGING

It is all too easy to conceive of English theatre at the end of the
century as a site of radical ideas and innovative performance. It was
indeed an exciting time of rejuvenation: Pinero and Jones (following
Ibsen) raised hot debates about their unconventional women, the
Independent Theatre encouraged a generation of young writers
(including a few women), and George Bernard Shaw was flexing his
writerly muscles in the wings. It was the era of the New Drama, a
time during which the proliferation of problem plays encouraged
playwrights to tackle new issues, though the fate of women remained
notably orthodox. The New Woman is deflated in the guise of
Pinero's Mrs. Ebbsmith, for example, a woman whose public
commitment to sexual equality is slowly, painfully strangled and
whose power as a public speaker conveniently remains offstage.
While Agnes Ebbsmith pays a tragic price for transcending gender
roles, the New Women in Henry Arthur Jones's *The Case of Rebellious
Susan* and Sydney Grundy's *The New Woman* are belittled and rejected
in a comic mode. Jones's suffragist Elaine Shrimpton is first ridiculed
and then jailed, to the glee of all the other characters; Grundy's New
Women are similarly derided by those who claim New Women "only
want one thing – the one thing every woman wants – the one thing
that no woman's life is worth living without. A true man's love"
(Grundy 1894: 89–90). While there were those in the theatre
community who were wary of such restrictive staging, these three
writers – whose "supremacy at the West End theatres" had "long
passed beyond dispute" (Shaw [1896] 1993: vol. II, 550) – were
setting the dominant discourses about gender on the late Victorian
stage. As Tracy C. Davis notes, the times remained "deeply conservative" (T. Davis 1992: 111).

Ironically, this resistance to ideological change came hand-in-
hand with rapid changes in theatre venues at the end of the century.
Thus, while mainstream representation of women remained relatively stable, both men and women writing for the stage were thrown
together in new ways. A proliferation of theatre building in the West
End, culminating in the building of Her Majesty's (1897) and
Wyndham's (1899), established Westminster as a magnet for would-

be writers – men and women – hoping to appeal to the middle-class
audience. In the suburban outskirts, building was equally intense.
Often the same theatres which targeted commercial success also
staged the (mostly) noncommercial plays by women. The Comedy
Theatre, for instance, where Grundy's *The New Woman* (1894) had its
immensely successful run, was also home to the limited playing of
Lady Florence Bell's *Time is Money* (1890a) and Eva and Florence
Bright's *Tabitha's Courtship* (1890). The Garrick Theatre was host to
Pinero's *The Notorious Mrs. Ebbsmith* in 1895 and also to George
Fleming's (Constance Fletcher's) *Mrs. Lessingham* a year earlier, in
1894. In other words, the male writers whose aesthetic sensibilities
have dominated our thinking about late Victorian theatre were
working alongside female writers whose work is, literally, disinte-
grating in the British Library. As George Bernard Shaw noted,
aesthetic and economic forces were working against these women
playwrights. Although Shaw grumbles about the "ladylike plays"
taking over the stage in 1898, he applauds women writers who, "as
purveyors of the newest new drama, are breaking down the male
monopoly of dramatic authorship in all directions" (Shaw [1896]
1993: vol. III, 980). Given the high cost of commercial success (he
estimates that one must play to 75,000 people to succeed financially),
Shaw also explains why such new drama was so quietly received
(vol. III, 1077–82).

WOMEN'S COMEDY

The burgeoning theatre accounts, in part, for the expanding
number of women who were writing plays at the end of the century.
As they had their plays produced for one, maybe five, and only
rarely more performances, women playwrights present a stubborn,
insistent presence. Caught between their conflicted politics and their
often confused attempts to find a home in traditional genres like
comedy, these women offer an apprentice-like move into public life.
I have chosen to focus on women's comic playwriting efforts since
comedy's investment in social protocol and issues of relationship
encouraged these women's attention to social power and its theatrical dimensions.

I will first examine plays in which a comic formula relentlessly
points women towards marriage; I think of these as the "marriage *de
rigueur*" plays. Second, I will turn to plays in which central women

characters experiment with new roles and ideas, to learn, overwhelmingly, that their traditional roles, in most cases their roles as wives, are preferable. Finally, I will look at a group of plays in which the comic formula itself is challenged. This final group of plays puts on stage women who contest conventional narratives of womanhood and most obviously play out the conflicted politics of their time. In all three groups of plays, however, the writers present a world in which the conflicts and compromises of gender politics of the 1890s are integral. My organization of these groups assumes, of course, the illusion of evolution, the illusion of a progress in women's understanding of their political and cultural positionality. In actuality, all three modes I describe exist simultaneously, not in chronological succession. Yet by managing the plays this way, I can point to varying degrees of playwriting skill and a variety of political commitments.

Group 1: marriage de rigueur

I begin with *Tabitha's Courtship*, a representative one-act written collaboratively by Eva and Florence Bright and originally produced for a single performance at the Comedy Theatre in 1890.[1] In a play consisting of a standard mix of witty banter, deception, and love games, the most notable quality is the insistent presence of marriage. Young lovers Kate (originally played by Florence Bright herself) and Harry concoct a plan to bring his father and her Aunt Tabitha together romantically: both couples are engaged by the end of the play. What emerges from the experience of this play, however, is not the audience's attachment to any one of the stereotypical characters, but the recognition that marriage takes the place of a main character. Whether she is young and vital or middle-aged and weathered, a woman will find her best home in marriage. Florence Bright's single-authored play, *Caught Out* (1888), likewise shows a writer pressing all of her skills into the service of a conventional contentment with marriage.

I am speculating that Florence Bright would not agree with such an assessment of her work. Writing much later, in the heat of pre-World War I suffrage upheavals, she notes that her support for "the cause" (women's vote) has been present from her "girlhood" (Bright n.d.: 2). She further prophesies that women's "detestable competition for man's admiration will no longer be the be-all and end-all of a woman's life" (4). In other words, Bright is on record as a woman committed to militant suffragism, committed to a world no longer premised on heterosexual desire and its institutionalization in marriage. I have no direct knowledge of Bright's politics in the years when she wrote *Caught Out* and *Tabitha's Courtship*, but I would speculate that she remained unaware of the way her women characters' spunk and liveliness diminish in the long shadow marriage casts in her conventional comedies. The disjunction between politics and playwriting is even more pronounced in the work of Madeleine Lucette Ryley.

In the 1890s, American-born Ryley had several stage successes in London, all comedies cleverly plotted, linguistically adept, and free from direct engagement with progressive politics. In *Jedbury Junior* (1896), for example, the prodigal son (Junior) travels the world, finagles his way around a demanding father, and finds that a rushed marriage to an unknown woman in Trinidad has actually coupled him with his soul-mate. I find Ryley's plays of particular importance because in the next decade she became a central figure in the English suffrage campaign as a vice-president of the Actresses' Franchise League. For some time she had also been a prominent and successful dramatist (one of few women who could make that claim). The connection between her theatre writing and her politics is far from direct, however. Profiled in 1910 in the London suffrage newspaper, the *Vote*, she comments on her involvement with women's issues in a way strikingly parallel to that of Bright: "I have always been a suffragette without knowing it. Since the agitation commenced five years ago I have formulated my views, but I had always held them unconsciously" ("Mrs. Madeleine Lucette Ryley" 1910: 256). But in her plays, such "unconscious" identification with the plight of women remains only spectrally present; Ryley writes comedies ruled by standard generic harmonies, not political consciousness.

Other examples of cautious yet playful dramas like those of Bright and Ryley abound, plays in which the trajectory towards marriage consumes the energies of nearly all the characters and is binding for old and young alike. The determination with which these plays are plotted around marriage is nowhere clearer than in Maud M. Rogers's *When the Wheels Run Down* (1899). Ironically, however, the desperation with which two sisters desire marriage reveals the tyranny of a universal drive for marriage. Miss Lavinia Dormer (age sixty) and her younger sister Priscilla (age forty) live in a country cottage along with their still younger maid, Kate. When it is hinted that Kate is being courted by the postman, never-married Lavinia belittles marriage; but almost simultaneously, she also lets us see how severely she feels her own missed chance. While Lavinia admits that her unhappiness stems from a life of waiting *for a man*, to the maid Kate she condemns living *with a man* as an equal source of misery: "But don't imagine that you are going to be happy, ever after, like the fairy tales, even if you do marry him" (1.12).

However, Kate's match is only the background to Priscilla's romantic history. Years ago Priscilla's fiancé set sail for the Cape, releasing her from their engagement. After fifteen years without a single word from him, suddenly he returns. After Priscilla meets him offstage, she announces her forthcoming marriage:

LAVINIA [*as* PRISCILLA *is sobbing in her lap*]: My poor, poor child!
PRISCILLA [*raising her head suddenly*]: Poor! [*Her face is radiant*]
   I am not poor!
LAVINIA [*eagerly*]: What do tou [*sic*] mean – do you mean that –
PRISCILLA: Oh, Lavinia! He just took my hand, and said, "Have I come
   too late Priscilla?" – and I said "No!"
                                               (1.14)

The play ends on this conflicted note. On the one hand, there is Priscilla, whose long wait has paid off, whose narrative conforms to the cultural norm, finally. Marriage certifies her worth as the rest of her forty years of life have not. On the other hand, we have Lavinia, whose bitterness is likely to be intensified with the loss of her life-long companion but whose eagerness for her sister's marriage prevails at the end. While the stage directions suggest that Rogers views this end as joyful, Lavinia remains alone, a testament, perhaps, to the human waste left behind in the cultural hegemony of marriage.

These plays in which marriage defines women's lives, whether married or not, are marked by the appearance of women who display their intelligence and wit only in a quest for marriage as well as by the conspicuous absence of timely political issues. At a time when most politically active women were uncritical of the institution of marriage, the prevalence of such plays is hardly surprising.

Group 2: independent women in comedy

Those women playwrights who gave their heroines an awareness of timely political issues produced a notably different kind of comic

play. These are plays in which protofeminists are frequently making
choices, often expressing their ideas on issues of the day, but almost
as often, still settling on marriage.

In many plays, women test more independent selves, clearly
influenced by the social debates around them. The New Woman on
her bicycle, for example, is the central trope in Kate Dixey and Lilian
Feltheimer's *A Girl's Freak* (1899), in which the freedom emblematized
by bicycles motivates the actions of the young heroines. In Annie
Hughes's *A Husband's Humiliation* (1896), Mrs. Wildfire negotiates her
dissatisfaction with marriage by using bicycling to challenge her
husband. While the bicycle threatens disruption in both of these
plays, it represents a temporary liberty for women who return to
conventional marriages at the plays' ends. Playwright Hughes played
the character of Mrs. Wildfire; but while her liberty may have been
curtailed onstage, her decision to write plays simultaneously marks a
challenge to tradition offstage. This mixture of a New Woman's
freedom with a married woman's restraint is also dominant in Estelle
Burney's *Idyll of the Closing Century* (1896), in which an engaged couple
free one another to pursue marriage in other relationships. As the
play's title points to the end of the century, it also gestures to the
decade's aura of progress. The choices in this play are, however,
much more limited for the woman than for the man. In reviewing
Burney's play, *Settled out of Court*, a year later, George Bernard Shaw
notes a central contradiction in her work which is representative of
many of these comedies by women – a contradiction between "up to
date" characters and "the morality they [playwrights] inherit from
their grandmothers" (Shaw [1896] 1993: vol. III, 875).

I consider Gertrude Warden Jones and J. Wilton Jones's *Woman's
Proper Place* (produced 1896) something of a paradigmatic play in its
containment of New Women and their political zeal.[2] Richard and
Mary Montague Robinson have agreed to trade traditional male and
female roles; but the play immediately establishes the foolishness of
the swap. Richard is irritated by supervising dinner menus and Mary
spends her day debating frivolous ideas – the latest Paris fashions
and the social acceptability of a divorcee. So when Mary delivers her
defense of women's new social and political independence to her
husband, it has already been undercut:

How little interest you take in the burning questions of the day – in
Woman's Suffrage, Woman's Independence, and her right to assert herself?
But the World of Woman is moving fast! Very soon she will take her place

on the Stock Exchange, for which her marvellous business capacity specially fits her; in Parliament – to make the laws; at the Bar, to plead them; on the magisterial bench, to enforce them. With women judges and magistrates, as well as women doctors, where will you *men* be? (Jones and Jones 1896: 7).

Predictably, Richard engineers her back to the traditional wife's role. Mary vows to leave her club life behind and the play ends with Richard and Mary agreeing on Woman's Proper Place:

MRS. M. R.: Ah! [*With a sigh of satisfaction, puts her head on his shoulder as they turn up stage and then looks up laughing.*] If people saw us, wouldn't they consider this dreadfully sentimental?

MR. M. R. [*putting her head down again on his shoulder*]: What would it matter? Don't take your head away, dear. A little closer – yes, that's it. *This* is Woman's Proper Place!   (1.14)

In short, the play demonstrates the unnaturalness of women in the public sphere. But like Burney's drama, Jones and Jones's play is rattled by the contradictions of theatrical politics. By 1896, Warden had established herself as an actor of New Women, having performed both the sympathetic Mrs. Linden in *A Doll's House* and the unsympathetic Vivian Vivash in Grundy's *The New Woman*. In other words, Warden participated in the expansion of woman's role in the Drama at the same time she was instrumental in the onstage belittling of the New Woman. Her play's run of performances (fifty-three nights at Terry's Theatre) suggests, however, that it was the reigning in of the New Woman that struck the strongest chord with audiences.

Three additional plays take the changing political climate of the 1890s more seriously. While in each play the characters ultimately privilege personal happiness over political commitment, marriage does not stand as such a universally suitable goal for women. Not surprisingly, the comedy is also less buoyant.

Honesty: A Cottage Flower (1897), by Margaret Young, is distinguished by its connection to the New Century Theatre and was originally produced for the group by Elizabeth Robins and William Archer. Such literary prominence is earned by Young's subtle character portraits as well as by her efforts to mix issues of political import with a clear-eyed recognition of class distinctions. There are two women of very different backgrounds at the center of the play. One – Clorinda – is the loving maid to John Wentworth; the other – Lucy – is his beloved. As chance would have it, both Clorinda and

Lucy belong to the SMIS – Spinsters Mutual Improvement Society – a group which has the object "of bringing into direct contact the classes and masses" (Young 1897: 10). When Lucy shows up to meet Clorinda, their class-conscious discussion complicates the play's romantic entanglements. Clorinda presses Lucy to do what her heart tells her (to claim her love for John); Lucy urges Clorinda to be wary of her vulnerable sexual position as a maid. In this relationship, as in others, Clorinda is the most articulate character. But in the end, the novel connection of these two women is truncated as Lucy and John are united and as Clorinda and another servant, Tom, are left to their shared domestic duties. In part, this play operates as did *Woman's Proper Place*, to demonstrate that women's investment in politics is wrong-headed and that their place is at home; but also, in part, the play offers an effective critique of women's class positions by showing two very different female positions in those homes. Marriage cannot resolve all the social issues that this play opens up.

Lady Florence Bell is already known to many students of late nineteenth-century drama for her collaboration with Elizabeth Robins on the grim *Alan's Wife* (1893). Yet earlier, in 1890, she had published a hefty volume of her own plays including the unproduced *A Woman of Culture*, which contains one of the most notable portraits of the decade's New Woman. The action pivots around Diana Chester, "a woman of culture," who is consumed with politics, especially the politics of women's rights. While she is more sympathetic than Grundy's New Women, Chester's zeal is familiarly tempered by the plot. Chester shares with Major Symonds the guardianship of Evelyn Barrington. While she wants to persuade Evelyn to take up political activism, he wants Evelyn to find happiness in love. It is clear from the opening of the play, when Evelyn and Symonds make fun of Chester's causes – Vivisection, Women's Suffrage, Sanitary Dustbins, and Psychical Research (Bell 1890b: 82) – that the split between the two guardians will be resolved in Symonds's favor.

When young Herbert Sandford, Chester's political protégé and (unknown to her) the young man in love with Evelyn, comes to visit, she foolishly assumes that he is in love with her, not Evelyn. She is "bewildered" when she first understands that Evelyn is the true recipient of Sandford's love, but within seconds she is "recovering herself" (1.120), and even denying her need for love: "a man who can consecrate his life to a girl of that type is not worth having ... I am well out of such follies" (1.121). The upshot of Chester's brush with love is that this activist and reformer is shown to welcome love, but to be unworthy of it. Women's involvement in intellectual pursuits is given a generally sympathetic image here; after all, Chester proudly retains her politics. That has not been an option in other plays I have surveyed to this point. But Bell clearly tells us that in privileging her politics, Chester has lost touch with her femininity. While other plays by Bell were staged, *A Woman of Culture* was not performed in its day, as far as I know; one can only speculate whether its politics were too progressive or too stagnant.

Like *A Woman of Culture*, Lucy Clifford's *A Woman Alone* (1915)[3] focuses on a woman caught between intellectual and political pursuits on the one hand, and emotional attachments on the other. Clifford provides an understanding portrait of her independent woman, Blanche Bowden, but during the play Blanche realizes that her independence is only important as an aid to her spousal duties: "but that's what the woman-movement means, for as women reach high they will want men to reach higher, so that they may love them still" (Clifford 1915: 72). In her preface, Clifford defends this rediscovery of the centrality of marriage: "I wanted to draw a woman full of intellectual energy and ideals who, since she was not strong enough to carry them to achievement alone, longed to see them take shape in the life that was clearest to her" (vii). Clearly responding to charges that she had disappointed progressive women by co-opting her heroine's power, Clifford explains that her character merely discovered her natural place beside her husband. And with the remnant of a happy ending (Blanche rushes back to her husband's arms after four years of turbulent separation), Clifford suggests the inevitability with which such politically vocal characters rediscover the suitability of marriage. Yet the tone of the ending is strained: as in Bell's play, the stronger and more politically committed the woman, the less assured the comedy.

It is no coincidence that Clifford's play valorizes not only the ragged prevalence of marriage but also the grounding of the status quo in a racially segregated empire. The white characters – both male and female – draw from a common source of colonial power, most obvious in Blanche's use of companionable hierarchies of both gender and race to reclaim her spot as a loving wife: "The leopard cannot change his spots nor the black man his skin, nor woman her nature ... Women may reach out to the world with pride and joy feeling their capacities – and they *have* them – but in the end they come back to their own for happiness" (Clifford 1915: 71). As authors like Clifford and Bell stage the social conflicts of women's political activism, their shared class and race mark a common purpose.

By speculating for a moment about the audience for these plays, I can explore further the way such political ideology is reflected in their stagings. Consider, for example, that plays like *A Woman Alone*, *An Idyll of the Closing Century*, *A Husband's Humiliation*, and *Tabitha's Courtship* were mounted only as matinees. Shaw describes some such occasions as coterie venues at which women with "huge towering hats" obstruct sight lines and – I would venture – progressive politics. In describing a matinee performance of comedies by both Clifford and Bell in 1896, Shaw's obsession with obstructing hats, together with his bemused analysis of the plays ("a couple of Mrs. Hugh Bell's drawing room pieces, trivial, but amusing enough on their side, and a one-act piece of hardly greater pretension, but of much more serious merit by Mrs. Clifford" [Shaw [1896] 1993: vol. II, 545]) points to the notable class and gender dimensions of such performances. These are middle-class female audiences flocking to women-authored plays. Three other plays I have discussed (*Caught Out*, *When the Wheels Run Down*, and *A Girl's Freak*) were performed at St. George's Hall, not a licensed theatre but a concert hall at a Marylebone address where such female prosperity was also likely to have been on show. The plays I am surveying throughout this chapter were performed at a wide variety of venues, from the most opulent theatres of the West End to local halls. Generalizations are hard to draw, yet as this book proves again and again, knowledge of venues and audience helps to clarify issues of politics and genre. Much research remains to be done on the details of such stagings.

Group 3: testing the boundaries of comedy

In my third group of comic plays, women challenge the status quo. In some cases this means a new commandeering of power by women, in some cases a redefinition of women's place in marriage. But in all cases, the authors refuse conventional comedy in either small- or large-scale ways; in the most extreme cases, an author's attempt to tell her story as comedy completely breaks down. But while women maintain strong relations to one another, few of the central women characters are politically active.

Clotilde Graves's *The Wooing* (1898) is a disturbing example of a play in which the creation of a strong woman character is clearly at odds with standard comic plotting. Set at the height of Renaissance Florence, the narrative is focused on Dianora, daughter to Lorenzo de Medici, a young woman who is navigating her way through a varied group of suitors. In the first two acts, we experience Dianora's dazzling display of wit, chicanery, and daring. Her character has a depth and originality rare in plays of the 1890s. But she is reduced to a sobbing heap by the end of the second act, worn out by her draining attempts to maintain control of her life. Subsequently, the last two acts transfer power from Dianora to those around her (mostly men), and in her marriage she becomes a character of diminished power and articulation. It feels as if Graves's only option is to return to a destructively potent plot formula after experimenting with the promise of a different kind of comic life for Dianora.

In two additional plays, traditional comic teleology is also blocked as the women characters reject conventional thinking about friendship, fallen women, and marriage. In Constance Fletcher's ("George Fleming's") *Mrs. Lessingham* (1894), Lady Anne Beaton exercises her notable freedom in the personal realm, not the public or political realms. It nevertheless shakes the foundations of social behavior. With Walter and Anne on the brink of what everyone assumes will be a smashing marriage, Mrs. Lessingham unexpectedly shows up to tell Walter that she is ready to marry him and legalize a long affair. Walter weakly attempts to dismiss Gladys Lessingham, but when Anne gets a whiff of this intriguing woman from Walter's past, she takes command of the action and plots the middle section of the play herself.

While Anne and Gladys are similar to stereotypical characters appearing in many prominent dramas of the 1890s, what sets them apart is their intense, warm interaction in Act 2, enticingly labeled "The Future." In Gladys's rooms, Anne is forthcoming about the dilemma they share: she ignores the shame others attach to Mrs. Lessingham. In fact, she feels a deep bond with her since they have both loved the same man. Anne even sacrifices her love for Walter and shames him into marrying Gladys. While both the men and women around her attempt to put the situation in conventional terms, Anne operates without relying on socially acceptable protocol. Her openness, sensitivity, and toughness are notable for their lack of the melodrama so dominant in other similar plays. But her magnanimous actions, her ability to think past social decorum and envision a more equitable world is, indeed, but a vision of "The Future", for in Acts 3 and 4, the play collapses under the weight of her social heresy. Walter and Gladys are miserable in their marriage, Gladys kills herself in desperation, and Anne retreats to a marriage with Major Edward Hardy, the most conventional man in the play.

Fletcher subtitles the play "an original comedy." Shaw corroborates the originality, finding the play an example of experimental theatre that should be encouraged (Shaw [1896] 1993: vol. II, 462). William Archer, though more ambivalent in his response, notes that Fletcher "writes well" and credits her with developing the sensational plot of *The Second Mrs. Tanqueray*, even before Pinero (Archer [1895] 1971: 99, 102). Indeed, thirty-three performances at the Garrick Theatre make this "one of the more successful productions of a woman's play in the late Victorian period" (Powell 1997: 135). But the originality of Fletcher's play cannot be sustained, and in the play's last two acts, Fletcher seems to be working against herself. The contest between the conventional ending and the play's efforts at political comment were perhaps amplified in performance as the parts of Walter and Gladys were taken by Johnston Forbes-Robertson and Elizabeth Robins, both progressive thinkers who would play large roles in the early twentieth-century suffrage campaign.

In Dorothy Leighton's *Thyrza Fleming* (1895) another young woman attempts to integrate the woman-with-a-past into her own life. In its day, this play achieved a distinction received by few other women's plays when it was produced by the Independent Theatre. The woman-with-a-past is again the titular character, Thyrza Fleming, an independent middle-aged woman who has had a long-term relationship with Colonel Hugh Rivers. It is her letter to Colonel Rivers that separates Rivers and his new wife Pamela. Both Thyrza and Pamela are a source of strong feminist sentiment as the play develops. Thyrza believes in "perfect freedom of speech and conduct between men and women" (Act 2: 26) and is articulate about the suffocating orthodoxy she suffered in living with her husband. She left him as well as a baby daughter to reclaim her self and soul. Pamela also refuses to see situations from a male point of view: "It is just that [looking at issues with a male point of view] which has wrecked women's lives for generations ... weak pandering to the man's view of life is the cause of women's enslavement" (Act 3:

56). With this shared, progressive understanding of gender relationships, both Pamela and Thyrza search for the information that will help them understand and resolve their mutual attachment to Hugh Rivers. Thyrza has no intention of claiming him, and in fact goes to Pamela to explain that she is no threat to the new marriage. The women's connection is more complicated, however; for, during the visit, Thyrza discovers that Pamela is the baby she left behind in her quest for selfhood. Later, when Thyrza attempts suicide, Pamela saves her by wrapping herself around her mother. Despite the heavy-handed melodrama, the two have etched out a new kind of relationship for women admidst an array of generally unsympathetic men.

Perhaps more a drama than a comedy, *Thyrza Fleming* nevertheless ends on an upbeat note, and hints at the possibility of women finding an autonomous identity with impunity, of women caring for one another. While Kerry Powell sees the play as a variation on Oscar Wilde's *Lady Windermere's Fan* (Powell 1997: 137), Shaw notes of the original production that Leighton's play is "a courageous attempt at a counterblast to *The Heavenly Twins* [Sarah Grand's 1893 novel]" (Shaw [1896] 1993: vol. I, 249). Of significance in both comments is the notion of Leighton's drama in dialogue with prominent genres and writers of her day. But like *Mrs. Lessingham*, Leighton's play breaks down; Archer describes it as a degeneration from a "spirited, natural, and entertaining" first act to an ending of "irrelevance and embarrassment" (Archer [1896] 1971: 12, 14). I would describe it as a battle of genre. Leighton's rich female characters and their intimate connections are not at home in comedy.

Women's comedy does not always collapse under the weight of such innovation, however, and I will end with my own comic upturn by looking finally at a representative play in which the women refuse to be confined by the narrow dictates of convention, a play in which a woman's independence creates a marriage based on her fully fledged agency.

While in *The Wooing* Clotilde Graves was unable to sustain her assertive heroine in a comic plot, in her earlier *A Mother of Three* (1896), a mother and her three daughters make their merry way in dealing with the mother's absent husband, the daughters' skittish lovers, and the family's modest means. Mrs. Emmeline Murgatroyd has been on her own for years as her husband is the long-time employee of an observatory in Peru, and is, as his wife explains "wedded to science" (Act 1: 29). He has been home in England so little that he does not even know he has three daughters, not one; and in his absence his wife has developed into a fun-loving and resourceful woman. Her daughters like to hear stories of her life, and when it becomes clear that the daughters may lose yet another set of beaus (the men leave when the absence of the father cannot be explained to their satisfaction), she presses her narrative imagination into active service and assumes a disguise as the girls' newly returned father.

As the mother enjoys her assumption of male dress and behavior and uses her mantle of power to poke fun at gender roles, the real Professor Murgatroyd has secretly returned. He too assumes a disguise, as a boarder in the home, hoping to test the loyalty of his wife. His wife finds it difficult to sustain her disguise, however, and just as she is beginning to doubt its effectiveness, the Professor reveals himself and humbly recounts how wrong he has been to stay away. His wife Emmeline then resumes her favored place as mother and wife: "Let others call me fond, foolish, doting if they will, you at least will say – 'What she has done she did because she was a mother' ... and I'm a wife in a thousand" (Act 1: 22). While Emmeline accepts a return to conventional roles here, her spirit – unlike the many spirits whose smashing I have described – is undaunted. She engineers her husband's confession, she assertively claims distinction as a wife, and while she reclaims her petticoats, nothing suggests that her high jinks are over. The overall effect of this play is to demonstrate that comedy can be the home of female agency and that even a return to marriage need not cancel that control.

The play "drew large crowds to the Comedy Theatre night after night" (Powell 1997: 143); and while reviews were begrudgingly positive, the play marks the possibility that women writing comedy – even in their apprenticeship – could influence the English stage. Graves met with considerable success as a writer (Powell 1997: 122–46); and her career as well as her play offer evidence for what Archer sees as the growing comic presence of women: "The English comic stage may look forward with confidence, not to a Renascence (we have done with such pedantries), but to a new Restoration, in which the Wycherleys and Congreves, as the spirit of the age decrees, shall yield precedence to the Aphra Behns" (Archer [1897] 1971: 152). Graves was not alone in building on many of the qualities Behn set at the center of her drama: strong women who honor their friendships and are allowed to dabble in various degrees of love for men, a foolish exposure of the men, a clear sharing of power between the sexes, and an assertion of women's sexual desire.

In a New Woman novel named *A Husband of No Importance*, a young wife gives up her own writing career to be the stay-at-home model for her husband's plays about New Women (Ardis 1990: 153–54). In this ironic plot twist, the public life of the stage is relinquished to men. The women writers I have studied refuse such a polite retreat and choose instead to wrestle with the challenges of genre, production, and public life. With a few exceptions, these writers are not in the vanguard of what many scholars have studied as the ideologically vibrant decade of the 1890s. Nevertheless, they are courageous thinkers who seem to be reflecting on stage the lives they know; and the transactions of private life which these writers put on stage offer revealing portraits of women's roles and commitments. At the end of the century, women could be seen to be writing more complex plays, as Powell asserts (1997: 133); they are certainly – as the prominent responses of Archer and Shaw attest – being noticed as a force on the stage. Now, 100 years later, the study of the women writing comedy in the 1890s is wide open – their abundant work calls out for more negotiation with dusty texts, letters, and archives; for investigation of forgotten venues; and for continued theorizing about their authorship. Future study will no doubt show that the work of these late-century women is best understood as the work of women who make the theatre a tool in their response to a specific place and time, as the contributors to this volume show.

The lesson I have learned again and again from the study of these plays is that the politics of the 1890s are very different from those a century later. In fact, the lens of my own feminism has often threatened to distort my evaluation of this work. The writers I have surveyed are not literary heroines with progressive agendas; by and large, they are recognizable as ordinary women with a drive and talent to go public – startling enough in their day. We must accept them on their own terms. In the end, what I have found in this theatre of the 1890s is that women's comedy does both challenge *and* validate the status quo, and that these writers have various degrees of success in recognizing and negotiating the delicate balance between a woman-conscious theatre and a literary genre – comedy – renowned for its reconciliations to the status quo.

NOTES

1   Many of the plays in this chapter are available only in the Lord
    Chamberlain's Plays at the British Library. I have no biographical
    information about some of the authors and thus no confirmation that
    all of these are plays by women, not pseudonymous plays by men.
    Many production details come from Wearing (1976).
2   The play is coauthored by a man and a woman, yet the play is one of
    few (by women) published in its day, and in that, an unusual example of
    how women's work came to the general public.
3   The play was published in 1915, but in her preface, Clifford notes that
    the play was first performed in the nineteenth century.

REFERENCES

Archer, William [1895] 1971, "Mrs. Lessingham," *The Theatrical World of
    1894*, New York: Benjamin Blom, 95–103.
Archer, William [1896] 1971, "Thyrza Fleming," *The Theatrical World of
    1895*, New York: Benjamin Blom, 12–14.
Archer, William [1897] 1971, "A Matchmaker," *The Theatrical World of 1896*,
    New York: Benjamin Blom, 150–55.
Ardis, Ann 1990, *New Women, New Novels: Feminism and Early Modernism*, New
    Brunswick: Rutgers University Press.
Bell, Florence, and Elizabeth Robins [1893] 1991, *Alan's Wife*, in *New Woman
    Plays*, ed. Linda Fitzsimmons and Viv Gardner, London: Methuen, 1–25.
Bell, Mrs. Hugh [Florence] 1890a, *Time is Money*, Lord Chamberlain's
    Plays, Add. MS 53460, British Library, London.
Bell, Mrs. Hugh [Florence] 1890b, *A Woman of Culture*, in *Chamber Comedies:
    A Collection of Plays and Monologues for the Drawing Room*, London:
    Longman, Green, 123–36.
Bright, Eva, and Florence Bright 1890, *Tabitha's Courtship*, Lord Chamber-
    lain's Plays, Add. MS 53446C, British Library, London.
Bright, Florence 1888, *Caught Out*, Lord Chamberlain's Plays, Add. MS
    53407, British Library, London.
Bright, Florence n.d., "An Outsider's View of the Woman's Movement,"
    London: Women's Social and Political Union, Suffragette Fellowship
    Collection, Museum of London.
Broomfield, Andrea, and Sally Mitchell (eds.) 1996, *Prose by Victorian Women:
    An Anthology*, New York: Garland.
Burton, Antoinette 1994, *Burdens of History: British Feminists, Indian Women,
    and Imperial Culture, 1865–1915*, Chapel Hill: University of North
    Carolina Press.
Burney, Estelle 1896, *Idyll of the Closing Century*, London: Samuel French.
Caird, Mona Alison 1890, "The Morality of Marriage," in Broomfield and
    Mitchell (1996), 625–53.

Campbell, Constance 1914, *One of the Old Guard*, London: Samuel French.

Clifford, Mrs. W. K. 1915, *A Woman Alone*, London: Duckworth.

Davis, Jill 1992, "The New Woman and the New Life," *The New Woman and Her Sisters*, ed. Viv Gardner and Susan Rutherford, New York: Harvester, 17–36.

Davis, Tracy C. 1992, "Indecency and Vigilance in the Music Halls," *British Theatre in the 1890s: Essays on Drama and the Stage*, ed. Richard Foulkes, Cambridge: Cambridge University Press, 111–31.

Dixey, Kate, and Lilian Feltheimer 1899, *A Girl's Freak*, Lord Chamberlain's Plays, Add. MS 53679, British Library, London.

Fawcett, Mrs. Henry (Millicent) [1887], "Home and Politics: An Address delivered at Toynbee Hall and Elsewhere," Central and East of England Society for Women's Suffrage, Suffragette Fellowship Collection, Museum of London.

Fleming, George [Constance Fletcher] 1894, *Mrs. Lessingham*, Lord Chamberlain's Plays, Add. MS 53546, British Library, London.

Grand, Sarah 1898, "The New Woman and the Old," in Broomfield and Mitchell 1996, 667–76.

Graves, Clotilde 1896, *A Mother of Three*, Lord Chamberlain's Plays, Add. MS 53594, British Library, London.

Graves, Clotilde 1898, *The Wooing*, Lord Chamberlain's Plays, Add. MS 53664, British Library, London.

Grundy, Sydney 1894, *The New Woman: An Original Comedy in Four Acts*, London: Chiswick Press.

Hannam, June 1995, "Women and Politics," *Women's History: Britain, 1850–1945. An Introduction*, ed. June Purvis, New York: St. Martin's Press, 217–45.

Hughes, Annie 1896, *A Husband's Humiliation*, Lord Chamberlain's Plays, Add. MS 53605F, British Library, London.

Jones, Wilton, and Gertrude Warden 1896, *Woman's Proper Place*, London: Samuel French.

Leighton, Dorothy 1895, *Thyrza Fleming*, Lord Chamberlain's Plays, Add. MS 53565, British Library, London.

"Mrs. Madeleine Lucette Ryley" 1910, *Vote*, 26 March, 256.

Powell, Kerry 1997, *Women and Victorian Theatre*, Cambridge: Cambridge University Press.

Rogers, Maud M. 1899, *When the Wheels Run Down*, Lord Chamberlain's Plays, Add. MS 53683E, British Library, London.

Ryley, Madeleine Lucette 1900, *Jedbury Junior*, London: Samuel French.

Schiff, Emma 1882, *The Rights of Woman*, Lord Chamberlain's Plays, Add. MS 53092B, British Library, London.

Shaw, George Bernard 1993, *Bernard Shaw: The Drama Observed*, 3 vols., ed. Bernard F. Dukore, University Park: Pennsylvania State University Press.

Simcox, Edith Jemima 1887, "The Capacity of Women," in Broomfield and Mitchell 1996, 583–97.

Taylor, Helen 1866, "Women and Criticism," in Broomfield and Mitchell 1996, 454–62.

Wearing, J. P. 1976, *The London Stage 1890–1899: A Calendar of Plays and Players*, 2 vols., Metuchen NJ: Scarecrow Press.

Young, Margaret 1897, *Honesty: A Cottage Flower*, Lord Chamberlain's Plays, Add. MS 53645, British Library, London.

Plays cited in this volume

Listed below by last name are the women playwrights and plays cited in this volume. The date indicates the first mention we have of the script: either the year in which the play was written, or the first time the play appeared in print or in production. In cases where the play was never published, the date is usually taken from the year in which an application for a license was made (regardless of whether it was allowed or refused). This list is only a fraction of the plays written by women in Britain during the entire nineteenth century. For more detailed information about where to find surviving manuscripts, printed versions, anthologies or facsimile versions, consult chapter notes and lists of references. The main sources for manuscript material in particular are the Lord Chamberlain's Plays held by the British Library in London, the Larpent Collection held by the Huntington Library in California, and the promptbooks of the Frank Pettingell Collection at the University of Kent at Canterbury, which are available as microform through Harvester Press Microform Publications.

Baillie, Joanna

> *De Monfort*, 1798
> *Constantine Paleologus; or, The Last of the Caesars*,
>   1804
> *The Family Legend*, 1810
> *Witchcraft*, 1836

Bell, Florence

> *Time is Money*, 1890
> *A Woman of Culture*, 1890

Boaden, Caroline

> *Fatality*, 1829
> *The First of April*, 1830

A Duel in Richelieu's Time, 1832

Bright, Eva and Florence
Tabitha's Courtship, 1890

Bright, Florence
Caught Out, 1888

Burney, Estelle
Idyll of the Closing Century, 1896
Settled Out of Court, 1897

Campbell, Constance
One of the Old Guard, 1914

Cavendish, Lady Clara
A Woman of the World, 1858

Clifford, Lucy
A Woman Alone, 1915

Crauford, Charlotte
Paul the Showman; or, A Dead Mother's Letter, 1864

Cumming, Lucy Caroline (trans.)
*Sappho, a Tragedy. From the original by Franz
Grillparzer*, 1855

Dacre, Lady (Barbarina Wilmot)
Ina, 1815

Dixey, Kate and Lilian Feltheimer
A Girl's Freak, 1899

Fletcher, Constance (George Fleming)
Mrs. Lessingham, 1894

Godwin, Catherine
Sappho, 1824

Gore, Catherine Grace Moody
School for Coquettes, 1831
The Maid of Croissey, 1835
A Tale of Tub, 1837
Dacre of the South, 1840
Quid Pro Quo; or, The Day of Dupes, 1844

Graves, Clotilde
A Mother of Three, 1896
The Wooing, 1898

Hall, Caroline
The Will and the Way, 1853

Hemans, Felicia
The Siege of Valencia, 1823

The Vespers of Palermo, 1823

De Chatillon; or, The Crusaders, 1840

Hill, Isabel

The First of May; or, A Royal Love Match, 1829

Brian the Probationer; or, The Red Hand, 1842

Holt, May (Mrs. R. Fairbairn)

Every Man for Himself, 1885

Hughes, Annie

A Husband's Humiliation, 1896

Jones, Gertrude Warden and J. Wilton Jones

Woman's Proper Place, [1896?]

Lane, Sarah

Taken from Memory, 1873

Dolores, 1874

Albert de Rosen, 1875

The Faithless Wife, 1876

St. Bartholomew; or, A Queen's Love, 1877

The Cobbler's Daughter, 1878

Red Josephine; or, A Woman's Vengeance, 1880

Devotion; or, The Priceless Wife, 1881

Leighton, Dorothy

Thyrza Fleming, 1895

Lewis, Estelle

Sappho: A Tragedy in Five Acts, 1876

Medina, Rose

Ernest Maltravers, 1874

Mitford, Mary Russell

Julian, 1823

Charles the First, 1825

Foscari, 1826

Rienzi, 1828

Penhorn, Mrs. Edward

The Merchant's Daughter of Toulon, 1856

The Wife's Tragedy, 1870

Planché, Elizabeth

The Welsh Girl, 1833

The Sledge Driver, 1834

The Handsome Husband, 1836

The Ransom, 1836

A Hasty Conclusion, 1838

Polack, Elizabeth
> *Esther, the Royal Jewess*, 1835
> *St. Clair of the Isles*, 1838

Randall, Mrs. W.
> *Formosa*, 1870

Roberts, Valentina
> *The Young Recruit*, 1860
> *Jack Mingo, The London Street Boy; or, Try Again*, 1866

Robins, Elizabeth and Florence Bell
> *Alan's Wife*, 1893

Robinson, Emma
> *Richelieu in Love; or, the Youth of Charles I*, 1844

Rogers, Maud
> *When Angels Run Down*, 1899

Ryley, Madeleine Lucette
> *Jedbury Junior*, 1896

Sandford, Edith
> *The Firefly*, 1869

Schiff, Emma
> *The Rights of Woman*, 1882

Scott, Jane Margaret
> *The Animated Effigy*, 1811
> *The Vizier's Son and the Merchant's Daughter; or, The Ugly Woman of Baghdad*, 1811
> *Asgard the Demon Hunter*, 1812
> *Broad Grins; or, Whackham and Windham*, 1814
> *Camilla the Amazon; or, The Mountain Robbers*, 1817
> *The Old Oak Chest; or, The Smuggler's Son and the Robber's Daughter*, 1816
> *The Lord of the Castle*, 1817

Wortley (a.k.a Stuart-Wortley), Emmeline
> *Moonshine*, 1843

Wilton, J. H.
> *Uncle Peggoty's Darling; or, The Flight from the Ark*, 1871
> *Miss Brown*, 1874

Wilton, Kate
> *Pearl Darrell*, 1883

Young, Margaret
> *Honesty: a Cottage Flower*, 1897

Young, Melinda (Mrs. Henry)

> *Pride, Property and Splendour; or, The Seamstress and the Duchess*, 1856
>
> *The Dark Woman*, 1861
>
> *The Fatal Shadow; or, The Man with the Iron Heart*, 1861
>
> *The Man with an Iron Heart; or, The Woman with Golden Hair*, 1861
>
> *The Beggars' Banquet; or, Beneath the Lights of London*, 1862
>
> *The Death Fetch; or, The Pauper's Child*, 1862
>
> *Jessie Ashton; or, The Adventures of a Barmaid*, 1862
>
> *The Life and Adventures of George Barrington; or, One Hundred Years Ago*, 1862
>
> *String of Pearls; or, The Life and Death of Sweeney Todd*, 1862
>
> *Woman of the World*, 1862
>
> *Ben Child; or, The Swallow's Nest*, 1863
>
> *The Bravoes of London; or, The Stain on the Glass*, 1863
>
> *Drip Drop; or, The Secrets of the Vulture's Nest*, 1863
>
> *Ida Lee; or, The Child of the Wreck*, 1863
>
> *The Mescican [sic] Bandit; or, The Silver Digger of Perate*, 1863
>
> *The Poor Girl; or, Il Idiour the Wanderer*, 1863
>
> *Catherine Hayes*, 1864
>
> *Left Alone; or, The Footsteps of Crime*, 1864
>
> *Fair Lilias; or, The Three Lives*, 1865
>
> *Britomart the Man-Hater; or, Will He Win Her?* 1866
>
> *Eyes in the Dark; or, The Graves in the Sand*, 1866
>
> *Nobody's Son; or, Half a Loaf Better Than None – A Night in a Workhouse*, 1866
>
> *The Pick-Lock of Paris*, 1866
>
> *The Light of Love; or, The Diamond and the Snowdrop*, 1867
>
> *Twenty Straws*, 1867
>
> *Jonathan Wilde; or, The Storm on the Thames*, 1868

Young, Mrs. W. S.

> *The Black Band; or, The Mysteries of Midnight*, 1861

APPENDIX 2

Plays by women dramatists in East End theatres
1860s–1880s

Compiled by Heidi J. Holder

LCP   Lord Chamberlain's Plays
P   Frank Pettingell Collection of Plays
Licensing copy call numbers provided in some cases. Dates indicate
   night of opening in East End theatres.

Lady Clara Cavendish
A Woman of the World. Melodrama. Queen's Theatre, 13 November
   1858. LCP 52978D.
Charlotte Crauford
Paul the Showman; or, a Dead Mother's Letter. Melodrama. Britannia
   Theatre, 16 April 1873. P, LCP 53031N (licensed 1864).
Caroline Hall
The Will and the Way. Melodrama. City of London Theatre, 16 May
   1853. P.
May Holt (Mrs. R. Fairbairn)
Every Man for Himself. Melodrama. Pavilion Theatre, 24 October
   1885. P, LCP.
Sarah Lane
Albert de Rosen. Melodrama. Britannia Theatre, 1875. P, LCP 53151F.
The Cobbler's Daughter. Melodrama. Britannia Theatre, 1878. P, LCP
   53200H.
Devotion; or, The Priceless Wife. Melodrama. Britannia Theatre, 1881. P,
   LCP 53249L.
Dolores. Melodrama. Britannia Theatre, 6 April 1874. P, LCP 53135B.
The Faithless Wife. Melodrama. Britannia Theatre, 1876. P, LCP
   53164H.
Red Josephine; or, A Wife's Vengeance. Melodrama. Britannia Theatre,
   1880. P, LCP 53241C.
St. Bartholomew; or A Queen's Vengeance. Melodrama. Britannia Theatre,
   1877. P, LCP 53185C.

Taken from Memory. Melodrama. Britannia Theatre, 10 November 1873. P, LCP 53119C.

Rose Medina (American)

Ernest Maltravers. Melodrama. Britannia Theatre, 28 September 1874. P.

Mrs. Edward Penhorn

The Merchant's Daughter of Toulon. Melodrama. Standard Theatre, 10 March 1856. LCP 52957H.

The Wife's Tragedy. Melodrama in verse. Standard Theatre, 12 October 1870. LCP.

Mrs. W. Randall (with W. Randall)

Formosa. Melodrama. Britannia Theatre, 5 December 1870.

Valentina Roberts

Jack Mingo, The London Street Boy; or, Try Again. Melodrama. Possibly coauthored with C. H. Hazlewood. Britannia Theatre, 11 August 1866. LCP, P.

The Young Recruit. Melodrama. Pavilion Theatre, 28 November 1860. LCP 52998G.

Edith Sandford

The Firefly. Equestrian melodrama. Surrey Theatre, 17 May 1869; Britannia Theatre, 3 June 1870.

J. H. Wilton

Miss Brown. Comedy. Britannia Theatre, 11 May 1874. LCP, P.

Uncle Peggoty's Darling; or, The Flight from the Ark. Britannia Theatre, January 1871. P.

Kate Wilton

Pearl Darrell. Melodrama. Britannia Theatre; Sefton Theatre, Liverpool, 17 September 1883. LCP, P.

Mrs. Henry (Melinda) Young

The Beggar's Banquet; or, Beneath the Lights of London. Melodrama. Effingham Theatre, 17 October 1862. LCP 53016Y.

The Bravoes of London; or, The Stain on the Glass. Melodrama. Effingham Theatre, 8 October 1863. LCP 53026F.

Britomart the Man-Hater; or, Will He Win Her? Melodrama. Marylebone Theatre, 9 June 1866; Effingham Theatre, 2 July 1866. LCP 53051S.

Catherine Hayes. Melodrama. Effingham Theatre, 29 July 1864. LCP 53033L.

The Dark Woman. Melodrama. Effingham Theatre, 17 May 1861. LCP 53004H.

The Death Fetch; or, The Pauper's Child. Melodrama. Effingham Theatre, 23 June 1862. This may in fact be Henry Young's *Bertha Gray, the Pauper Child; or The Death Fetch* (staged at the Bower Saloon, 15 July 1851, LCP 43036), produced under Mrs. Young's name.

Drip Drop; or, the Secrets of the Vulture's Nest. Melodrama. Effingham Theatre, 6 April 1863; City of London Theatre, 10 August 1867. LCP 53021L.

Eyes in the Dark; or, The Grave on the Sands. Melodrama. Effingham Theatre, 8 December 1866. LCP 53055I.

Fair Lilias; or, The Three Lives. Melodrama. Effingham Theatre, 22 May 1865. LCP 53042J.

The Fatal Shadow; or, The Man With the Iron Heart. Melodrama. Effingham Theatre, 16 February 1861. LCP 53000Q. (Probably same as *The Man with the Iron Heart*.)

Ida Lee; or, The Child of the Wreck. Melodrama. Effingham Theatre, 28 August 1863; Britannia Theatre, October 1863; East London Theatre, 31 May 1868. LCP 53024T.

Jessie Ashton; or, The Adventures of a Barmaid. Melodrama. Effingham Theatre, 21 April 1862; revived 16 February 1867. LCP 53013S.

Jonathan Wild; or, The Storm on the Thames. East London Theatre, 13 July 1868. LCP 53069P.

Left Alone; or, The Footsteps of Crime. Melodrama. Effingham Theatre, 30 November 1864. LCP 53037N.

The Life and Adventures of George Barrington; or, One Hundred Years Ago. Melodrama. Effingham Theatre, 2 August 1862. LCP 53015I.

The Light of Love; or, The Diamond and the Snowdrop. Melodrama. Effingham Theatre, 25 February 1867. LCP 53057I.

The Man with the Iron Heart; or, The Woman with the Golden Hair. Melodrama. Victoria Theatre, 29 April 1861; Britannia Theatre, 31 August 1870.

The Mescican [sic] Bandit; or, The Silver Digger of Perate. Melodrama. Pavilion Theatre, 26 October 1863. LC 53026K.

Nobody's Son; or, Half a Loaf Better Than None – A Night in a Workhouse. Melodrama. Effingham Theatre, 12 February 1866. LCP 53048K.

The Pick-Lock of Paris. Melodrama. Effingham Theatre, 27 October 1866. LCP 53054R. (Licensed under the title *Adele d'Escars; or, The Picklock of Paris*.)

The Poor Girl; or, Il Idiour The Wanderer. Melodrama. Effingham Theatre, 8 July 1863. LCP 53023R.

Pride, Poverty, and Splendour; or, The Seamstress and the Duchess. Melodrama. Victoria Theatre, 1 November 1856; Effingham Theatre, 9 June 1862. LCP 52962K. (Note: first licensed 1856.)

The String of Pearls; or, the Life and Death of Sweeny Tod [*sic*]. Melodrama. Effingham Theatre, 11 July 1862.

Twenty Straws. Melodrama. Effingham Theatre, 7 March 1865; City of London Theatre, 2 November 1867.

Woman of the World. Melodrama. Effingham Theatre, 8 September 1862.

Mrs. W. S. Young

The Black Band; or, The Mysteries of Midnight. Pavilion Theatre, 25 September 1861.

Index